W9-AHV-005

THE GREAT WALL

THE GREAT WALL

FOREWORD BY
JACQUES GERNET
COLLEGE DE FRANCE

TEXTS BY
LUO ZEWEN
DAI WENBAO
DICK WILSON
JEAN-PIERRE DREGE
HUBERT DELAHAYE

DESIGNED BY
EMIL BÜHRER

McGRAW-HILL BOOK COMPANY
NEW YORK ST. LOUIS SAN FRANCISCO

THE DEPICTION OF THE GREAT WALL OF CHINA AND ITS HISTORY
PRESENTED IN THIS BOOK
IS THE RESULT OF CLOSE COOPERATION BETWEEN THE PUBLISHERS,
MCGRAW-HILL BOOK COMPANY, NEW YORK,
AND THE CULTURAL RELICS PUBLISHING HOUSE, BEIJING,
AND PARTICULARLY THE LATTER'S EXPERTS, EDITORS, AND ORGANIZERS:
WANG FANGZI, WANG DAIWEN, HAN ZHONGMIN,
SUN BANCHANG, LUO ZEWEN, AND YU JIN.

A McGraw-Hill Co-Publication

Copyright © 1981 by McGraw-Hill
Book Company (UK) Limited,
Maidenhead, England. All rights
reserved. Except as permitted under the
Copyright Act of 1976, no part of this
publication may be reproduced, or distributed in any form or by any means,
or stored in a data base or retrieval system, without the prior written permission of the publisher.

Library of Congress Cataloging in
Publication Data

Zewen, Luo.
    The Great Wall.

    Bibliography: p. Includes index.
    1. Great Wall of China (China) I.
Wilson, Dick, 1928–   II. Drège,
Jean Pierre. III. Title.
DS793.G67Z48   951   81-6067
ISBN 0-07-070745-6   AACR2

Editor: David Baker

Managing Editor: Francine Peeters

Assistant Editor: Simon Fear

Production Manager: Franz Gisler

Graphic Artist: Franz Coray

Picture Researcher: Rosaria
    Pasquariello

Picture Procuration: Ruth Rüedi

Translators:
Dorie Brodie (texts by J.P. Drège).
Alison Martin (captions by
    H. Delahaye)

Printed by:
Courvoisier S.A., La Chaux-de-Fonds,
Switzerland

Bound by:
Schumacher AG, Schmitten,
Switzerland

Photolithography by:
4-color sections: Hego, Littau,
Switzerland, 1-color sections: Räss,
Bern, Switzerland

Printed in Switzerland

A military parade on the Great Wall. This rubbing made from a low relief contains many iconographic details that are typical of the Han and earlier periods (the chariot, arms, horses, birds in the sky), but the general style of the composition suggests that it dates to an earlier era. In this book we shall encounter many of the architectural elements depicted here —walls, crenellated fortifications, which follow the rise and fall of the terrain, small forts, watch towers, signal fire towers—as we study the defensive works that culminated in the Ming wall (1368–1644).

CONTENTS

JACQUES GERNET

"Jiayuguan Pass": inscription on the western-most fortress of the Great Wall. Situated in the Gansu corridor, west of the present-day city of Jiuquan, the pass of Jiayuguan was the near-obligatory entranceway into China for caravans traveling eastward on the Silk Road.

FOREWORD

Proclaimed as the only man-made structure that can be seen from the moon, the Great Wall of China is a subject of astonishment to westerners. No one but the Chinese, we tend to think, could have conceived and executed a project so ambitious and so mad. Suppose that Europe had wanted to protect itself from the great invasions and the Mongol raids by building a wall that extended in an unbroken line from the northern Urals all the way to the Persian Gulf or the Mediterranean! But such an undertaking, which is inconceivable in the human and geographical context of Europe, seems somewhat less illogical in the Far East. The two worlds of the nomadic herdsmen and the settled farmers are more clearly differentiated there than anywhere else in the world, owing to the distinct latitudes and to the peculiar rainfall patterns. Anyone traveling by air in clear weather from Irkutsk (in eastern Siberia) to Beijing (Peking) will be struck by the contrast between the gray expanses of Mongolia and the greenness of the first Chinese plains. This country so rich and populous, which was the mother of learning, of arts and sciences, in eastern Asia, had to defend itself throughout almost the whole course of its history against the incessant incursions or the threat of invasion from the Asian interior beyond its northern borders. The Chinese scheme to construct these imposing fortifications was not inspired by any desire to isolate themselves—contrary to the belief of certain historians who accuse China of lacking the western spirit of "openness" and "enter-

prise." Rather, the Chinese were guided by experience. The history of the Great Wall—or rather of the Great Walls, since construction went on at so many different periods and in such diverse places—is inseparable from the history of China in the period extending from the first attacks by nomadic mounted archers around the middle of the first millennium B.C., up to the development of modern artillery and the enormous task of settling the nomadic tribes under the Manchu dynasty beginning in the seventeenth century.

As long as they were divided, the tribes of nomadic herdsmen posed no serious threat to northern China: they merely launched periodic raids to seize crops, livestock, or people. This state of affairs was to change when the tribes were joined, at various epochs, into great federations. The best-known of these groupings were the Xiongnu (perhaps the ancestors of our Huns) in the third to second century B.C., the Kirghiz Turks in the sixth and seventh centuries A.D., and the Mongols in the thirteenth century. These Mongols, so famous for their far-flung conquests (as recounted in this book in the chapter "Why the Wall Was Built"), eventually occupied all of China. The Chinese tried throughout the centuries to ensure their peace and safety and the integrity of their borders: vigorous military offensives aimed at destroying the nomads or driving them farther north, various attempts to destroy the unity of these tribes, such as through gifts of silks, creation of buffer states consisting of coopera-

At its eastern end, the Great Wall reaches the seacoast at the border between Hebei and Liaoning provinces. The Ming emperors (1368–1644) christened this fortress "the First Pass on Earth" and restored it as a defense.

When the Europeans finally forced their way into China near the end of the nineteenth century, many travelers were astounded to discover the immensity of this great architectural marvel. Marco Polo, according to his reports, had not visited the Great Wall, and a few missionaries in the late Ming period, and under the Qings (1644—1912), were the only visitors who had glimpsed it. This engraving shows a German expedition inspecting the wall in the vicinity of Nankou, approximately 30 miles (50 km) north of Beijing. This is close to the very spot where hordes of Manchu horsemen, just before 1644, crossed into China to establish the Qing dynasty.

Right: This panoramic view of the Great Wall, continuing over the next few pages, takes in the best-known segment, at Juyongguan near Nankou, north of Beijing. Juyongguan is a pass and fortress mentioned in the oldest preserved written sources. It occupies a site that has been of vital strategic importance throughout the centuries. The walls of the fort are inscribed with texts in Chinese, Manchurian, Mongolian, Arabic, and Jürchen (Tangut).

The Great Wall has often been compared to a dragon. With its head at the east, its tail to the west, it winds its way over thousands of miles of rugged contour. In China the dragon is an auspicious protective divinity, not destructive as in the Western tradition. It is synonymous with springtime and vital energy.

Indeed, China's earth is filled with dragons which give shape to mountains and form the curves of rivers. These creatures form the sinew of the land relief and partake of the earth's divinity.

tive and coopted nomads, peace treaties supplemented by matrimonial alliances and exchanges of hostages—and on one occasion, in the year 1004, China was even forced to purchase peace from her conquerors at a considerable price. The lines of fortresses and the Great Walls were just one of the means to which the Chinese resorted to protect themselves from their turbulent northern neighbors. And thus, contrary to the popularly held view, the Great Wall is not a line of demarcation fixed once and for all between China and the outside world. Between the wall completed by the First Emperor of the Qin dynasty at the end of the third century B.C., and the wall that can be seen today north of Beijing (and shown on these pages), built in the fifteenth century, many changes occurred in construction methods, war technology and weaponry, social conditions and political organization, and even in mentality. To provision their armies encamped in the fortresses of southern Mongolia, the Hans in the second and first century B.C. installed military colonies, systematically irrigated and settled whole regions (which went fallow in the succeeding

Below: The arched gateway of the Cloud Terrace at Juyongguan closely resembles many other gates along the Great Wall. The arch is surrounded with high-relief carvings of figures of protective divinities.

periods) because the Great Wall of Qin, extended toward central Asia by the Han rulers, lay much farther to the north than those built in later periods. In the fifteenth and sixteenth centuries, the Mings preferred to entrust the provisioning of their northern armies to salt and tea merchants. The Tangs, on the other hand, staked everything on military offensives, the creation of major horse-breeding installations, and the use of auxiliary troops recruited among allied nomads. In each

period, the general conditions and the solutions adopted were to vary considerably.

The Great Walls, in any event, testify to the administrative genius of the Chinese people. It is far from a simple task to mobilize several hundred thousand men, to see that they are fed, organized in units, and to direct their work in the prevailingly mountainous, desert-like, inhospitable regions where these

impressive fortifications were erected. Many are known to have died at the task. (A popular old legend tells the story of Meng Jian, wife of a farmer press-ganged into the construction of the Great Wall under the Qin empire. After struggling, at enormous hardship, to cross the snow-covered mountains to bring him warm clothing, she arrived at the worksite only to learn that her husband had just died. Meng Jian wept until the wall collapsed at the point where her husband had been buried.) Nor could it have been a simple matter to maintain, as the Ming rulers were later to do, an army of one million men along the 6,000 kilometer (4,000 mile) stretch of wall all the way from Manchuria to the area south of the Gobi Desert. We find evidence of the Chinese organizational genius even in the humble documents discovered at the turn of the twentieth century in western Mongolia, dating to the period between 100 B.C. and A.D. 100. These documents found in the ancient fortifications built by the Han dynasty, include fragments of calendars, legal texts, soldiers' letters, as well as official reports, communiqués, and precise inventories drawn up by garrison officers. (An illustration of these finds is shown on page 38.)

The Great Walls never impeded contact and exchanges between the Chinese and the populations speaking Turkish, Mongolian, and Tangut languages who roamed the regions between Korea and the Tianshan mountains, and between the Baikal and the provinces of north China. The steppe empires

Waves at the western end of the wall, waves also where it ends in the east: here, waves in the sands of the Gobi Desert; there, in the waters of the Yellow Sea. This contrast is brought home to us in two photographs, the one at right and the other on the following page which shows the sea at Shanhaiguan.

Between the two ends lies a distance of more than 6,000 kilometers (4,000 miles) of winding wall, with a variation in elevation of more than 2,000 meters (6,500 feet)—and an unlimited diversity of landscape features, natural species—human, animal, and vegetative—and artistic and architectural forms.

Uranus, or Tianwang, who was the personification of Heaven, is frequently portrayed on the reliefs found at strategic points and passes of the wall. This detail is from a relief over the west wall of the arch at Juyongguan pass.

The sands of Chinese Turkestan preserve for us the China of the barbarians better than any solid walls could have done. And yet, in these vast desert stretches of Gansu there are still to be found remains of defensive walls that go back some two thousand years, to the time when the Han generals came here to fight the Xiongnu tribes.

could never have taken shape without having borrowed heavily from China and without the help of Chinese advisers, administrators, artisans, and farmers. And northern China for its part, which had already intermingled with barbarian peoples at many periods, continued to receive influences from the steppe. Northern China learned a great deal from the nomadic herdsmen concerning animal farming, horse breeding, use of draught animals, and the arts of war. The "barbarian" influence is even seen in certain recipes of Chinese cookery and in the use of the tunic and trousers which became the standard Chinese garb. Indeed the many products (silks, tea, salt, and silver from China; horses, camels, cattle, and sheep from the steppe) were not the

only commodities exchanged by way of the passes through the Great Wall opened up for the use of ambassadors and merchants. Just as was the case everywhere else in the Old World, the paths opened up by trade were soon to be traveled by technology and religion. The nomadic herdsmen were to serve as intermediaries between the two extremes of Eurasia. It was they who, in the Mongol period, introduced Europe to two major Chinese innovations—the use of gunpowder, and wood engraving, ancestor of modern printing.

And thus the history of the Great Wall provides an introduction to the history of Chinese civilization in general, and its close and constant relations with the world of the steppe in particular. The publication of this handsome volume—the first book to treat this important subject in a manner at once so attractive and so thorough—is a happy event indeed.

JACQUES GERNET
Professor, Collège de France

Chinese cities never had any fortifications other than those inspired by good sense to all nations prior to the usage of artillery: a trench, a rampart, a strong wall, and, and some towers. But ever since the Chinese took up the cannon, they ceased to follow our military model, for not content to fortify their fields of battle, the Chinese have fortified their entire empire.

Voltaire, Essay on the Manners and Spirit of Nations (1756)

JEAN-PIERRE DRÈGE

Far to the west in the rough Chinese hinterland, in northwestern Gansu province, this tower still stands, witness to a period of intense activity that has long since ended. Beside it, passes the road traveled by the Buddhist monk Xuan Zang on his return from India at the beginning of the seventh century A.D.

THE WALLS BEFORE THE WALL

According to a story still told in China today, a young woman named Meng Jiang in the third century B.C. came in search of her husband who had been sent to work on the building of one of the early Chinese walls. Learning that he had perished, like so many others, in this hazardous work, Meng Jiang killed herself. These rocks near Shanhaiguan, at the eastern end of the Great Wall, are said to serve as her tomb.

The Great Wall that we know from the famous remnants near Beijing is not, in terms of Chinese history, very old. It dates only to the Ming dynasty (1368–1644), a period when widespread invasions from the north required the construction and maintenance of an enormous rampart stretching for thousands of miles across Chinese territory. Yet this was not the first China wall by any means. As early as the fifth century B.C. a number of smaller walls were built, sometimes several of them at practically the same time, at sites often far removed from the present Great Wall; there was not yet any single unifying plan, as there would be under the Mings.

The first walls were themselves no more than a rough form of connection between even smaller units—fortifications and watch towers—that had formerly been isolated here and there in the countryside. But soon these walls came to designate a kind of frontier, if only over relatively short distances. Their first purpose was protection from the constant threat of invasion. In the northern regions of China, however, the wall or walls were to assume another function, as a line of demarcation between two types of culture or society. On the one side was a settled population practicing agriculture, while the other side was peopled by nomads who raised animals. Whereas the interior walls disappeared once China was unified under the power of Qin Shi huangdi ("the First Emperor," 221–210 B.C.), the border

walls were eventually linked up to form the "Great Wall of 10,000 *li*."

The first centuries of the empire were marked by the futile but nonetheless determined effort to separate two worlds, the civilized and the barbaric. The stability of such a border can only be a fiction, and so it was that the course of the Great Wall, through the centuries, would often vary. The most striking example is in the Ordos region defined by a great loop of the Yellow River, where Chinese conquests were not always of long duration.

The mixing of populations in the border regions was a reciprocal process whereby the barbarians were made more Chinese, while the Chinese themselves became more like the barbarians. This is the reason that assimilated barbarians, who went on to found new dynasties in China, were able to claim as their own the legacy of ancient Chinese rulers. These infiltrations and encroachments by the nomads were later to be replaced by real wars of conquest in which the Great Wall proved ineffective. The progress of military technology and the development of strategy made it possible again and again for the nomads to create empires in the north of China. The Mongols finally had their turn at occupying all of China, and it was only when they were pushed back to their original territory that the colossal enterprise of rebuilding the Great Wall as an effective defense was undertaken.

17

THE WARRING KINGDOMS

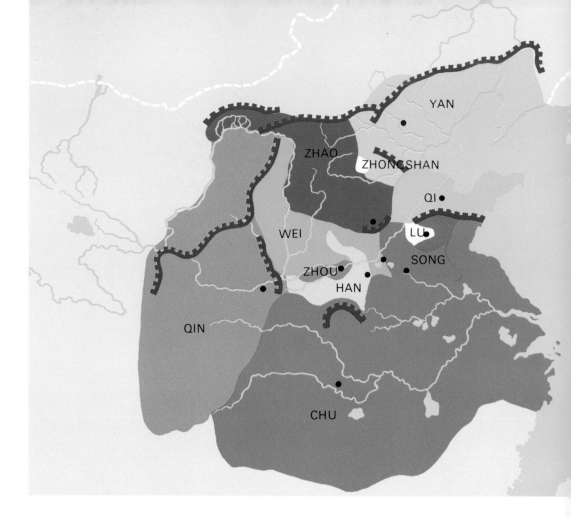

The fragments of walls erected before the third century B.C. correspond to the frontiers of kingdoms or principalities which were at that time in a near-permanent state of war. Although most of these segments of wall are impossible to locate on the terrain today, some of them (particularly in the kingdom of Qin) were used again in later times. In addition, the fortifications built in that period, as a rule, bore little resemblance to the Ming wall so well known to us today. They were instead, especially in the north, primarily far less imposing walls than the Ming. The states mentioned on this map did not all coexist at the same time. Moreover, the site of many of the capital cities indicated here can only be approximate.

The Warring Kingdoms have left bronzes which are often decorated with scenes of hunting or warfare. The figures seen here, from a fourth-century B.C. bronze vessel now in the Beijing Museum, depict an attack upon a walled city. Despite the archaic, somewhat stiff style, we can make out with some clarity the postures and weapons of the belligerents and the vividly evoked heat of battle.

During the period known as the Warring Kingdoms (ca. 500–221 B.C.) a host of principalities were superseded by vast kingdoms. A kind of confederation of "kingdoms of the center" (zhongguo) was established, along the Yellow River and in the Central Plain, as opposed to principalities farther away in the northwest (the Wei valley) or the south (the Yangzi valley). By this time the royal power of the Zhou dynasty (eleventh to sixth century B.C.) which perpetuated the traditions of the Shangs (eighteenth [?] to eleventh century) had lost its moral and religious authority.

The building of the first walls, in the fifth century, was part of a whole complex of technical, economic, social, and ideological innovations which marked a real break with the past. First, this was the beginning of cast iron: the earliest reference to this method, specifically the molding of caldrons, dates to 512 B.C. This new technique made possible the large-scale production of a wide range of utensils for use in agriculture as well as earthwork. Land clearing, drainage, irrigation of wide expanses of virgin land, soil preparation, and the use of fertilizer all led to a considerable increase of agricultural production. A direct consequence of this was the levying of a grain tax, at a fixed rate of ten percent of the annual production, which was a prevalent practice from the sixth century on. Concomitantly the population, which was still so sparse during the "Spring and Autumn" era (seventh to sixth century), had a significant spurt of growth.

Cities too grew up, to assume a vital eco-

Civil strife within, barbarian attacks from without: this entire period was marked by violent conflict. The state of Zhao, with its center the present city of Taiyuan in Shanxi province, suffered the most from incursions by the Xiongnu nomads. The Zhao general Yan Guang, shown here, won glory in many battles against these invaders.

nomic role, bringing a concentration of the means of production and a kind of nationalization. An inevitable side effect was a degree of social upheaval. As commercial exchanges intensified, several types of metallic currency appeared. Politically, fiefs disappeared; territories were divided into districts administered by functionaries who were paid in grain and were subject to removal by the central authorities. The creation of a system of punishments and rewards, which evolved from necessary military discipline, contributed to a transformation of attitudes. The very hierarchical structure of Zhou society was endangered. The leaders of the kingdom rejected such institutions as oaths of allegiance and other rites that had been handed down from the archaic era. Wars of conquest came to replace the old confrontations arising from family disputes; displays of heroism yielded to decimation of the enemy; honor gave way to trickery. Thus were the great kingdoms set up at the expense of the small principalities founded by the Zhous.

In the name of efficiency the instruments of warfare must change to keep step with the evolution in the nature of war itself: hence the advent of the sword, the crossbow, the catapult, and the creation of a real infantry. Undoubtedly the infantry was first deployed in the southern kingdoms of Wu and Yue because the swampy areas there were impassable to chariots. At Jin the mountains necessitated the use of infantry. The lowly crew that once only served the chariots were now promoted to a fighting force. In earliest times, before heavy chariots had been replaced by the cavalry, the advance of the invader is said to have been impeded by furrows dug perpendicularly across his path. King Wuling of Zhao (325–298 B.C.) was, apparently, the first to organize, in 307, a cavalry based on that of the *Hu* nomads, and to adopt

their costume: a tunic and trousers instead of a single long garment. The mounted archers were an elite corps. As the kingdoms conquered more territories, military expeditions began to range farther afield and garrisons had to be maintained far from the royal capitals. Tactical and strategic theories abounded, as the celebrated *Art of War* of Sunzi still bears witness. An entire arsenal of offensive weapons was developed. Siege warfare spawned special equipment such as ladders, towers, and saps, which in turn were countered by a spate of fortification-building.

Formerly a city was composed of a walled town surrounded by cultivated fields which were in turn protected by other walls. After the outer ramparts had been extended, as the conquests themselves spread farther the king would build up fortifications in the area between the walls. And whenever two territories of the great kingdoms came into contact, walls were erected over long distances to protect them from each other. In all probability these fortifications were not continuous, for where natural obstacles could serve to repel the enemy there was no need of ramparts.

A multitude of small walls were erected throughout China during this pre-imperial period, reflecting the local kings' mutual mistrust. This wall stands in the ancient country of Chu, present-day Henan, about 1,000 km (600 miles) south of the Great Wall.

Xiang Yu *(above)*, famous for his cruelty, was instrumental in putting an end to the reign of China's first emperor (end of third century B.C.).

The king commanded Nan Zhong to go build a wall at Fang. They brought forth chariots in great number, standards and flags flew in the wind. "The Son of Heaven has ordered me to build a wall out there in Shuofang."

SHIJING *(The Book of Odes)*

Ah, what misfortune for us living at the frontier. Three times in one year, he served in the army. Three of his sons have gone to Dunhuang, two to Longxi, all five have gone to do battle far away.

ZUO YANNIAN, *third century* B.C.

The Wei kingdom, in the central Yellow River valley, put up a wall in a vain effort to withstand their western neighbors, the Qin. These ruins, 6 meters (20 ft) high and 8 meters (26 ft) wide, are still in evidence today.

Above right: Restored terrace at Handan (southern Hebei) with a double roof, said to have been built under Wu, the Zhao ruler during the Warring Kingdoms period.

Here and there along the ancient course of these internal walls, a tower still rises *(as below)*.

Along the rivers, floodgates were reinforced and fortified. These were made of tamped earth like the city walls, though at times stones were used as well. They were flanked by small forts distributed here and there.

We do not know with any certainty whether the walls were built to set the definitive limits of conquest, or rather as protection against encroaching neighbors. In fact, a distinction must be made between two types of walls according to the type of people they were designed to keep out: on the one hand, walls between Chinese or quasi-Chinese kingdoms, and on the other, walls separating northern kingdoms from the nomads of the steppes. During the period when the first long ramparts were built, seven "powers" formed alliances or fought with each other by turns: Han, Wei, and Zhao in Shanxi-Henan, as a result of the division of the Jin kingdom in 453; Qi in Shandong; Yan in

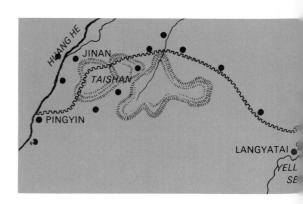

Hebei; Qin in Shaanxi; and Chu, partially "civilized" by the Chinese, on the banks of the Yangzi. The first kingdom to build a defensive wall was apparently Qi, which needed protection against incursions from Chu. According to some sources this occurred at the beginning of the fifth century, while others place the event at the end of that century. The next wall was built by the Chu kingdom, which had to protect itself from the encroachments of

This ancient terraced building at Zhenbei, near Yulin in northern Shaanxi province, is one of the many large-scale paramilitary structures that were found in the vicinity of the ancient walls. Beyond this promontory stretched the vast, menacing Inner Mongolia.

The maps on these two pages show five of the walls built during the period of the Warring Kingdoms:
1 Qi wall, fifth century B.C., in Shandong province

2 Chu wall, mid-fourth century B.C., Henan province
3 Wall of the Qin kingdom, fourth to third century B.C., Shaanxi and Gansu provinces
4 Yan wall, fourth to third century B.C., Hebei
5 Wei wall, second half of fourth century B.C., Henan

Qi as well as Qin. This wall may well have been constructed as early as the fourth century, probably before 328. Then came Wei, defending itself against Qin, Qi, and Chu; then Yan, against Qi; and Zhao, against Wei. Even the tiny principality of Zhongshan, situated on the border between Hebei and Shanxi provinces, managed to put up a wall of its own.

But the neighboring kingdoms were not the only danger: the northern kingdoms of Zhao, Yan, and Qin also built walls to keep out nomads. Mention is made in the *Book of Odes (Shijing)* of a wall being built in the northern regions as early as the seventh century, but its exact location and length are not known. The tactical reason for erecting these walls was to prevent raids by the nomads from the steppes and the Manchurian plains, but in the long range they served to establish a limit between what was Chinese and what was not, between civilization and barbarism.

If the kingdoms learned certain military arts from the nomads, these outsiders also began to erect fortifications. In his book of *Historical Records (Shiji)* Sima Qian (135?–93? B.C.) tells how after the division of Jin into three kingdoms (453), the Yiju barbarians constructed a double wall in Ordos as protection. Nevertheless, little by little the kingdom of Qin encroached on their territory and King Hui seized twenty-five of their walled towns. As soon as Qin had managed to push them far enough back, a wall was built—possibly incorporating the ramparts already constructed by the Yiju themselves—to contain them. And this line of defense between the Chinese and the nomads of the steppes was to become what is now known as the Great Wall.

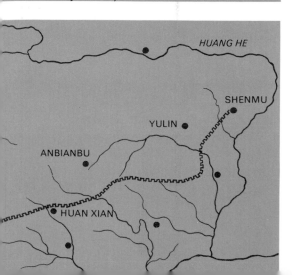

The period of the Warring Kingdoms came to an end with the conquest of the last one of these kingdoms, the Qi (221 B.C.), by Qin Shi huangdi, the ruler of the Qin empire, who had acceded to the throne in 247 B.C. With this conquest the unification of China had finally been achieved in the shape of the First Empire.

Qin Shi huangdi is not only remembered as having been, in 221 B.C., China's first emperor: during the ten preceding years, he conquered and annexed six rival kingdoms—all of what was then considered China. His short reign, so crucial to Chinese history, put an end to the era of the Warring Kingdoms. This engraving shows him giving the command for the attack upon the neighboring states.

THE FIRST EMPEROR

The king of Qin is a man with a prominent nose, large eyes, a chest like a bird of prey; with the voice of a jackal; a man of little kindness; a heart of tiger, or that of a wolf.... He finds it easy to act humble toward people: as soon as he obtains what he wants, he finds it just as easy to devour them.

SHIJI *(Historical Records)*

The first Qin emperor claimed descent from the line of Huangdi (the Yellow Emperor), a mythical ruler of remote Chinese antiquity. He and a few other legendary sovereigns were believed to have brought order into the world, and he supposedly had the secret of eternal—or at least very long—life. Qin Shi huangdi undoubtedly longed to claim for himself the attributes of this supposed ancestor.

A bitter fate lay in store for anyone who dared oppose the authority of the first emperor. One of the few persons known to have defied this law was none other than his mother, Zhao Ji, shown at right in this engraving *(below)*. One day she publicly denounced her son's despotic character. When the emperor's eldest son tried to do the same, he fell victim to assassination.

The first emperor, Qin Shi huangdi (ruled 221–210 B.C.), is often considered the builder of the Great Wall, but in fact he destroyed as many fortifications as he put up. But this is not the only paradox we encounter in studying Qin Shi huangdi; he is a figure who has always generated discussion, and as recently as the "cultural revolution" of the 1960s, so critical of Lin Bio and Confucius, he still aroused a controversial fascination. This fascination stems from his radical transformation of the Chinese world, first within the state of Qin and then, with the unification of all Chinese territory, on a national scale.

An entire mythology grew out of the remarkably active life of Qin Shi huangdi, beginning with his birth. The son of the king of Qin, Zichu, had been sent as a hostage to the kingdom of Zhao. In the city of Handan (Hebei) where he lived, he made the acquaintance of a rich, aggressive merchant by the name of Lü Buwei, who had taken as concubine an extremely beautiful dancer. Zichu also took a liking to her and ended up claiming her as his own. Extremely perturbed, but undoubtedly hoping to profit from the deal, Lü Buwei yielded his concubine. Zichu married her not knowing that she was already pregnant. Sometime later Zichu succeeded his father as king of Qin. The child of the concubine, named Zheng, himself succeeded to the throne at the age of thirteen. Thus the future emperor, though acknowledged as the son of the king of Qin, was actually the natural son of the merchant Lü Buwei. Lü Buwei himself became the king's counselor.

All of this took place during the wars of conquest waged by the kingdom of Qin, in the course of which the neighbor states fell, one after the other, under its yoke. All possible tactics were adopted to win the support of, or do away with, the leaders of these other kingdoms, including corrup-

The sovereign emperor has extended his rule;
His bravery has rallied together all the princes;
He is the first to have established universal
*   peace.*
He has thrown down and destroyed the inner
*   and other walls....*
He has leveled all obstacles and removed all
*   difficulties.*

SHIJI *(Historical Records)*

秦始皇

如其才如其智

士橫議不坑無儒長城裁三亘古中外長淮悠三黔首傲賴武署

遠播文運重開誠罪之首六功之魁鳴呼欲和人先論世嗟彼始皇

姬籙運衰紀綱中墜天相有秦厥功維偉文勝則史不憖焉無書虞

tion and assassination. With the fall of the last adversary, Qi, in 221, unification was complete.

The first step taken by the king of Qin was to give himself a title. The antiquity of legend had three sovereigns *(huang)* and five emperors *(di)*: hence Zheng designated himself the "sovereign emperor" *(huangdi)*, first *(shi)* of a line that was to comprise 10,000 generations, but which in fact stopped at two.

A vast political, administrative, and social reform was launched—first tried out in Qin and later extended throughout the empire. The first emperor was certainly not himself the originator of all these innovations. A great number of them must be attributed to the Chief Counselor, Li Si. His authoritarian realism, in the tradition of Chinese Legalism, inspired this no doubt apocryphal anecdote: "While he was still only a young underling, he saw some rats in the latrines of municipal buildings gorging themselves on refuse. Whenever people or dogs approached, they would recoil in fear. Li Si then went into the storehouse where he saw rats

devouring the stock of grain. Living in the depths of these side buildings, they had to fear neither dog nor man. Observing this, Li Si exclaimed: 'A man's potential is exactly like that of rats. It all depends on where he is'." Finding no kingdom other than Qin worthy of his talents, Li Si entered the service of Lü Buwei. It was he who advised the future emperor to deliver the fatal blow to the other kingdoms that were already weakened. He was soon elevated to the rank of Chief Counselor, thus replacing Lü Buwei.

Under his aegis the reforms picked up speed. It proved necessary to stamp out regional influences and allegiances of whatever kind, to leave no traces of the old

Corruption, assassination, and finally the force of arms brought the first emperor, Qin, absolute power over the whole of China. The three portraits of him in his imperial role shown here bear little sign of the cold determination that guided him on his ambitious path—the founding of a centralized state, standardization of all currency, weights, and measures, law codification, as well as the installation of merciless police controls and moral conformism. To the Chinese of the period, he was less the glorious emperor than the tyrant of the state of Qin, considered at the time very backward, nearly barbarian.

秦李斯

Four likenesses of important figures in the First Emperor's court. If Qin Shi huangdi had not had these talented men at his disposal, it is doubtful that he would have succeeded in his radical transformation of China's political, economic, and social structure. *Left to right:* Li Si, his adviser; Shang Yang, who undertook important judicial reforms; Lü Buwei, prime minister; and General Meng Tian, undone by his own military ambition—he was executed for alleged conspiracy to seize power. None of these portraits are contemporary, and thus the persons' facial features are quite imaginary.

kingdoms. The empire was divided instead into 36 administrative zones (later 48), each headed by an appointed civil administrator and military governor. All weapons throughout the empire were confiscated, brought to the capital, Xianyang (not far from the present city of Xi'an in central China), and melted down to make bells as well as twelve immense statues which were placed in the imperial palace. City ramparts and defensive walls constructed by the former kingdoms were systematically destroyed. The "rich and powerful," representing 120,000 families, were brought by force to the capital. A network of new roads covered the empire, laid out in straight lines, assuring efficient service for the military as well as for commerce. The width of carriage axles, previously varying with each kingdom, was now standardized; dry and liquid measures and units of length were made uniform; and currency was reduced to a single type:

the round copper sapeke with a square hole in the middle. Pearls, jade, silver, or tin were no longer used in transactions and thus became purely decorative commodities.

The draconian rigor of the criminal justice system, inspired by the theories of Shang Yang, was reflected in the punishments inflicted: flogging, branding with hot irons, deportation, confiscation of possessions, forced labor, execution with the body put on display in the market place, decapitation, quartering, live burials, dismemberment, cutting off the nose and feet, cooking in a caldron, and so on. The principle was one of deterrence, even for minor crimes. All travel or migration was subject to police control, and inns had to register their guests with the police. Idlers, vagabonds, and other parasites were drafted into the army and consigned to the periphery of the empire. Functionaries unlucky enough to have their integrity

呂不韋
大賈面目假父
衣冠招
禮賢士成
一家言
爭名
於朝
爭利
於市令
之駆
僧如其智

Shown below is the supposed course of the Great Wall as built under Qin Shi huangdi. The emperor probably wanted to protect his country in the north as well, by building a wall along the bend of the Ordos region, but there is no

placed in doubt were deported; indeed, the Great Wall was built by such prisoners. With internal pacification now assured, the interior walls, which stood in the way of centralization, were destroyed. The external borders, however, were not stable. In the south, the war against the barbarians continued, and new administrative precincts were created all the way into what is now northern Vietnam. In the north, troubles with the nomads were not over. Our sources offer few details on the building of what is known to subsequent generations as the Great Wall: "When Qin had unified the empire, Meng Tian was sent at the head of 300,000 men to put down the Rong and Di barbarians in the north. He seized the area south of the Yellow River and built a large wall which followed the terrain and made use of natural obstacles and passes. From Lintao in the west, it went all the way to the east of the Liao River—more than 10,000 *li*."

The construction of the Great Wall was primarily the work of General Meng Tian. Born into a top-ranking military family, Meng Tian had been appointed in 221 to head the troops engaged against the kingdom of Qi and had scored a victory. A few years later, he repelled the barbarians in the northwest, and it was in this region that he

solid archaeological proof that such a structure ever existed. The roads shown here extend like spokes from the hub of Xianyang, capital of the empire. (After Jonathan Fryer, *The Great Wall of China*, New English Library, 1975.)

The adherents of Taoism, whose founders were Zhuangzi and Laozi *(right)*, did not fare much better than the Confucians under the First Emperor. The only Taoists to be spared were those who were well versed in the magic of longevity: the despot's obsession.

太上老君

先師孔子行教像

德侔天地道冠古今
刪述六経垂憲萬世

"Confucius as itinerant teacher," a print taken from a nineteenth-century engraving. Confucius had long been dead, but his followers suffered terrible hardships under the reign of Qin Shi huangdi.

He who killed by the sword had to die by the sword, in the manner illustrated here. This murderer *(below)* had concealed his weapon in some maps in order to trick the vigilant guards.

荊軻
秦武陽

前石士

spent the rest of his career. Here he was entrusted with overseeing the building of the wall and the communication routes. The northern walls of the Yan and Zhao kingdoms were joined up. The old Qin wall appears to have been relegated to secondary position, because, according to the *Historic Records,* a wall was built along the Yellow River farther north.

We know little of the life and activities of Meng Tian except that the invention of the paintbrush has been attributed to him—wrongly, as it turns out. At the death of Qin Shi huangdi, a conspiracy was mounted against Meng Tian and he was condemned to die. He is said to have declared: "Yes, I did commit a crime, and I must die for it. From Lintao all the way to the east of the Liao River, ramparts and moats stretch for more than 10,000 *li.* Surely in that expanse of land I must have severed a vein of earth. That is my crime." Then he swallowed his mortal potion. A legendary story, no doubt, but interesting nevertheless because it is one of the first allusions to geomancy—the belief in the quasi-divinity of the earth, or the presence of occult influences in certain locations. Interest in the subject has continued in China until contemporary times.

Aside from radical social changes and the great building projects, Qin Shi huangdi and especially Li Si are still known for two cultural events: a new form of writing, and the destruction of books. The famous burning of the books, in 213 B.C., is said to have come about as follows. One day, during a celebration, a learned man upbraided the emperor for not taking the ancient world as his model. Li Si, hearing this, responded angrily: "Today, when such great things are being accomplished, you intellectuals prefer to study the ancients and to scorn the present, little caring how you corrupt men's minds." Having seized the initiative, he went on to propose that all official histories be burned (with the exception of Qin's annals), along with the *Book of Odes,* the *Book of History (Shujing),* and the Resolutions of the Hundred Schools (i.e., philosophical works). These books were to be available only to the most learned scholars. Whoever failed to execute this order within thirty days would be condemned to forced labor, and any discussions of these banned books would be punishable by death. Draconian though this step was, its long-range consequences were less catastrophic than has been claimed. But it was a move that earned the most vehement reaction from the followers of orthodox Confucianism.

If thinkers, moralists, and individualists

This rather late painting depicts the two great sins of Emperor Qin, which were unpardonable to the Chinese: the burning of the books (that is, nontechnical books) and the condemnation to death of intellectuals, philosophers, and other troublemakers in 213 B.C. Although not as many books were burned as has been claimed, the execution of classical scholars was an anti-humanist atrocity. Twenty centuries later, the eyes of the tyrant in this painting were defaced as though they were the devil's own.

The explorer W.E. Geil (whose notes and sketch are shown here) was among the first to furnish us with precise details of the funerary tumulus of Qin Shi huangdi. He was convinced that excavations would someday reveal many archaeological marvels at the site.

The Afang palace (below), here depicted by an artist several centuries later, was where Qin Shi huangdi lived—or where he hid, since in his fear of assassins he went so far as to disguise himself as a servant. Whoever recognized the disguise was put to death.

This reconstruction of a palace in the kingdom of Qin near Xianyang (Shaanxi) is more authentic, since it is based on very precise archaeological data. Even if this is not the imperial palace, it must have looked much like this.

Near the funerary tumulus of the first emperor were found life-size clay statues of soldiers, horsemen, peasants, and various sorts of people—a microcosm of the real world. What is most surprising about these treasures is the extraordinary technical and aesthetic quality of figures so well preserved at the time of their discovery in 1974.

were hunted down, indeed exterminated, books on divination were spared. Magicians abounded in the entourage of the emperor, who was so interested in drugs offering immortality. The quest for such substances had begun as early as the fourth century, in the former kingdom of Yan. The story was told that immortal beings dwelt on three supernatural mountains rising up in the middle of the Bohai. During one of his many journeys, Qin Shi huangdi went to the seacoast and decided to send someone in search of the islands. Three thousand young men and women were dispatched, never to return. Legend has it that these same young men and women landed in Japan and colonized it. Many further attempts were made to find the mountains, but all without success. It was even said that some being was thwarting the project, and that to overcome evil spirits one would have to become invisible. Thus the emperor had the 270 palaces of Xianyang and environs connected by covered, walled paths. In this way he could wonder about in secret and without his subjects' knowing in which palace he was to be found. Nonetheless the quest was a failure, and many magicians fled in fear.

Magic and authoritarianism increased the unpopularity of Qin Shi huangdi, who was the object of several attacks, including three attempts on his life. In the end, he died of illness, while on a trip to Hebei. His death remains tainted with mystery. At Li Si's instigation, the succession was diverted to the emperor's second son, but the death was not announced immediately for fear of a revolution. The body was taken in a carriage to the capital. After some time, the decomposing corpse started to attract attention—so the carriages of the funeral cortege were loaded with salted fish for concealment. The burial finally took place with full pomp in the mausoleum that Qin Shi huangdi had built during his own lifetime. Seven hundred thousand men who had reportedly been subjected to castration were forced to work on this mausoleum. Automatic cross-bows assured the emperor's protection; there was a ceiling representing the heavenly bodies, and a map of China in which the rivers were made of mercury that could be set in motion by means of concealed machinery.

With the first emperor dead the dynasty soon crumbled. The short reign of the second emperor (210—206) was rife with ever-increasing insurrections; it was one of the rebel leaders, Liu Bang, who founded the new dynasty of Han.

Recent excavations have led to the discovery, in 1974, of the mausoleum of Qin Shi huangdi. An entire funerary army, guarding his tomb, has come to light, consisting of nearly seven thousand terra-cotta soldiers

Qin Shi huangdi had of course not been able to attain the immortality after which he had so passionately striven. Nevertheless, in a sense he has indeed lived on for more than two thousand years. For his name acquired a new sparkle when, in 1974, farmers who were drilling for water to the west of the district capital town Lintong, in Shaanxi province, unearthed the gigantic burial site of the First Emperor. It was the most spectacular archaeological find of the century: there were painted clay figures of warriors and horses in full life size in a quantity which set the whole world in amazement. This army of clay figures, which was assembled here some two thousand years ago, and which must be considered as the huge personal bodyguard of the emperor, has been estimated

and ten thousand weapons, in an enclosure measuring 60 by 210 meters (198 by 693 feet). The columns of statues, with horses and chariots, are arranged in three groups: front guard, main body of troops, and rear guard.

as numbering seven thousand men. This in so many respects splendid emperor, one of the most fascinating figures in Chinese history, thought and dealt in "superhuman categories and dimensions, which set completely new standards, and which might well be measured against the yardstick of eternity. Against this background one must also see how his enormous bodyguard, presently being brought to light little by little, made this man, who was only defeated by death, still invincible against every opponent in the life to come." These were the words of Professor Helmut Brinker in the catalog of the exhibition "Art Treasures from China," which brought the name of Qin Shi huangdi to the whole world.

Ever since its discovery in 1974, the clay army buried near the funerary tumulus of Qin Shi huangdi has continued to be unearthed. It consists of armored archers and foot-soldiers with and without armor—all of different ranks and in different positions. They are a tall (over six feet) and fearsome lot. Each one has his own individual facial expression: they are mute and unarmed, calm and threatening. So far only a portion of them have been found. Their faces and costumes were painted, and the smallest details such as the uniform buttons and shoes, which have been restored, make us wonder at the amount of work these figures must have generated for thousands of anonymous artisans. Even after hundreds of the soldiers are uncovered, the mystery will still remain: the existence of these statues is completely incomprehensible in terms of what is known about the stylistic evolution of Chinese statuary.

FROM THE HANS TO THE MONGOLS

The Xiongnu were a long time a source of trouble for the Chinese. They are described in traditional history as a people very different from the Chinese themselves. They were nomadic herders, with strange customs and way of life, living almost exclusively on meat, dressed in animal skins and living in felt tents. Fine horsemen, they excelled at the use of the bow and arrow. When a man died, his son would marry all the father's wives, except his own mother. They prayed to the sun and moon. To ratify a treaty, they would drink blood from the skull bone of an enemy chief.

Above: Another vestige of vanished economic splendor, this ruin of an ancient warehouse near Dunhuang (Gansu) is ample evidence of the importance of the markets established in central Asia at the entrance to the Silk Road.

Opposite: Liu Bang, founder, under the name of Gaozu (206—198 B.C.), of the western Hans. Although less ferocious than his rival Xiang Yu, he was more competent, managing to take full despotic advantage of a military and administrative structure based on that of Qin Shi huangdi.

Below right: A fine example of late Han art is this small bronze horseman, full of verve, from Lei T'ai.

Above: The Empress Lü, wife of Liu Bang, became the empress regent on the death of her husband. She eliminated any possible pretenders to the throne including her son.

The Han emperors (206 B.C. to A.D. 220) pursued a dynamic expansionist policy—extending their sphere of influence southward (into southeast Asia and to the Indian Ocean), to the east (Korea), the north (Manchuria, Mongolia), but above all in the west (central Asia) where they erected a new branch of the wall that it was impossible for their successors to maintain.

The Hans inherited a rather shaky Chinese state. With the demise of the Qins, there came a slackening of the border controls which had been strongly enforced along the Great Wall and the first of the Han sovereigns, Liu Bang or Gaozu (206—198 B.C.), after a defeat by the Xiongnu around the year 200, pulled his forces back well within the wall and resigned himself to a policy of "peace and friendship."

With Emperor Wu (140—87 B.C.) all this was to change. He set out to contain the Xiongnu by making new alliances. In 139 he sent a delegation of one hundred, under Zhang Qian, to woo the Yuezhi in central Asia, a people who had fled far to the west after their defeat by the Xiongnu in 165. But no sooner had Zhang Qian and his party left China than he was seized by the Xiongnu. He stayed on among them for ten years, married, and had children.

Managing to escape at last, he resumed his mission.

Now, as soon as one piece of territory was conquered, a command post was set up and colonists installed. Immediately an extension of the Great Wall was built in Lingju, where it had previously ended. It was pushed westward as far as the Yumen pass. By this time the Xiongnu had already been driven north of the great loop of the Yellow River and a wall had been rebuilt, probably along the river itself. Other fortifications went up in Mongolia and Manchuria.

The small states of the oases were either won over or subdued, but the expansion was not without setbacks. The emperor

漢高祖

漢祖生來肌骨奇龍顏
隆準聖神後誅殘代暴
登天位龍造炎劉四百基

repeatedly sent emissaries to the kingdom of Tayuan in pursuit of the famous "divine horses" which were reported to sweat blood. But relations with the people of Tayuan deteriorated, and in 104, General Li Guangli, already decorated in anticipation of victory, was sent to bring them under control. When he failed in his mission, the emperor refused to admit him back through the Jade Gate (Yumen), named for the jade imported there from Khotan. Li Guangli settled outside the wall in Dunhuang, and then in 102 set off again for Tayuan with reinforcements. This time victory was his, and the route to the west was opened up. In order to protect convoys and emissaries, the Great Wall was extended beyond the Jade Gate, although not in one continuous stretch. Fortresses were also built along the way from Dunhuang to Lobnor, as early twentieth-century archaeologists such as Aurel Stein have shown. The wall in this area was apparently just one element in a complex system that could be compared to the Roman *limes,* the defense line that ran for

hundreds of miles along the Germanic-Roman border. Of course, the wall—or *agger,* in the precise terminology of Aurel Stein—was the cornerstone of this fortification line. It would come to a halt only whenever natural obstacles could be relied on as impenetrable barriers.

Auxiliary military colonies grew up in the border area, responsible for clearing and developing newly won territory and for the supply of provisions for the troops and any diplomats passing through. Groups would be resettled en masse in these western regions—180,000 peasant soldiers, for example, were imported to the command zones of Jiuquan and Zhangye (Gansu) where they raised wheat, millet, and hemp. And so for the Han dynasty, the Great Wall had as much to do with dynamic commercial conquest as it did with passive military defense. All this activity along the wall developed throughout the first century B.C. and the first century A.D., uninterrupted by the turbulent reign of the usurper Wang Mang (9–23) and the restoration of the Hans.

MAJOR DYNASTIES 3RD C. B.C.—14TH C. A.D.

The Han Dynasty (206 B.C.– A.D. 220)
Having taken over the centralized system of government of Qin Shi huangdi, the Hans reigned another four centuries, always expanding the empire and strengthening the institutions.

From the Three Kingdoms to the Suis (220–618)
The Chinese "Middle Ages" began with the division of the Han empire. An opposition soon became established between the often short-lived dynasties of the north (barbarians who had become assimilated into China) and the south. Political reunification did not occur until the sixth century, when the Suis instituted profound economic and administrative reforms.

The Tangs (618–907)
Taking advantage of the vast effort at unification and reform launched by the Suis, the Tangs strengthened both the central power and the army, at the same time stimulating commerce and the expansion of the empire. Nevertheless the peace of the three centuries from 618 to 907 was severely shaken by the rebellion led by General An Lushan in the mid-eighth century. After that crisis the empire never again regained its initial splendor: the tenth century in particular was rife with power struggles and partitions of the territory.

The Northern Songs (960–1127)
By adopting and developing the politico-economic scheme of the Tangs, the Songs brought a high degree of civilization to China. But when the threat of the northern barbarians (Khitan, Jürchen) became more and more serious, the Songs withdrew to the south before being totally liquidated by the Mongols. The Jürchen founded the Jin dynasty (1115–1254) in the north.

The Yuans (1277–1367)
The Mongols were the first barbarians to reign undivided in China. Nevertheless, they were unable to deal with the rebellions resulting from economic turmoil, and they were swept away in 1367.

Molded polychrome statues of divinities—Buddhas, guardians, disciples—in the shrine hall of grotto no. 45 at Mogao. These works display the stylistic high point of Chinese Buddhist iconography such as it was transposed to Japan beginning at this time.

This person seated under a canopy has non-Chinese facial features, but his clothing and the surrounding decor show that Buddhist painting during the Tang period had been shaped by Chinese influences to a considerable degree. This painting is from grotto no. 103 at Mogao, near Dunhuang (Gansu).

Meanwhile, trade with the barbarians, particularly the Xiongnu, increased on both sides of the Great Wall. The Han rulers, and many before them, found it useful to bestow gifts on the barbarians, with one particular goal in mind: divisiveness. With the neighboring tribes appeased, a wedge was driven between them and the barbarians living farther away. Little by little, thanks to this strategy, a fringe group was formed known as the "dependent king-

A general view of the southern part of the Buddhist site at Mogao. Into these cliffs were carved hundreds of grottoes which contain superb wall paintings, most of them made from the seventh century onward. The construction and decoration of these grottoes coincided with the economic prosperity of the region: merchants grown rich on trade with central Asia often proved to be generous donors.

A view of the ceiling in the shrine hall of grotto no. 361, Mogao. Despite the repetitive representations of Buddha and of other stylized and geometric subjects, the infinitely varied shapes and colors form a most decorative ensemble.

doms," a buffer zone of settled nomads who were allowed to maintain their own customs. With their progressive integration into the empire, the Chinese succeeded in "fighting barbarians with barbarians." In fact, it sometimes happened that border walls were moved outward in order to separate the external barbarians from those within. But despite these barriers, contacts continued, in two basic forms: first, tribute paid by one state to another, and second, public or private commercial exchanges. The gifts presented to the *shanyu* actually resembled a form of economic foreign aid, distributed at the request of the Xiongnu—whose attacks

The ancient gateway to the city of Dunhuang, an important post on the Silk Road famed for the impressive Buddhist grottoes located here.

Below: A fantastical figure on painted silk, from Dunhuang. Artworks in a variety of media have been found at this site.

This miniature in a Buddhist manuscript from Dunhuang shows the Buddha in the center, with offering bearers at either side and below him. This was a theme often seen illustrated at the various Chinese Buddhist sites, along with figures of other divinities.

ceased when their demands were met. In turn, the *shanyu* sent emissaries as hostages to the Chinese court bearing tribute, usually just symbolic in form but sometimes consisting of many head of cattle. The *shanyu* Huhanye sent his own son as hostage in 53 B.C. and even surrendered himself to the court in 51 in order to pay homage to the emperor. Princess Wang Zhaojun, who was later celebrated in literature, was given to Huhanye in marriage. All this trafficking back and forth helped to bring the people living near the Great Wall into the Chinese fold. It also converted the nomads into unpaid serfs. Harsh conditions of exploitation at the hand of Chinese administrators soon led the nomads to revolt. The general disintegration of imperial power under the later Hans around the end of the first century was hastened by these popular uprisings. Troops sent to crush these rebellions included barbarians, in particular Cao Cao who, when the empire was breaking up in A.D. 220, established one of the so-called Three Kingdoms.

Shortly after the founding of the Western Jin dynasty (265), which reunified China for a short time, a veritable war broke out. The barbarians, who had served in large numbers in the armies of the embattled imperial families, rebelled and formed independent kingdoms. During the fourth century northern China was broken up into sixteen kingdoms, ruled by peoples who had achieved various degrees of assimilation into Chinese culture, known as the Five Barbarians. Eager to give their states a distinctively Chinese flavor, they went so far as to adopt the names of ancient Chinese dynasties. Thus the leader of the Xiongnu in Shanxi, Liu Yuan, took the name of the Han sovereigns, and consequently felt no qualms about creating a new Han dynasty (304–329).

A truly striking example of barbarian assimilation into Chinese culture is provided by the Northern Wei dynasty (386–534), founded by a Tabgatche (Tuoba) tribe descended from the Xianbei of Manchuria which settled in northern Shanxi. Dissatisfied with the arid and already crowded region in which they had settled, the Northern Weis extended their territory into more fertile regions, until little by little they had reunified all of northern China. Using Chinese advisers, they pursued a harsh rule, enforced by Chinese functionaries. Anything of Xianbei origin, including language, family names, and clothing, was prohibited—with predictably depressive effects on local morale. The flourishing of Buddhism at the time inspired widespread, and costly, building of monasteries, statues, and bell towers. The most impressive testimony to the flowering of Buddhism is seen in the famous Yungang grottoes near Pingcheng (modern Datong), the original capital of the Wei.

Because of the commercial importance of the city of Dunhuang beginning in the seventh century, and the variety of contacts established from there, foreign influences become apparent in the stylistic diversity of the artworks found here. *Above:* Wall painting in one of the grotto shrine halls. *Left:* The clay statues of Buddha, well preserved despite twelve centuries of exposure to the elements, can still be admired in the niches carved into the rock.

"Chinese cavalryman facing a barbarian horseman in deadly combat": Under the Han dynasty, this conflict tended to favor the Chinese, since in the second and first centuries B.C. the Chinese armies for the first time pursued their advantage throughout central Asia.

These fragments of paper and of wooden slats dating from the Han dynasty were found near the Great Wall at the beginning of the twentieth century. They are documents

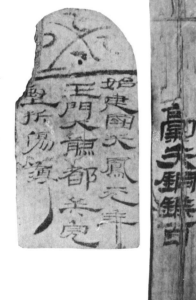

transmitting military orders, accounts, rank insignia, or money—as in the example, top center, with a pierced coin with knifelike protuberance, which was dated first century A.D.

Assimilated for the most part into the Chinese world, the Tuoba were soon threatened in turn by the peoples who had remained nomads. Wall construction once again got under way. From the beginning of the fifth century, the Weis began repairing and reinforcing the old wall of the Hans, from western Shaanxi to Hebei; then around 446 they undertook to build a line of defense more than 500 kilometers long (300 miles) to protect their capital city of Pingcheng.

After the uprisings of the army, which was largely composed of barbarians, and the revolts of the poorly assimilated tribes, the empire split up into two factions, giving birth to two new dynasties: the Northern Qi (550–577) in the east, and the Northern Zhou in the west. In 552 the Qis began to build a new wall in the west of their territory, spanning more than 400 kilometers (250 miles), which was supposed to protect them against their constant enemy, the Zhous. Faced with the same problems that the Weis had had with their northern neighbors, the Qis undertook the construction of a wall along the entire border: from the western wall, which for the most part followed the Yellow River, to Shanhaiguan on the Bohai Gulf, a distance of some 1,500 kilometers (nearly 1,000 miles). For good measure, they even duplicated their defenses with a second wall, about 200 kilometers (130 miles) long, farther to the south. The Mings were later to follow this same course in building their Great Wall. When the Zhous, having at last conquered the Qis, reunified northern China, they resumed the building or repair of the wall.

A new group of people promptly emerged along the northern border, bringing a new series of invasions of Chinese territory. These were the Turks (Tujue), a loose confederation of tribes that soon split into two groups, the eastern and western Turks. The Qis and Zhous as well as their predecessors, in their perennial striving for supremacy against one another, had each at various times sought alliances with the Turks. Later dynasties found them more of a threat. When the Sui dynasty was founded in 581 as the result of a coup d'état, the emperor immediately resumed

Han personalities (left to right): Cai Yong (133–192), an eminent intellectual ruler under the Eastern Hans, whose daughter was married to a barbarian king with whom she stayed for twelve years. Zhou Yafu, outstanding politician, in the service of emperors Wendi and Jingdi (from 179 to 139). Wei Qing, general of the Eastern Hans.
Along with tribute money and gifts,

work on the restoration of the Great Wall, but could not prevent the eastern Turks from breaking through, starting in 582. The Suis did not give up. In 585 a force of 30,000 men built a wall of more than 350 kilometers (230 miles) through the Ordos region. In 607 another Sui, Yangdi, ordered a new construction near the northeast corner of the Yellow River. This project took only a week to complete, but required one million men, only half of whom survived. But for some time it managed to stem the invasions. Diplomatic measures followed: a Chinese princess offered in marriage to a Turkish khan, and more significantly, efforts by the Chinese to sow dissent among the Turkish tribes. Even so, Turkish pressures along the borders did not really ease until 630, during the Tang dynasty (618–907), when the Chinese gained control of the Ordos and dealt the eastern Turks a crippling blow from which they were a long time recovering.

Defeat of the eastern Turks marked the beginning of the Tang expansion in both east and west. The king of the Koguryo in Korea, who lived in fear of a Chinese invasion, had a defense wall put up: more than 500 kilometers long (300 miles), it ran from what is now northern Jilin province all the way to the sea. It could not stop the Chinese, who not only invaded the Koguryo, but pushed farther south into the Silla kingdom. In central Asia, meanwhile, expansion continued unabated throughout the century, all the way beyond the Pamir Mountains (in the U.S.S.R.).

From the beginning of the eighth century, Chinese expansion began to meet resistance—from the Arabs, the Turks (now being called the Uighurs), and the Tibetans. After a rebellion led by General An Lushan in 755–756, the empire disintegrated into separate regions. Five dynasties followed one another in quick succes-

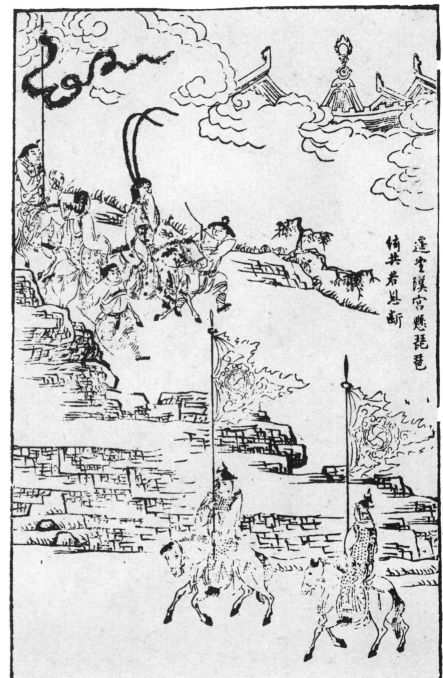

sion (907–960) in the north, while the south was ruled by ten different kingdoms. The northern dynasties had to face new threats from nomads who were relatively assimilated and sedentary. First were the Khitans, descendants of the Kiabei, who

the best way to cement relations with the Barbarians, and thus to keep the peace, was to give them a Chinese "princess" in marriage—and not all of these young women were of royal blood. In this picture the fair Wang Zhaojun sets out for her marriage to a Xiongnu chief.

Li Shih-min (below), though not the first official emperor of the great Tang dynasty, was nevertheless its true founder. As Emperor Taizong (626–649) he instituted an important reconstruction of the army, especially the cavalry, along with major developments in economy and international commerce.

established a state in the northeast (Liaoning) and by the beginning of the tenth century were already masters of an empire. They quickly extended their dominion to include Mongolia, the Beijing region, and the entire northern area of Shanxi. A defensive wall, modeled on the Chinese example, was built in the area of the Liao River. Their deadly attacks forced the new Song dynasty (960–1127) to buy them off with heavy tribute in silks and silver. So famous were the Khitans that even today a cognate of their name is used for "China" in several Slavic languages. And another derivate of "Khitan"—Cathay—was Marco Polo's term for northern China.

China remained very much on the defensive for some time. The creation of the Western Xia empire (1032–1227) by the Tangut (of Ningxia and Gansu) posed a new threat to the Chinese, who had to offer tribute of silk, silver, and tea in appeasement. But soon both these assimilated empires, the Khitan and the Tangut, were threatened in turn by tribes of northern Manchurian provenance, the Jürchen. These ancestors of the Manchus soon founded their own dynasty, the Jin (1115–1254). Allied to the Songs, they liquidated the Khitan Liao empire (1125), and then turned on the Songs themselves, conquering all of northern China up to the Huai valley.

Still there was no end to the upheavals. The Jin empire, having become well assimilated into Chinese culture like so many peoples before, was attacked by new conquerors, the Mongols, in the beginning of the thirteenth century. Of course several walls were erected to contain them—all to no avail. It was on the crest of the Mongol wave that Genghis Khan (ca. 1167–1227) took Manchuria and the region of Beijing, swept aside the Xia empire, and at the same time drove into northern India and westward as far as Poland. Upon his death the Mongol empire was divided up, and his successors pursued their conquests in eastern Asia as well as in the west. It was Kublai (1260–1294) who founded the Yuan dynasty in 1277 and finished off the conquest of China. The Mongols, who were impervious to Chinese influences, practiced a discriminatory policy. They were eager to stimulate insurrections on all sides. Ironically, these movements soon led to the liberation of Chinese territories and the founding, in the year 1368, of the dynasty of the Mings.

Left: The Northern Wei, who were of barbarian origin like the Western Jins and some others, became one of the most powerful dynasties of these turbulent centuries. Their emperor Taiwudi (424–451) sits enthroned here among his ministers who each bear a jade tablet as a sign of his function.

Portrait of an empress, wife of Shenzong of the Northern Song dynasty, whose reign of nearly twenty years (1068–1086) was little more than a series of disastrous compromises aimed at appeasing the menacing Khitan and Jürchen tribes in the north.

His grandson, Huizong, at the beginning of the twelfth century, dealt the death blow to the prestigious 167-year Song dynasty following a period of gradual decline. In 1126 the Songs were forced to retreat from northern China and content themselves with a much diminished kingdom.

DAI WENBAO

OIRATS BURIATS UIGHO
KIRGHIZ
NAIMAN KARAKORUM
KERAITES

WESTERN LIAO (KARAKITAN)
1218

WESTE
1209

15th c.

WHY THE WALL WAS BUILT

Periodically throughout the ages, northern China has been overrun by nomadic horsemen, who thus became a perennial theme in Chinese art.

From the foregoing, it is clear that walls were built in and around Chinese kingdoms for century after century since early times. The fundamental reason for all this defensive construction was quite simply the conflict between the people in the Central Plains who lived on agriculture and the nomads to the north of China who relied on the raising of livestock.

Farmers are of course confined to their croplands—since farming, managing, and harvesting all require settled conditions—while herdsmen move about in search of grassland and water. These nomadic tribes would harass and plunder the stable areas of agricultural production, coming and going at will, making farming impossible unless some way were found to stop them. In order to protect agricultural development—the guarantee of stability in their lands—rulers in the Central Plains had tried various expedients, which could almost all be grouped under one of the following headings: (1) preemptive raids on nomadic tribes (difficult because of their exceptional mobility); (2) cultivation of peaceful relations with these northerners (expensive, sometimes a blow to Chinese pride, and in most cases short-lived at best); and finally (3) the erection of barriers to slow invaders and allow for systematic military defense. From the time of Qin Shi huangdi (third century B.C.), through the Han dynasty, especially under Emperor Wu, and the successive dynasties discussed in the previous chapter, the building of walls was the solution most consistently relied upon, the one best suited to the defense systems.

During the reign of Emperor Wen of the Han dynasty (second century B.C.), for example, a noted minister named Chao Cuo, in an essay on defense against the Xiongnu nomads, stated: "The Xiongnu

live on meat and cheese, wear furs, and possess no house or field. They move like birds and animals in the wild. They stop only at places which abound in grass and water, want of which will start them moving again. Today the Xiongnu are herding at several places and hunting along the frontiers, confronting Yandai, Shangjun, Beidi, and Longxi, waiting for a chance to make an intrusion once the garrison troops are decreased. Your Majesty is concerned about the border troubles. It will be profitable to you to dispatch generals and officials together with troops to govern the frontier areas. People should be selected to

MERKITES

MONGOLS

TARTARS

Two millennia of invasions from the north are schematized on the map below. The third-century B.C. Qin empire, with its capital at Xianyang, erected a wall against Xiongnu, Rong, and Di tribes (blue arrows). Under the Han dynasty (206 B.C. to A.D. 220), ruling from Chang'an and later Luoyang, wars were fought against encroaching Xiongnu and Xianbei tribes (blue), who were to remain a threat for nearly four more centuries. Turkish tribes—Uighurs, Khitans, Tanguts (Tungus) among them— invaded at various times during the Tang dynasty (618–907), and the Khitans (orange) settled near Beijing in 938 taking the name Liao. The Jürchen (green) in the twelfth century supplanted them and founded the Jin dynasty (1115–1254), only to be overrun in their turn by the Mongolian tribes (red) under Genghis Khan. The Mongols also conquered the

TUNGUS

MANCHU

XIONGNU 3rd c. B.C. to A.D. 87

XIANBEI

JÜRCHEN 1122/23

KHITAN 920

XIONGNU 4th c. A.D.

LIAOYANG

A (XIXIA)

15th c.

938

BEIJING

JIN 1215

Xixia kingdom that had been established in the northwest. The Mings drove the Mongol Yuan dynasty rulers out of China (1368) but were themselves to yield in 1644 to another northern ruling group, the Manchus (Qings).

1258

1126

XIANYANG

LUOYANG

KAIFENG

CHANG AN

During the Han dynasty (206 B.C. –A.D. 220), the Chinese applied the name Xiongnu (Huns) to all the proto-Turkish nomadic tribes living in the steppes. These fearsome horsemen, a torment and an obsession to the northern Chinese populations, were finally repelled by the Hans after many military campaigns.

settle along the border areas permanently, who can set up families and grow food grains while getting prepared against possible invasion by the Xiongnu. Then we can have high walls built with deep ditches dug, and we can prepare boulders and road blocks inside the walls. At strategically important points and passes we can set up minor cities with a thousand households each."

Some seven centuries later, in A.D. 487, in almost the same terms, an official named Gao Lu offered advice to Emperor Xiao Wen of the Northern Wei dynasty:

"The Northern Di people are brave but ignorant. They excel at field operations, but their weak point is the assault on cities. We must avoid their strong point while taking advantage of their weakness. The Di people live scattered in the open country by ponds and they are often on the move in search of grass and water. We ought to build the wall along the terrains north of the six strategical posts in order to stop the northern tribes. This wall, once completed, will bring profit for centuries. At the strategic points we can set up passes, beside each of which we shall build a small city. When the Di people come, we can defend the frontiers making use of the city

From ancient times [The Xiongnu] have left only
whitened bones in fields of yellow sand.
The house of Qin built the Wall
as protection from the Hu,
the house of Han has added signal fires.
These fires that never cease burning...

Li Bo (705–762)

The Quanrong barbarians, at the end of the eighth century B.C., conquered King You of the Zhou dynasty, a ruler famed for his frivolity and incompetence. They are shown here attacking Gaojing, the capital of this feudal state. The Zhou then retreated to the east and continued their rule.

Below: Twenty-five centuries after the Quanrong, the Jürchen, residents of what is now Manchuria, once more swept into China. Their leader Nurhaci, founder of the Qing dynasty, is shown here on a campaign.

Below right: Battle scenes at the Great Wall. It was no mean feat to penetrate the great barrier, especially if the barbarian force was of modest size and the Chinese guards were well trained. Many would-be invaders reached the wall but were stopped there.

and the garrison troop. If they do not come to take the city, they will get nothing; they will surely leave when they find themselves short of grass."

This same Northern Wei dynasty, incidentally, were themselves originally from northern barbarian stock. As soon as they settled in the Central Plains and ended their migrations, they too demanded stability. And as a defense against the new invasion threat, their chief resort was to build the wall.

With the coming of greater stability under the powerful Tang dynasty (beginning in A.D. 618), we find not only a slackening of interest in great walls, but—even more surprising—a scornful attitude toward the construction of such defenses. Li Shihmin, who came to power in 626, called a halt to patrols along the wall, described the structure as a monument devoid of strategic value, and when one of his generals routed the Turks, said to him "You are a better Great Wall than the one built by Yangdi" (an earlier emperor). The Tangs believed that only strong military offensives, and not defensive walls, were effective against troublesome neighbors.

Chinese princesses often became pawns in their country's diplomacy, and would be offered in marriage to leaders of neighboring barbarian states. The nomadic chieftain who received such a bride was usually honored by the chance to obtain such a token of Chinese glory and civilization, and the resulting goodwill could prove useful in maintaining truces. But China's princesses were also abducted at times by such suitors and a number of these women have become famous in Chinese art, drama, and literature, as in the two examples portrayed here. The young Han noblewoman shown mounted on a horse *(left)* is being

How then did the Mings come to revert to the ancient (and to the Tangs quaint and superstitious) tradition of wall-building? Under their strong rule (1368–1644), the wall came to assume a greater importance than it had done for centuries past, as the Ming emperors restored the wall over its entire length and maintained it in a state of military readiness for mile after mile, more consistently, more effectively, and for a longer period than any previous rulers had done. In order to explain their commitment to the Great Wall, we must review the history of the period leading to the Ming era, paying particular attention to the crucial invasions that left such enduring memories on the Chinese national consciousness.

The stability of the Tang rule was undermined beginning in the eighth century by a series of invasions from the west and north. Both the Tibetans and the Uighurs sacked Chinese cities in the year 763, and although they withdrew to their homelands, the Uighurs and other proto-Turkish peoples remained a threat until the 840s. The Tang dynasty was followed by a chaotic period period (907–960) in which various generals and petty despots ruled in quick succession, often controlling only small domains. Then there came

a split, which was to endure for two centuries, between north China, ruled by the Khitans, and southern China with its cultured life under the Song dynasty.

These Khitans, like so many of the nomadic herders through the centuries, invaded the area of Beijing (938), settled in the Central Plains, and assumed many Chinese ways, calling themselves the Liao dynasty. These people of Xianbei origin, speaking a Mongolian language and residing in Manchuria, found themselves gradually weakened by their more sedentary life

led off a captive by the Xiongnu in the year A.D. 195. Cai Wenji *(above)*, daughter of the scholar Cai Yong, is seen in captivity in the Xiongnu camp in Inner Mongolia in the late second century B.C. A cultivated young widow, a poetess and musician, she was married to a barbarian leader and bore him two children. The story says that she then was able to return to China.

It was Genghis Khan, 1167—1227 *(right)*, who gathered together the full force of the Mongols. By the beginning of the thirteenth century, his empire extended from Samarkand to Korea, and all of China north of the Yellow River was within his domain. His posthumous title was Taizu, the "Great Ancestor." He is seated here *(far right)* on the imperial throne with his wife and consort.

The Jürchen barbarians had ended the reign of the Northern Songs in founding the Jin dynasty. They were themselves swept away by the Mongols, who are depicted in this Mogul painting attacking a Chinese city. The canon in the foreground is an unlikely addition.

in China. Their borders did not long remain quiet. In the west, the Tangut, a Tibetan or Western Xia people, settled the Gansu area and collected tribute. By the early twelfth century the Khitans fell prey to new invaders, the Jürchen (or Nuzhen) under Akuta—a people whose descendants were the Manchus who ruled China centuries later. Not content with the northern Chinese kingdoms, these Jürchen (who established the Jin dynasty at their capital city of Yanjing near Beijing) also seized the Song emperor and court in 1125 or 1126.

All these invasions, related in compressed form in a brief survey such as this, tend to make one forget that there were long intervals of relative calm in between. There is no denying, however, that by the twelfth century these incursions by nomadic peoples were assuming a new character. Invasions tended increasingly to become occupations, leading to the foundation of more or less Chinese-style dynasties (the Liao, the Jin) lasting a century or more. Moreover, the new rulers from the north were now extending their territory farther throughout Chinese territory; the Jürchen penetration of the Song kingdom to the south was a prelude to far wider conquests later under the Mongols.

With the rise to power of Genghis Khan, these Mongols were to bring the most wide-ranging and convulsive changes, marking a culminating point in the tide of invasions in China from the ninth to the twelfth century. More serious yet, the Mongols—unlike earlier invaders—remained foreign, resisting the civilizing influences of Chinese culture. The Chinese, in turn, continued to consider these rulers as aliens.

The emergence and expansion of the Mongol empire constitute a remarkable tale, known far and wide thanks to the legen-

The submission of the barbarians *(above right)* or to the barbarians *(above)* was the last episode in a continuing struggle.

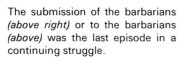

Even the barbarians had their heroine-princesses and their noble women. This warrior was from the Rouran, a particularly formidable tribe around the fifth and sixth centuries.

dary exploits of the terrible Genghis Khan. Born sometime between 1155 and 1167 as Temujin, he brought together a mass of proto-Turkish and Mongolian tribes and began to conquer large expanses of central Asian territory. By 1206 he was in a position to consolidate his rule over a confederation of peoples of the steppes, and in that year they met and conferred on him the title of Genghis Khan—"Greatest of Rulers," or "Emperor of All Men."

He seems to have had a thirst for glory which drove him to violent military conquest. The Mongols under this leader became an overwhelming military force, despite their relatively modest numbers (some 2.5 million total population, with an army of only about 250,000)—a result due partly to the terror inspired by their name alone. Many cities and kingdoms surrendered before an attack could even begin. Among the early Mongol victories was the conquest of the Tangut or Xia people at the western end of the Wall, in 1209. Two years later Genghis began his campaign against the Jin empire in north China.

The Great Wall proved an obstacle to Genghis Khan only at its most heavily fortified segment—at the gate of Juyongguan which led to the capital city of Yanjing. He penetrated the wall nevertheless, but could not take the capital, secure behind its forty-foot walls and its complex of towers and moats. After a prolonged siege, the

Mongols temporarily withdrew. They consolidated their position by winning wider territories in China, and finally, in 1215 —four years after their first attack—the capital city of Yanjing was theirs.

The Mongol expansion continued throughout China, Central Asia, and even beyond—undeterred by the death of Genghis Khan in 1227. By the end of the thirteenth century their empire stretched all the way across Asia, from Korea to Poland and Hungary in the north, and from south China to Turkey in the south. Their rulers vied with one another until the emergence of Genghis' grandson Kublai Khan as emperor in 1260. His vast domain was by then too great for effective control by one man, and he turned his attention to China, which he ruled with

great effectiveness. He united the whole of China, thanks to his conquest of the Song empire in 1279, and founded the Yuan dynasty. Until his death in 1295 the country was strong militarily and economically and saw considerable achievements in science and the arts. But the Yuan rulers nevertheless remained foreign, and under Kublai's successors the Mongol dominion suffered a decline, as the indigenous Chinese mounted increasingly powerful resistance movements. One of these, led by a certain Zhu Yuanzhang from southern China, drove the last of the Yuans from the capital city of Beijing, forced the Mongols back to the north of the Wall, and founded the Ming dynasty (1368).

The Mongols, having lost control of China to these southerners, nevertheless retained some of their former strength in the steppes and beyond and were able to mount offensives against the Ming (including a considerable attack in the year 1408). In the Mings' dynastic history we find this comment: "Once they had been driven out of China, the descendants of the Yuan dynasty (the Mongols) constantly endeavored to regain their lost domain. When the Yongle emperor [Zhu Di] moved the capital up north, the Great Wall was close by on three sides but the enemy became daily more troublesome.

Pursuing the conquest of southern China begun by Genghis Khan, Kublai Khan managed to complete the mission around 1278. He established his capital in Khanbalik (today Beijing), where he was visited by Marco Polo and where he proved himself to be an excellent—if somewhat severe—administrator. Despite his distrust of the Chinese, whom he kept as far away from government as possible, by the end of his reign (1294) he was already well assimilated into Chinese ways himself.

The defense of the Great Wall therefore became of leading importance as the Ming Dynasty wore on."

The Ming rule was thus threatened from the very beginning by these Mongol forces who had already overrun all of China in the past and whose century of rule was not yet forgotten. The need for strong military defense—particularly in the north—was thus, to the Mings, one of the basic facts of life, an essential element to their very survival.

Thus it was only to be expected that, during the Ming dynasty, yet another military adviser like those quoted from earlier periods at the beginning of this chapter, should have written yet another text urging his emperor, in terms by now quite familiar, to protect his northern frontier with a wall: "The minorities in north China who lead a nomadic life, and excel at horsemanship and marksmanship, often

The other great conqueror of China, Nurhaci, rallied the strength of the Manchurians to end the Ming dynasty. His task was made easier by the fact that the Mings had already been bled dry and undermined by intrigues.

The Chinese considered the court paid by foreign ambassadors, illustrated in this Tang fresco, as an acknowledgment of their sovereignty and proof of the power of their country.

The Manchu leader Nurhaci (below), 1559–1626, while pretending to be a loyal vassal to the Mings' "Celestial Empire," raised a nomad army and eventually declared war on China. Here he is seen, preceded by his musicians and surrounded by soldiers wearing the Manchu braided hair, entering a military campaign. Nurhaci died of wounds from one of these battles.

General Wu Sangui (below), during the last years of the Ming dynasty, led armies to defend the northeastern frontier against the most recent nothern enemy, the Qings of Manchuria who had often broken through the Great Wall and raided parts of the north China plain. Meanwhile, a rebel peasant

army under Li Zicheng, son of a village leader in Shaanxi, became an ever greater threat to the Mings. When the peasants seized Beijing, General Wu Sangui joined forces with the Qings. They defeated Li Zicheng and his rebel army and retook the capital in 1644. The Qing (Manchu) dynasty was thus founded.

attack and plunder the border areas, coming and going unpredictably. In the past dynasties troops were stationed there to guard the frontiers. We must make use of natural barriers such as mountains and rivers. Man-made barriers ought to be set up along the strategically important terrains. Our country has driven away the intruders, the Rong and Yuan, and is now unified. To hold our land together, we should set up a series of strategic posts—*zhen*—and station troops at each." And the writer, Wei Huan, concluded that it was essential to rebuild and lengthen the Great Wall.

This was not, however, the only method chosen by the Mings in their defense against the Mongols. They had recourse to all three of the defensive measures listed at the beginning of this chapter: preemptive raids, diplomacy, and wall-building. As an example of the first method, we find that Zhu Di, Emperor Chengzu, who moved the capital from Nanjing to Beijing to support his military maneuvers, personally led huge armies on northern expeditions on five different occasions to vanquish surviving Mongolian forces. In the autumn of each year he also sent out troops as far as two or three hundred kilometers (130 to 200 miles) north of the frontier, in order to set fire to wild grasslands and thus deprive the enemy of grazing land as well as fodder for their horses. Where diplomatic or peaceable efforts were concerned, we find that Emperor Chengzu in the early fifteenth century personally inquired into the customs and habits of the Jürchen tribes living in the northeast and seized every opportunity of exerting Chinese influence and control over them. Political and economic contacts were maintained with these people. This policy, indeed, had been adopted already by the first of the Ming emperors, Zhu Yuanzhang, who attempted to maintain good relations with the Mongolian princes and the Jürchen.

Along with these two basic methods, of course, the reliance on the defensive wall remained the major strategy of the Ming defense. The Great Wall assumed such importance that the first Ming emperor, Zhu Yuanzhang, dispatched nine of his own sons to the northern frontier to head the nine *zhen* or garrison divisions patrolling the defense line. Year after year, this emperor sent more troops northward and built more fortifications.

In view of the massive invasions the Chinese had experienced in the past, and particularly the Mongol domination that immediately preceded the Ming dynasty, it is not surprising that they resumed the age-old Chinese tradition of wall-building—and carried this effort to greater lengths than any previous rulers had done.

Nurhaci is also seen, in a more heated moment of battle *(left)*, leading his archers in a mounted attack. Upon his death in 1626, his son Abahai took command. Unable to take Beijing, which was so well fortified and defended, Abahai concentrated his efforts on Korea, which he subdued. But he was still unable, on returning to Manchuria, to wear down the Chinese resistance, and the Qings were kept out of China until 1644.

Above: A scene showing the storming of fortifications—one which would have been often experienced in the seventeenth century. Horses are even seen on the ramparts.

JEAN-PIERRE DRÈGE

GALLERY OF THE MING EMPERORS

TAIZU 1368–1398

ZHU YUANZHANG, otherwise known as Emperor Taizu, founder of the Ming dynasty (shown in the two portraits at right), was himself from very poor stock. Like many before him, he was quite adept at climbing the social ladder as far as the Imperial Dignity.

THE BUILDERS OF THE WALL

China under the Mings was similar to China today, with these notable exceptions: today's autonomous region of Inner Mongolia, the western regions of Qinghai and Xizang (Tibet), as well as the provinces situated more to the northwest—part of Manchuria. It was from these provinces that the Manchu armies emerged, although these territories had escaped from the clutches of the Mings long before their actual fall.

In the traditional history books, the Ming dynasty was often treated as a restoration, because it was a Chinese dynasty succeeding a period of Mongol rule over China.

It was during the ever-increasing rebellions at the beginning of the fourteenth century that Zhu Yuanzhang, destined to become the first Ming emperor, made his appearance. The rebel movements were organized around secret political-religious societies, the White Lotus, and, in particular, the Red Turbans. The leader of the Red Turbans, with whom Zhu Yuanzhang was allied, proclaimed himself emperor of a new, very short-lived, Song dynasty. After Zhu had succeeded in putting down rival movements, he founded the Ming dynasty in Nanjing. The very name "Ming," meaning "brilliance" probably has some Manichaean connotations. He took the name of Hongwu for the reign. The Mings and

later the Qings, unlike preceding dynasties, only used the single name for the era for each reign, thus becoming known by the name of the dynasty rather than by their own name.

The founder of the Mings, who would later be called Taizu, first applied himself to the task of expelling the Mongols. Indeed he chased them beyond the Gobi desert all the way to Karakorum. The reorganization of the empire, which was presented as a restoration, in fact depended heavily on certain institutions inherited from the Yuan dynasty. The population was divided into hereditary categories: peasants, soldiers, and skilled workers. When a member of one of these classes died, his family was obliged to supply his replacement. Military colonies, in which men worked at either agricultural or martial labor, were extended from the border regions to the interior of China. Segments of the population were transferred from the Yangzi region to the north, which was underpopulated owing to the ravages of war. Great projects were undertaken to recultivate, irrigate, and refoliate the land. But despite these efforts, grain provisions had to be sent all the way from the Yangzi valley, by the sea route along the Shandong coast. Unfortunately, the way was often impeded by violent storms and pirate raids.

SHAZHOU
GANZHOU
SUZHOU (JINQUAN)
YONGCHANG
LIANGZHOU
NINGXIA
XINING
TAOZHOU
XI'AN FU
MINZHOU
SONGPAN
CHENGDU FU
YUESUI
NINGFAN
YONGNING
HUICHUAN
GUIYANG FU
YUNNAN FU
GUILIN FU (JINGJIANG)
YULIN
TAIYUAN FU
SHUNTIAN FU
NINGYUAN
JIANZHOU
GUANGYANG
HAIZHOU
KAIZHOU
JINAN FU
KAIFENG FU
YINGTIAN FU (NANJING)
WUCHANG
HANGZHOU
NANCHANG FU
FUZHOU
GUANGZHOU FU
TAIWAN

HUIDI 1399—1403

Emperor Huidi (Zhu Yunwen) only reigned four years following his grandfather Taizu, and his reign was almost obliterated from history, or at least from the history books, by the successor who deposed him. (No portrait existing.)

CHENGZU 1403—1424

Emperor Chengzu (Zhu Di) was the uncle of Huidi. He took power in a veritable coup d'état. He installed the capital in Beijing, which he had reconstructed, and he was one of the chief architects of the northern border defense. In addition to being an excellent tactician

he was also a dynamic leader who managed to reestablish order in the affairs of state. In short, his reign (the Yongle era) was brilliant.

RENZONG 1425—1426

The emperor Renzong (Zhu Gaozhi) only reigned a year. He hardly had the time to relax the strong political and administrative pressure that his father had imposed on the country for over twenty years.

XUANZONG
1426–1436

YINGZONG
1436–1450/1457–1464

XIANZONG 1465–1487

XIAOZONG 1488–1505

WUZONG
1506–1521

EMPEROR XUANZONG (ZHU ZHANJI) initiated some successful reforms in the management of the empire and continued the reinforcement of the Great Wall begun by Chengzu.

The presumed son of Emperor Xuanzong. YINGZONG (ZHU QIZHEN) reigned for almost thirty years. He had a second line of defense (the interior Great Wall) constructed. Having been kept a prisoner for a year,

in 1450, by the Mongols after an unsuccessful expedition in the north, he was sequestered for several years on his return to Nanking.

DAIZONG (ZHU QIYU) was the provisional emperor during the capture and sequestration of his elder brother, Emperor Yingzong, from 1450 to 1457. Although he was often well advised, he was irresolute and could not deal with the events

unleashed by the restoration of his elder brother. (No portrait shown).

EMPEROR XIANZONG (ZHU JIAN-SHEN) was the eldest son of Yingzong. His control remained weak despite the brilliant military campaigns of the 1480s. It was around this period that southern China experienced an economic flowering.

Of simple, even ascetic, tastes,

EMPEROR XIAOZONG (ZHU YUTANG) was a rather diffident person. He undertook very little, both within the country and at its borders, but he was successful at thwarting intrigues.

EMPEROR WUZONG (ZHU HOUZHAO) was by temperament quite the opposite of his father: He was not very interested in state affairs, preferring often costly pleasures; in decision

Above: Wei Zhongxian was one of those eunuchs who played such an important role in the collapse of the Mings. He created a reign of terror while Xizong was emperor, but he was exposed and put to death by Zhuangliedi in 1627.

The government of Taizu was centralized and totalitarian, reflecting the origins of the emperor himself. From peasant stock, having neither personal resources nor family connections, Taizu could not bring himself to trust the high-ranking functionaries who were part of the intelligentsia. He even went so far as to distrust his own comrades in arms. He launched a systematic campaign of suspicion in which massive purges were carried out—such was the case of Hu Weiyong in which 15,000 people were implicated. His brutality found expression in the "court floggings," where out-of-favor public servants were publicly humiliated. A veritable secret police, the 'Brocade Brigade,' who spied, made arrests, tortured, and killed without trials, was created in 1382. Thus the entire power structure of China was concentrated in the hands of Taizu. The activities of public servants as well as members of the palace were strictly codified. Women and eunuchs who traditionally benefited from

their intimacy with the emperor to exert a secret influence over him, were kept far from political affairs by Taizu. Eunuchs were only recruited in small numbers from among the uneducated classes. However, these precautions were to prove in vain, since the eunuchs soon came to command almost all the control levers of power.

After Taizu's death in 1398, his grandson Huidi could not succeed in establishing his authority over his uncles, particularly Zhu Di, the Prince of Yan. After three years of civil war, Huidi was deposed and his uncle began a new reign known as Yongle (eternal joy). The new emperor, who was later called Chengzu, was most probably the son of a Korean concubine of Taizu. Huidi had done his best to weaken the power of the imperial princes, and Chengzu in his turn, did the same. The first emperor of the Mings had set up his principal capital in Nanjing and had made Kaifeng (Henan) the capital of the north and Fengyang (Anhui), where he was from, the central

SHIZONG 1522–1566   MUZONG 1567–1572   SHENZONG 1573–1620   GUANGZONG 1620   XIZONG 1620–1627

making he was rather capricious and handed over the control of state completely to a eunuch.

When Wuzong died without a direct heir, his cousin (ZHU HOUZONG) succeeded him, assuming the name SHIZONG. Authoritarian, but unlike his predecessor little disposed to take charge of the government, he did nothing to impede the Mongol incursions in the northwest and raids by Japanese pirates on the coast. His reign accentuated the decline of central power, and he himself was almost assassinated in 1542.

The reign of MUZONG (ZHU ZAIHOU) only lasted five years. It was largely thanks to his minister Zhang Juzheng that the empire enjoyed both a real peace and an economic boom.

The reign of SHENZONG (ZHU YIJU), which was at first very prosperous, began to crumble in 1580. An inability to cope either with threats from abroad or with financial, socio-political crisis was characteristic of the end of the sixteenth century.

GUANGZONG (ZHU CHANGLUO) reigned only two months and died most probably from poisoning.

The years that XIZONG (ZHU YOUXIAO) reigned were a series of retreats in the face of internal disorders and the mounting threat at the borders.

Although ZHUANGLIEDI, the last of the Ming emperors (1628–1643), showed greater resolve than his predecessors, he was too late. He died in captivity in 1646. (No portrait shown.)

Below: Emperor Yingzong inspecting his army.

capital. The new emperor transferred the principal capital to Beijing, which had until then been called Beiping (northern Peace). But this transfer only took place progressively as the Grand Canal from the Yangzi to the Yellow River was restored. The move helped to improve the transport of grains to the north which had been endangered on its sea route.

At Beijing, the emperor had the palace formerly occupied by the Yuans completely resurrected. This project lasted fourteen years and enlisted the labor of several hundred thousand workers. At the same time work on the mausoleum of Chengzu to the north of Beijing began. The first emperor had had his tomb constructed near Nanjing; Chengzu and his successors—with the exception of Daizong who was dethroned—were all buried in the same necropolis, known as the Thirteen Tombs (Shisan ling).

The reign of Chengzu was marked by an intensification of diplomatic and commer-

More than at any other time, occasional art—portrait painting—made great strides. This portrait *(opposite)* is of Empress Xiaolie, the wife of Shizong. It was she who saved her husband from the assassination attempted by the palace maids-in-waiting in 1542.

Under the Mings society experienced periods of great refinement. This was due to the emergence of a rather well-to-do urban bourgeoisie who arose on the crest of an economic, industrial boom. The traditional arts of intellectuals (poetry and painting) were somewhat neglected compared to those of the middle classes; in particular, novels had a great flourishing. Rich merchants aspired to the "good life" replete with grand-scale accoutrements, and consequently the art of decoration, synonymous with luxury, became more and more overdone and mannered.

cial activity on the seas. At the beginning of the fifteenth century the Chinese navy was still ahead of that of the Portuguese and Spanish. Seven expeditions were led by Zheng He, a Moslem eunuch from Yunnan who, between 1405 and 1433, made his way to Java, Sumatra, Ceylon, India, the Persian Gulf, and the ports of the Arab Peninsula. And he even managed to land on the coast of eastern Africa in the region of Mogadiscio.

During the reigns of Chengzu's successors, Renzong and Xuanzong, a period of lethargy set in, and a general retreat from

the seas as well as from the land began. The Mongol tribes, the Oirats or Wala, started to invade. In 1449 an expedition was launched by the eunuch Wang Zhen with the participation of the young emperor Yingzong. Owing to their total inexperience in the art of warfare, the expedition was a fiasco. The emperor was captured at Tuma (Hebei) by the leader of the Oirats, Esen. He remained a prisoner until 1457 when he was able, with great difficulty, to reclaim the title of emperor by unseating his brother who had replaced him.

From then on the factional discord unleashed by the eunuchs spread unabated. The influence of the eunuchs which the founder of the dynasty had gone to lengths to avoid had reached a height never before attained in the history of China. The only males to live in close proximity to the imperial family, they were able to benefit from the centralized and secret system to become the emperor's favorite agents. It was they who communicated all imperial decrees, either oral or written. Having collaborated with the secret police organizations instituted by the emperors, they

In imperial China, each dynasty had its share of new constructions ordered by the ruler: restoration or extension of the Great Wall, the creation of a new capital city, even the erection of dikes beside a river or other body of water. This last type of undertaking was often a matter of necessity rather than of royal ambitiousness, for Chinese rivers often follow lengthy courses across plains, and the loess silt which they carry can make high-water periods catastrophic. In this Ming copy of a painting that dates to the Yuan dynasty, we observe the various techniques used in the construction of dikes: stakes are sunk into the bank, while bundles of faggots are piled up as fill. The building of the Great Wall required the same kind of collective effort, and there is no doubt that the thousands of workers requisitioned for that defensive structure were as conscious of the danger from northern enemies as their country-men were of the disasters caused by overflowing rivers or those that changed course.

This map of Beijing, drawn up in the twenty-first year of the Wanli era (1593), is the oldest map of Beijing known today. The public works undertaken by Chengzu at the beginning of the fifteenth century when he made Beijing his capital are depicted here.

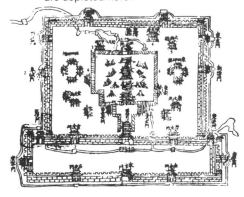

The military and animal statues which served as guards to some Ming imperial tombs do not have the same sculptural quality as the statuary of certain preceding epochs. They are no less spectacular, however, and the exotic and diverse nature of the animals was undoubtedly meant to convey the vast power of the defunct sovereigns.

Building palaces was a favorite and costly pastime of several Ming emperors. This one, seemingly suspended in the clouds as though in heaven, is in the same style as the Imperial Palace of the Forbidden City constructed by Chengzu.

ended up taking control of them. The number of eunuchs, which had been limited to 100 under the reign of Taizu, soon reached over 10,000; and with their increasing numbers came increasing power. The entire administration of the palace fell under their control. Xuanzong created a special school for the education of illiterate eunuchs, and recruited ten from this group to serve as his personal secretaries. Even outside the palace, the eunuchs led diplomatic missions and assumed military commands.

From the second half of the fifteenth century most of the emperors neglected the affairs of state. Social and economic changes came about with a development of trade and skill to the detriment of agriculture. The traffic in silks and porcelain bears witness to this fact. The last years of the Ming dynasty were particularly unstable: for in addition to the crises of political and financial management there were popular uprisings which ultimately allowed the Manchus to seize power.

And yet, more than the Great Wall still stands today as testimony to the truly resplendent years of the Ming Dynasty. The modern visitor to Beijing is overwhelmed by the magnificence and huge dimensions of the Palace of the Emperors, once called the "Forbidden City," and now the Palace Museum. Here it becomes especially understandable how the idea of a "Celestial Empire" could come into being—the idea that here was indeed the center of the universe. And not only in the city of the living emperors do we find work on such an enormous scale; for their tombs, 30 km (18½ miles) north of Beijing, are equally impressive witness to an ultra-aristocratic society whose members considered themselves to be the real Celestials of the Celestial Empire.

LUO ZEWEN

This map, which shows the line of the Great Wall on the Ordos Loop, was constructed on the initiative of the Jesuits living at the court of the Manchu emperor during the Kangxi period (early eighteenth century). The necessary surveys took no less than ten years, but the result was far superior to anything the Europeans produced in the West.

THE WALL ITSELF

These three tutelary gods were placed here to protect the Great Wall. Their sanctuary is at the

The Great Wall...a near-miraculous feat of engineering, eighth wonder of the world, its prodigious length is a record and a statistic. But where in fact does the wall begin, where does it end? This question is less easy to answer.

The Ming dynasty guard, in the period referred to as the Renaissance, might well have seen the wall as endless. At best, he would have imagined the possibility of two ends, one far away in the West, the other far, far to the East, both of them so remote as to lie at infinity. The sailor of old, making his way westward across the Yellow Sea, catching sight of the "Old Dragon's Head" tower, must have taken this for the beginning of the wall. For this is the place, a little west of the 120th meridian, where

Malanyu Pass, northeast of Beijing. They are not the only guards of such a long edifice, but their position could not fail to astonish: although they date from the Qing dynasty, they were placed at the very spot from which the Manchu invaders set sail.

the wall reaches the sea. And here the fortress of Shanhaiguan bears an inscription which can be translated "The First Pass in the World."

The wall looked different again to those in the far west, in the Yellow Desert on the

Chinese cartography, of which this book presents only the more recent examples (from the fifteenth century on), reached its high point at a very early period. Chinese rulers, under the strong impulsion of military and politico-economic requirements, never hesitated in mounting expeditions to perform geodesic research, which resulted in data of sometimes remarkable precision. Thanks to relatively sophisticated materials and mathematical knowledge that was quite advanced (especially in trigonometry), it was possible to create maps that would have been considered revolutionary in Europe at the time: from an early date Chinese maps had been using grid scales and symbols.

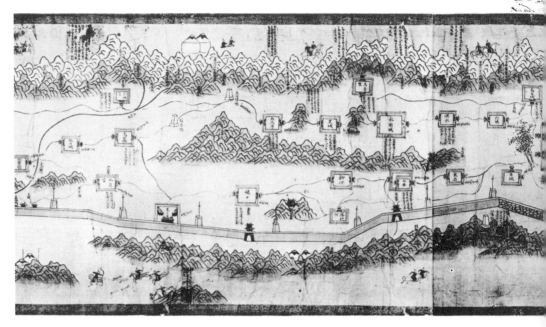

The origins of this map of the Great Wall, discovered in 1952 in the Lateran Museum, remain almost unknown. It was engraved during the Qing dynasty, and the part described in its six sections runs from Jiayuguan, the western end, to the Datong area in Shaanxi. The map points south; west is on the right. The Ordos Loop can be seen in the first quarter (starting from the right).

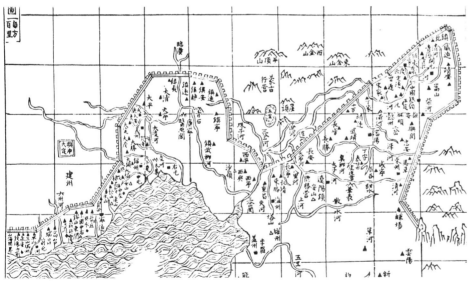

This extension of the Great Wall beyond Shanhaiguan towards the northwest appears in a sixteenth-century atlas of China. The wall follows the shoreline of the Bohai Sea and more or less encircles the central plain of Liaoning province. Written sources referring to this construction mention only earthen embankments planted with willow trees. (See also p. 127.)

89th meridian. To the pilgrims on the dangerous journey to the holy places of India the town and fortress of Jiayuguan ("the Jade Gate") was the end of the inhabited world, the limit of shelter and safety, the terminal point of the Great Wall. Beyond this gate lay a hostile world, a desolation inhabited by evil spirits. And yet, under the Han dynasty (third century B.C. to third century A.D.) the Great Wall had in

fact been prolonged three hundred miles beyond this "end"—though only temporarily.

The perspective was entirely different for the traveler coming in the opposite direction, along the Silk Road through central Asia, with a caravan from the distant lands of the West. For him the sight of Jiayuguan meant that he had survived the hardship, suffering, and danger of the journey. Here, on the far side of the wall, began the civilized, protected world, the goal of this journey: China.

At this point, too, begins the portrayal of the Great Wall in this book: at the western end/beginning, near Jiayuguan, beneath the icy peaks of the towering Qilian Mountains. The wall that we are tracing here— that of the Ming dynasty (1368–1644)— runs for some 12,000 *li* (6,000 kilometers or nearly 4,000 miles) through the most diverse geographical regions of north China.

Proceeding eastward from Jiayuguan, the wall makes its way through the 1,000 km (600 mile) long Hexi Corridor flanked by mountains. Though the wall rings the

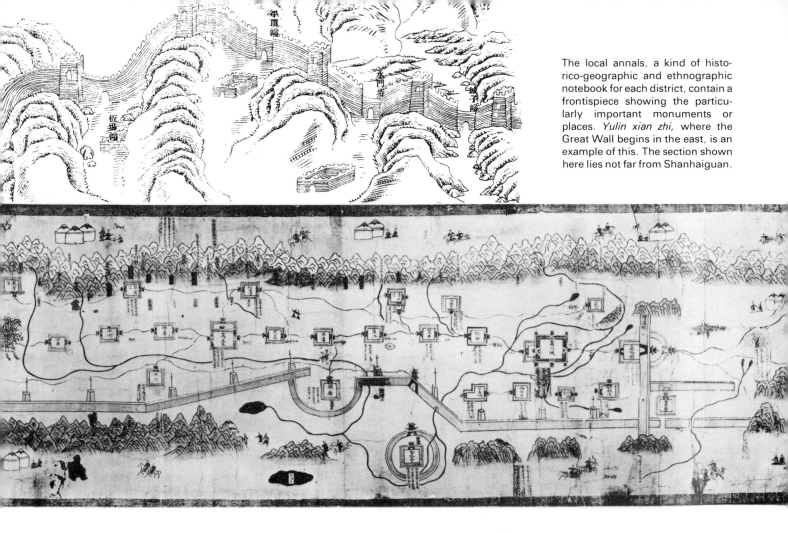

The local annals, a kind of historico-geographic and ethnographic notebook for each district, contain a frontispiece showing the particularly important monuments or places. *Yulin xian zhi,* where the Great Wall begins in the east, is an example of this. The section shown here lies not far from Shanhaiguan.

southern fringes of the Gobi Desert, the area is not entirely arid. The Gobi was once blessed with enough water to support belts of cultivated land as well as pasture ground and oases; and villages, towns, and cities sprang up from early times.

About thirty miles southeast of the town of Wuwei, a branch of the wall forks off to the south and forms the Yellow River loop, a giant arc which encloses the important town of Lanzhou, and then turns again to the northeast and, following the course of the Yellow River, rejoins the other branch of the wall at the point where it too reaches the Yellow River. There are various cartographic versions of the course of the loop at Lanzhou, as is the case with other stretches of the wall. The two walls meet again near the border between the province of Gansu and the Autonomous Region of Ningxia. Then the single wall turns northward along the Helan Mountains, crosses the Yellow River, which is here flowing north, and

The section of the wall shown on this map begins a bare 50 kilometers (31 miles) from the spot where the landscape drawing at the top of the page finishes. The numerous place names (principally military bases and passes) and the absence of information in the northern part can again be seen here.

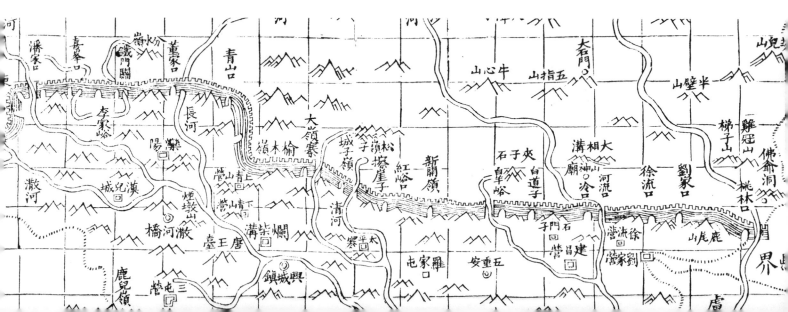

The map at right shows the Great Wall of the Ming dynasty in its full extent across twenty-one points of longitude. The map shows the sites, forts, garrisons, and cities which were, and many of which still are, important in China, with their rich artworks and architectural monuments. Still living in the vicinity of the wall are many ethnic groups with their diverse religious communities. There are countless sacred buildings, shrines, monasteries, holy mountains, and con-

secrated cities. In flora and fauna the region of the wall is particularly rich, including creatures such as this black-necked crane *(above)* native to the Qinghai highlands. *Below:* A typical garrison along the wall.

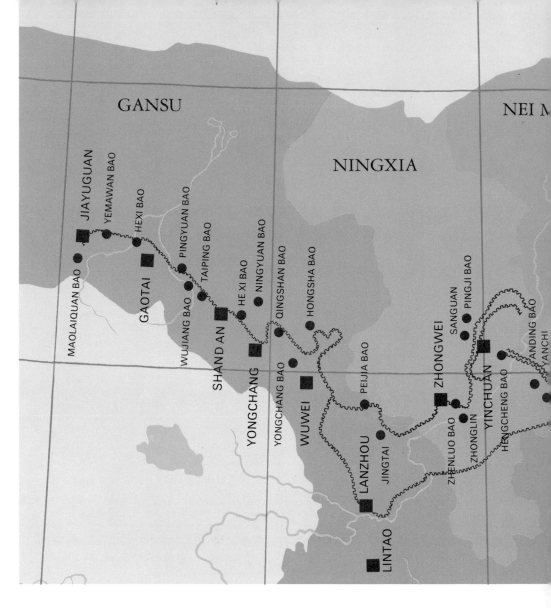

GANSU

NEI M

NINGXIA

JIAYUGUAN
YEMAWAN BAO
HEXI BAO
MAOLAIQUAN BAO
GAOTAI
WUJIANG BAO
PINGYUAN BAO
TAIPING BAO
SHAN DAN
HE XI BAO
NINGYUAN BAO
YONGCHANG
QINGSHAN BAO
HONGSHA BAO
YONGCHANG BAO
WUWEI
PEIJIA BAO
LANZHOU
JINGTAI
ZHENLUO BAO
ZHONGLIN
ZHONGWEI
SANGUAN
PINGJI BAO
YINCHUAN
HENGCHENG BAO
ANDING BAO
YANCHI
LINTAO

follows it southward again, to the northern boundary of the province of Shaanxi.

Here we are in the Hetao, or Ordos, area of the Yellow River valley, where the river runs a zigzag course. Over a stretch of some 2,000 km (1,200 miles) the wall snakes its way along the Yellow River and, as we have seen, crosses the river at several points. Then, after winding through the desert, the loess plateau and grasslands, and crossing the Yellow River, the wall divides into two parallel segments commonly referred to as the Inner and Outer Walls of the Ming dynasty. The north fork, crawling across the Fengzhen hills at the foot of the Yinshan Mountains (boundary between the Mongolian Autonomous Region and Shanxi province), comes to an end at Juyongguan near Beijing (Peking), north of the Taihang Mountains. The southern fork crosses the loess plateau of northern Shanxi, then the Taihang mountain range, before converging with the northern branch of the wall at Juyongguan.

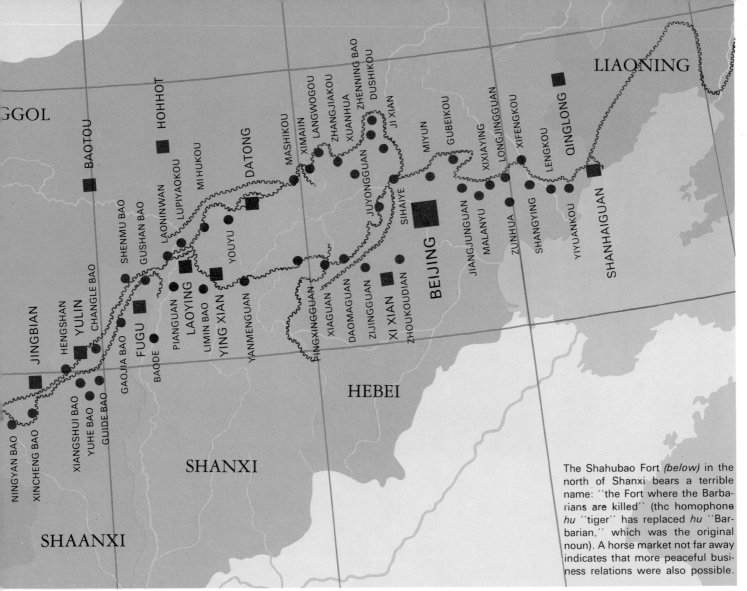

The Shahubao Fort *(below)* in the north of Shanxi bears a terrible name: "the Fort where the Barbarians are killed" (the homophone *hu* "tiger" has replaced *hu* "Barbarian," which was the original noun). A horse market not far away indicates that more peaceful business relations were also possible.

Between the area of Beijing and the sea lies the most magnificent, most solid, and best preserved section of the Great Wall of the Ming dynasty, a 600 km (400 mile) stretch extending eastward along the high ridges of the Yanshan Mountains to Shanhaiguan.

The wall was of course, first and foremost, a military rampart, a line of defense. And its 6,000 km length bristled with hundreds of gateways and passes, thousands of watchtowers, military stations, fortresses, and garrisons. During the Ming dynasty, when the defenses still functioned, the troop forces manning the wall were said to number one million. They were organized in nine areas of military jurisdiction, the so-called *zhen* (garrison posts), each of which controlled a number of guard stations which varied according to local strategic needs.

Anyone traveling the length of the wall in its entirety would find himself traversing not only the most diverse landscapes that China has to offer, but also some of the country's historically most significant areas. From the most ancient times until comparatively recently, these areas have witnessed the interpenetration, intermingling, and development of diverse nationalities which have come to constitute the peoples of China. Important discoveries have been unearthed by archaeological excavations on both sides of the Great Wall. From the tombs of the Jin dynasty near Jiayuguan, modern-day explorers have emerged with beautifully carved bricks painted in bright colors. The Neolithic painted pottery excavated in the vicinity of Lanzhou and in the Hexi Corridor is beautifully formed. Important relics of the Huns, dating back 2,000 years, have been brought to light along the Great Wall in the areas of Ningxia Autonomous

The section of the wall that winds over Mount Badaling to the northwest of Beijing is among the best preserved, and the one usually now shown to foreign dignitaries passing through. Standing on top of this construction, it would have been possible to see the Manchu armies passing in 1644 as they crossed the Juyongguan Pass to take Beijing.

The wall twists like a dragon; following the smallest irregularities of relief, it disappears and reappears on the horizon. The heavy task of the laborers, who had literally to work like ants, and the endless calculations the architects had to make may be imagined from this reconstruction.

There has been a revival of interest in the Great Wall in recent years in China. The scattered "little walls" have also been the subject of study, as for example here in the north of Huhehot (Inner Mongolia), where research has been carried out on a construction thought to date from the third century B.C. Shown in this photograph (second right) is Professor Luo Zewen.

Region, Shaanxi province and the Mongolian Autonomous Region. It was from these regions that the Qin kingdom was formed and the unification of China into the First Empire began—an event of the utmost importance for the country's history.

Local history—the stories of the many ethnic groups and political entities which have flourished along the wall—has also left behind eloquent artistic and archaeological testimony. The well-known ancient cities in northern Shaanxi, the Yunguang Grottoes of the Toba Northern Wei dynasty at Datong in Shanxi province, and the temples of the Liao and Jin dynasties are all immortal masterpieces. Many passes and ancient battlegrounds still remind us today of the often heroic resistance to the Liao invasion during the Song dynasty. And above all Beijing, which reigned as capital city of the dynasties of Liao, Jin, Yuan, Ming, and Qing during the final years of Chinese feudal society, is remarkably rich in archaeological discoveries and historic sites from those times. Throughout the segment of the wall running north from Beijing we encounter ruins of the Yan and Zhao states from the Warring Kingdoms period.

On both sides of the wall, too, are found cities and towns, many of them important trading centers in past eras. The counties of Wuwei, Zhangye, Jiuquan, and Dunhuang on the Hexi or Gansu Corridor province, figured as key points on the Silk Road which linked China with the West. Major provincial capitals neighboring on the wall include Lanzhou, Yinchuan Xi'an, Taiyuan, Huhehot, and Shenyang; and of course Beijing, capital of the People's Republic of China, stands just inside a strategically crucial segment of the Ming wall. For several centuries there were more than one hundred major trade centers along the wall for livestock, draft animals, and other goods.

A vestige from China's great past, testimony to the strength and durability of her people, the Great Wall repays a thorough study at close range, such as will be found on the diagramatic representation of it on the ensuing pages. Here it will be seen at a glance just how immensely different the wall is along its great length—to what enormous heights it climbs, how it crosses the Yellow River four times in all, and then plunges down again to sea level.

There are innumerable myths and legends connected with the wall, which are even to this day dear to the hearts of the Chinese people, and which have been immortalized in works of literature, and have enriched and enlivened the theater. Such, for instance, is the legend telling how a helpful dragon traced out the course of the wall for the workforce, over the mountains and across the valleys, and how the builders subsequently followed the tracks of this dragon. There are also many songs and poems—even Mao Zedong composed one once when he flew over it.

The careful scrutiny of this prodigious structure across its thousands of miles can tell us a great deal—can indeed unlock many of the secrets of China herself.

Opposite: This last bastion is both immense and luxurious. Carts could gain access to the pavilions built on the ramparts by means of the sloping ramp. *Below:* The sun sets on Jiayuguan, the last fortress to the west. This is the "Heroic Pass in the Sky," as the inscription on this stele shows. *Bottom:* The Qilian mountain range; in the foreground, Jiayuguan Fort itself.

THE WEST END OR THE BEGINNING

Jiayuguan Pass was a place of strategic importance at the western end of the Great Wall built by the Ming dynasty (1368–1644). The pass is located at the foot of Jayu Hill 25 miles (40 kilometers) west of Jiuquan in today's Gansu province. South of it lies Qilian Mountain, which remains snow-capped throughout the year. The Great Wall stretches west from Wuwei, Gansu province, through Qilian Mountain, up to Jiayuguan Pass. North of the pass are the Mabi Hills and deserts. An oasis, a clear spring, and farmland are in front of the pass. Thus it was possible for soldiers to have fresh drinking water and to grow crops.

The fort of Jiayuguan Pass stands in a valley 1,773 meters (5,817 feet) above sea level. Wide in the west and narrow in the east, it is also slightly ladder-shaped. It is 640 meters (yards) in circumference. Standing 10 meters high, the walls were durable, although built of rammed earth, except the gate towers, fortresses, and crenels, all of which were laid with bricks.

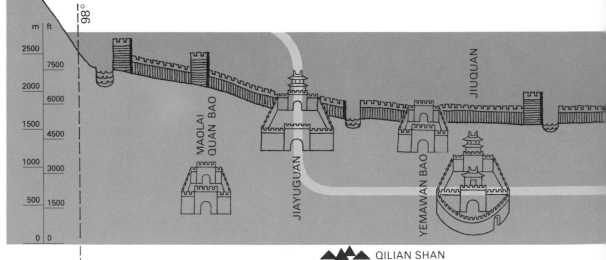

QILIAN SHAN

The pass has a fort with two gates: the eastern gate named Guanghua Gate and the west gate named Rouyuan Gate. On the top of each gate is a three-story tower seventeen meters high. The gate tower with painted pillars and carved beams has a roof with a single eave curled up at the corners, which blends the traditional styles of two-slope and four-slope roof. It looks more magnificent than the gate tower of Shanhaiguan Pass. Outside Rouyuan Gate is an outer gate which serves as the gateway to Jiayuguan Pass. On the top of this gate formerly was hung

a horizontal plaque inscribed with the words "First Fortified Pass on Earth." Jiayuguan Pass with this plaque and Shanhaiguan Pass with a plaque inscribed with the words "First Pass on Earth" stood at the western and eastern ends of the Great Wall, 5,000 kilometers (3,000 miles) apart. But it is a pity that the gate tower and its plaque at Jiayuguan Pass were destroyed in 1928. The monument inscribed with the words "Strongest Pass on Earth" now outside the west gate of Jiayuguan Pass was erected in the fourteenth year of the Jiaqing reign of the Qing dynasty (1809). Jiayuguan Pass was built in the fifth year of the Hongwu reign of Emperor Taizu of Ming (1372) but later was once abandoned. It was repaired and strengthened in the second year of the Zhengde era (1507) and eighteenth year of the Jiajing reign (1539). It was the first fortification commanding the Gansu Corridor. West of Jiayuguan Pass are the remains of the Han Great Wall which was built by Emperor Wudi (140–87 B.C.). In the early Western Han dynasty the Xiongnu, a minority nationality in northern China at that time, constantly harassed the domain of Han.

The emperor launched a war of counter-offensive against the Xiongnu by sending Zhang Qian as an envoy to the Western Regions. Many states in the Western Regions established friendly relations with the Han dynasty. In order to protect his domain against the invasion of the Xiongnu and to ensure the smooth traffic and security of the Gansu Corridor, the emperor sent workers to Hexi (in present-day Gansu province) to build a wall going west from the vicinity of today's Baotou through Jiuquan, Yumen, and Dunhuang up to Yanze (present-day Lop Nur). For more than two thousand years from the second century onward, large amounts of Chinese silk yarn and fabrics and other commodities were transported along the Gansu Corridor and across Congling (the Pamirs) and sold to central Asia and Europe. This route became known as the Silk Road. The Silk Road played an important role in history: it promoted friendly contacts between China and Asian, European, and African countries and economic and cultural exchanges between China and the West.

Left: a young Kazakh, member of an ethnic minority who traditionally settled around the western end of the Great Wall.

In these scantily wooded regions, every little thing counts: this plant has been used as fuel by the inhabitants of the Jiayuguan region for centuries.

This brick from a tomb dating from the third century A.D., discovered in Jiayuguan in 1972, shows that agriculture has always been an important part of the economy of north Gansu, as has animal farming *(far right)*.

Unshaded wall = less well-defined stretches

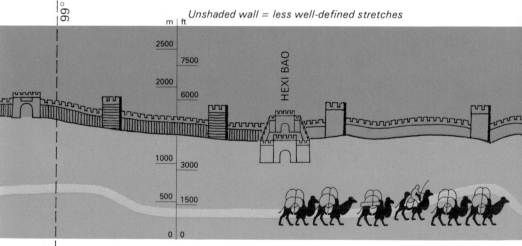

From time to time living evidence of past activities of the area are discovered, such as this stele bearing the names of the master masons at the time of the restoration of the walls (fourteenth century); and this motif *(right)* from the seal of a Ming general. The starting point of the Ming wall was in the jurisdiction of the Suzhou garrison, under the Gansu subcommand, one of the nine subcommands along the wall.

Far right: Another time, another place: oil-yielding plants are extensively cultivated in the Jiayuguan region.

THE RUINS OF LUOTO CITY

Within this area (99th to 100th meridian) the Great Wall stretches from Jiayuguan Pass across the Beida River to the south of Jinta county, then makes its course eastward from Gaotai county and reaches the ancient city of Zhangye. The county of Gaotai was a strong point along the ancient wall and even today one can find many historical remains in its adjacent areas. On the Gobi Desert southwest of the county seat are the citadel ruins of Luoto (Camel) city, Xusanwan city, and Yangtigou city, all of which were closely associated with the Wall. And Luoto is by far the biggest of the three. The site of Luoto lies on the Gobi Desert 22 kilometers (15 miles) southwest of the Gaotai county seat. At one time, it would have served as a post to station troops in order to open up wastelands or to protect the frontier.

According to archaeological investigations this ancient city had flourished for six or seven centuries since the period of the Han and Tang dynasties. However, it began declining after the ninth century

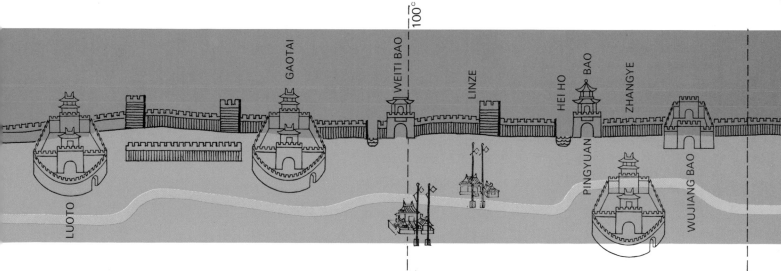

and was gradually deserted. Luoto city (which was of course not its original name) was named after the camel because it was haunted by herds of camels after it fell into ruins.

The ruins of Xusanwan are only 5 kilometers (3 miles) away from Luoto city. Measuring 66 meters from east to west and 84 meters north to south, it is much smaller than Luoto city. It seems to be a small-sized citadel attached to the latter for quartering troops. The exact date of its founding remains to be determined.

73

ZHANGYE: AN ANCIENT CITY

Within the area from the 100th to the 101st meridian, the Great Wall traverses its course from Gaotai county through Linze county to Zhangye county, goes eastward from Zhangye, and then reaches Shandan county.

Zhangye is located on the middle of the Hexi Corridor. Since Emperor Wu of the Han dynasty established the four prefectures on the Corridor, it was one of the politically and militarily important cities in western China and is now the seat of the prefectural government.

The section of the Great Wall here was built in the period of 121–111 B.C., which corresponded with the time when Emperor Wu sent his envoys to the Western Region. The Ming dynasty added another section to the wall in this area, thus enabling the city of Zhangye to become a militarily strategic point called Gansu Zhen—one of the Jiuzhen (the nine greater military areas during the Ming dynasty). It belonged to the defensive zone of Gansu and Suzhou (the modern Jiuquan) and had jurisdiction over the section of the wall on the Hexi Corridor. Naturally, this area is very rich in cultural relics and archaeological remains. Famous among them are the city of the Heishuiguo ("State of Black Water"), the Temple of the Great Buddha, the Bell Tower, and the Bronze Bell and Wooden Pagoda of the Tang dynasty. (In fact, only the two upper tiers of this are made of wood, but this alone qualifies it as one of very few such remaining.)

Since Zhangye city has existed for two thousand years on the vital communication line which links up China and the West, many relics concerning the city have been discovered in this area and some nearby places. For instance, the tally unearthed from Juyan (Edsen) in Echina Banner, Inner Mongolia, is a directive issued by a general residing at Zhangye city to the garrison troops that were stationed at Juyanhai (Edsen Git) to guard the wall during the Han dynasty. In addition, the local archaeological finds include bronze cannons manufactured in the Yongle era of the Ming dynasty (1399–1402) which were used to protect the wall. Some of the wall paintings at Dunhuang grottoes depict the tour of inspection of the prefectural officials in Zhangye.

The town of Zhangye, situated at the north entrance of the Gansu or Hexi Corridor, retains signs of its past history as a stage on the Silk Road and the road to Buddhism: mingled Buddhist and traditional mythological motifs decorate this Tang bell and bell tower. The tower, originally called Jinyuanlou and Gulou (Drum Tower), stands at the

Unshaded wall = less well-defined stretches

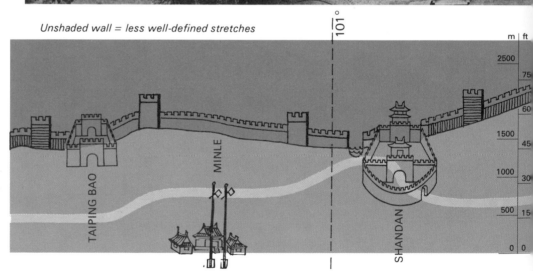

center of the city proper of Zhangye. It was set up in the second year of the Zhende era (1507) of the Ming dynasty, which occurred at the time when the Ming rulers strengthened the defense of the Great Wall in the Hexi Corridor. The two-storied bell tower is a structure with double eaves and a hip-conical roof.

The Zhangye Pagoda *(bottom),* built of bricks and wood, has defied the ravages of time with its eight stories, reaching a height of 50 meters (164 feet).

A large part of the Gansu wall, built simply of rammed earth, has not weathered well. The section to the northeast of Minle is the best preserved. A view of the wall in this area is shown below. Of course, this is not a part of the wall that is normally accessible to tourists.

Not far from Zhangye, the town of Minle also retains traces of Buddhist devotion, like this sanctuary built during the Yuan dynasty (1277—1368), a well-preserved work of impressive dimensions. The town of Minle stands slightly to the south of the Great Wall; in the county of Minle are found ruins dating to the Neolithic era.

SHANDAN AND YONGCHANG

The Great Wall between the longitudes 101° and 102°, which happen to coincide with the towns of Yongchang and Shandan, is a fairly well-preserved section in the Hexi Corridor. It stretches along, and sometimes crosses, the Lanzhou-Xinjiang highway, accompanied by beacontowers and beaconmounds. Both the wall and towers were built of rammed earth, which are solid and hard enough to challenge spade and shovel. Other archaeological sites and relics can also be found in the area nearby. Among them the Neolithic sites at Minle county, ruins of Yonggu city, tombs of the Han dynasty, and the Tongzisi Shangtianle cave temples which are of great archaeological significance.

The Great Wall skirts the county seat of Yongchang and then bends northward, following with the Shiyang River, into the desert. Around the county town is scattered with historical sites and cultural relics. Five kilometers away from the town stands a square, hollow brick pagoda dating from the Tang dynasty. At 1,200 years old, it is the earliest brick pagoda on the Hexi Corridor. About one kilometer from the city is a willow-lined spring pool called Beihaizi. The pool has long been

These white-lipped deer, a very rare and protected species today, live in mountain ranges above 4,000 meters (13,000 feet) to the south of the Great Wall, such as the Qilian Mountains. Their horns can grow to an imposing length of 1 meter (40 inches). The Chinese attribute great healing qualities to them.

The Gansu Corridor, or Hexi Corridor, is the name given to the long valley in northwestern China along which the westernmost portions of the Great Wall run. To the north are the Mongolian highlands; to the south, the spectacular Qilian Mountains *(right)* which reach a peak of 19,468 feet (nearly 6,000 meters) at their highest point. This region is also shown on the early eighteenth-century Lateran map *(above),* which is further described on page 62.

praised for its beauty. Buildings were set up around it including a pagoda 31 meters high still standing after five centuries.

Many sections of the Great Wall which travels through Yongchang county are in a state of good preservation. The wall near Beihaizi still measures 7 m high and 5 m wide (23 × 16 ft.), and moreover, the battlements on the wall are still existing—something seldom seen elsewhere on the 1,000-kilometer (600 mile) defense line of rammed earth in Gansu. Here also lie ruins of the beacon towers of the Han dynasty, some of which were still employed by the Ming garrison, together with those newly built.

WUWEI

Wuwei, in the central part of present-day Gansu province, is the convergence of the Lanzhou-Xinjiang railway and the Yinchuan-Xinjiang line. The Great Wall passes through this area in the north and the east. The Xiongnu were active here in the early days of the Han dynasty. Shuofang prefecture was established by the Han emperor Wudi in the second year of the Yuanshuo era (127 B.C.). On many occasions people were moved from elsewhere to reclaim the land and repair the Qin Great Wall on the northern banks of the Yellow River. After General Huo Qubing drove back the Xiongnu and obtained the vast areas west of the Yellow River (known as the Gansu Corridor), new fortresses were built along with political and economic construction. In 115 B.C. Jiuquan prefecture was created, followed by Wuwei prefecture. Soon afterward Wuwei prefecture was split into two— Wuwei and Zhangye—and Jiuquan prefecture into another two—Jiuquan and Dunhuang. These were known as the four prefectures along the Gansu Corridor. In Tang times, land was reclaimed on a large scale in these prefectures and ditches and canals were dug to water the fields. As a result, both animal husbandry and agriculture flourished.

In October 1976, many bronzes, gold objects, and silver seals were discovered in an Eastern Han dynasty (A.D. 25–220) tomb at Leitai north of the county seat of Wuwei. The bronze figures include 39 horses, 14 chariots, 17 warriors, and 28 maids and slaves—a splendid display indeed. The necks of some of the bronze horses were engraved with words reading:"A riding horse and a groom belonging to Mr. Zhang, Officer of a thousand soldiers in Zhangye." Some human figures are inscribed with such as "Mr. Zhang's slave" or "Mr. Zhang's maid." The inverted characters engraved on two silver seals were made out to be "Seal of General." These characters show that the host of the tomb was a Han official in defense of the Great Wall and the country.

In November 1972, volumes of medical books made of pine and poplar slips were excavated from an eastern Han tomb at Hantanpo in Wuwei county. These slips are generally 23 centimeters (9¼ inches) long. The contents include more than thirty complete prescriptions related to

acupuncture and moxibustion, internal medicine, surgery, the five sense organs (ears, eyes, lips, nose, and tongue), and gynecology. These prescriptions list more than one hundred varieties of medicines, including herbal, animal, and mineral substances. A rare find in China, these complete medical data also prove the cultural level attained in the Wuwei area. Above-the-ground relics in Wuwei include belltowers in the Great Wall built in the Ming dynasty. There is also a monastery on a loess terrace on the outskirts of the county town.

LINTAO AND LANZHOU

Mention of the Great Wall often reminds one of the name Lintao, for that was the starting point of the walls built in the Qin dynasty (221–206 B.C.).

During the Three Kingdoms (A.D. 220– 280) Jiang Wei, the Han general who succeeded to the will of the then late Prime Minister Zhuge Liang, made numerous offensives on the Kingdom of Wei. In A.D. 254 the general led his troops from Longxi (now Shaanxi) and defeated Wei forces after beseiging Gunwu.

The name Lintao (lin meaning "to reach") was derived because the township borders on the River Tao. The place was famous for the production of a fine stone which made excellent ink slabs, and for this reason the name "Tao Slab" had been a hallmark of fine quality, which had been cherished as one of the "four treasures in the scholar's studio"—paper, ink, writing brush, and ink slab. Highest-quality Chinese ink slabs include the "Duan Slab" made in Duanzhou and the "Han Slab" with its stone from Hanzhou. Coming into popular use in the Song dynasty (960–1279), long after the other two species had won widespread reputation, the Tao ink slab is of excellent quality. Of emerald color, the stone is very fine-grained. It is mostly quarried in the bed of the River Tao where the water is the

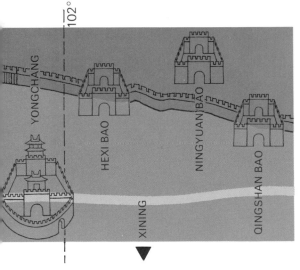

The Hans were the first to move the central Asian boundaries back and to spread Chinese influence there. The small-scale models of clay houses *(above)* that can be found in the tombs of this region are classic examples of funeral decoration. The aim of these objects was to provide the deceased with a familiar setting; now they are valuable material to study the way of life and architectural techniques of this period.

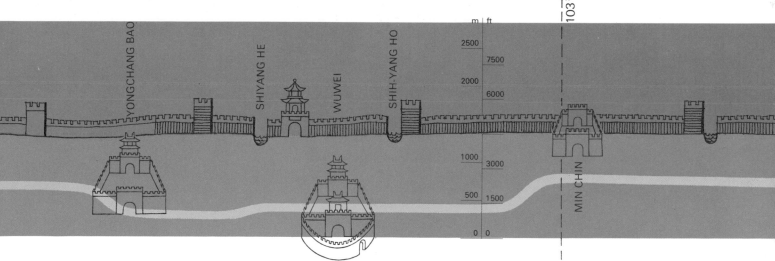

YONGCHANG BAO SHIYANG HE WUWEI SHIH-YANG HO MIN CHIN

These horsemen and horse-drawn carts *(above)*, which are also funeral trappings, are a mark of the high social rank of the occupant of the tomb. As this galoping horse *(right)* shows, funeral statuettes had reached an artistic peak by the end of the Han dynasty, even in the far-flung Gansu region where they were discovered. But did the large statuary equal that of the Qins four centuries earlier?

The present-day inhabitants of this region: Young woman of the Baoan ethnic minority of Gansu, and a Mongolian horseman from the Siziwang region, near Huhehot, the capital of Inner Mongolia.

Opposite: Before being put to death by the successor to Qin Shi huangdi, General Meng Tian won renown by building walls and defending the borders at the end of the third century B.C.

deepest. This involved high cost and limited the productivity, making the ink slab still more rare and valuable.

Though the Qin great walls started at Lintao, what now survives is a wall which snakes round the north side of Lanzhou, a city to the north of Lintao. Lanzhou, now the capital of Gansu province, was called Juncheng Jun (jun meaning "prefecture") in ancient times. It had been a major northwestern city since the Han dynasty (A.D. 206–220). From here one travels to Shaanxi province via Pingliang in the east, and beyond the Jiayuguan Pass on the west there is the Uighur Autonomous Region in Xinjiang (Sinkiang). Flanked by the Yellow River on its north, for two millennia the city had been a hub of east-west communication. In those days the only bridge available was a pontoon supported by boats or rafts, and this was what a poet called "the only bridge over the Yellow River under Heaven." Now the river is spanned by a giant steel bridge which takes busy traffic, both vehicular and pedestrian, overlooking the turbulent muddy waves.

From here the Yellow River goes through Ningxia province and the Inner-Mongo-

Unshaded wall = less well-defined stretches

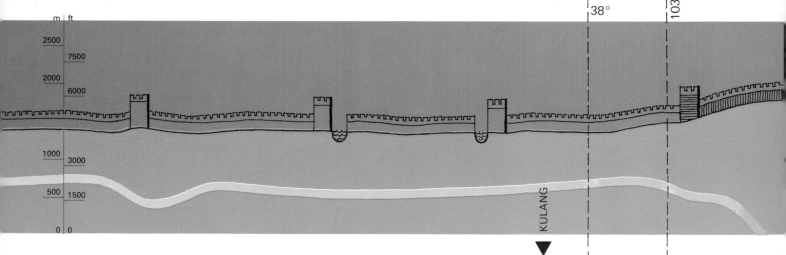

38°   103

KULANG

The town of Lanzhou experienced many tragic hours, by reason of its strategic position in the middle of the Gansu or Hexi Corridor. This position also provided its wealth, as the fine buildings in the city demonstrate. The surrounding region is noted for its animal farming. In this photograph *(right)* a southern Gansu herdswoman of Yugu nationality poses with a kid.

lian Autonomous Region, where it flows along the borderline between Shaanxi and Shanxi and enters Henan before making a loop. This is known as the "Bend of the Yellow River," or "the River's Bend." The region of the River's Bend, thanks to good irrigational facilities, is of rich soil and makes good farm yield. This has been referred to as "the only blessing of the Yellow River despite its 100 scourges."

Outside the city of Lanzhou lies a mountain called Gaolan, where the famous general Huo Qubing of the western Han

dynasty (206 B.C.–A.D. 23), in the wars against the Huns, encamped his troops and won a great victory. According to The History of Han, the general was richly rewarded for his feats by Emperor Wudi of Han.

A legendary tale has been told of General Huo Qubing's military adventures at Gaolan. When the army reached the hill of Mount Gaolan, tired and thirsty, they found the place devoid of any source of fresh water. This caused great anxiety and despair. In agitation General Huo hit the ground continuously with his whip. Presently five streams of spring gushed out from the spots the whip touched. Therefore the mountain was also known as the Mountain of Five Springs.

THE "LANZHOU LOOP"

Any invader who took Lanzhou would be master of Shaanxi province and the whole Chinese part of the Yellow River basin. All the successive Chinese rulers were aware of this danger and tried to make provision for it. The result today is an extremely elaborate system of walls in this region, as shown on these two maps.

Qin Shi huangdi, at the end of the third century B.C., was the first ruler to build a wall, which began at Lintao (see photograph) and joined the Yellow River and the Yinchuan region in the north. Today it is often impossible to detect the course of these walls. The smaller of the two maps is based on the work of Professor Jacques Gernet. At right is

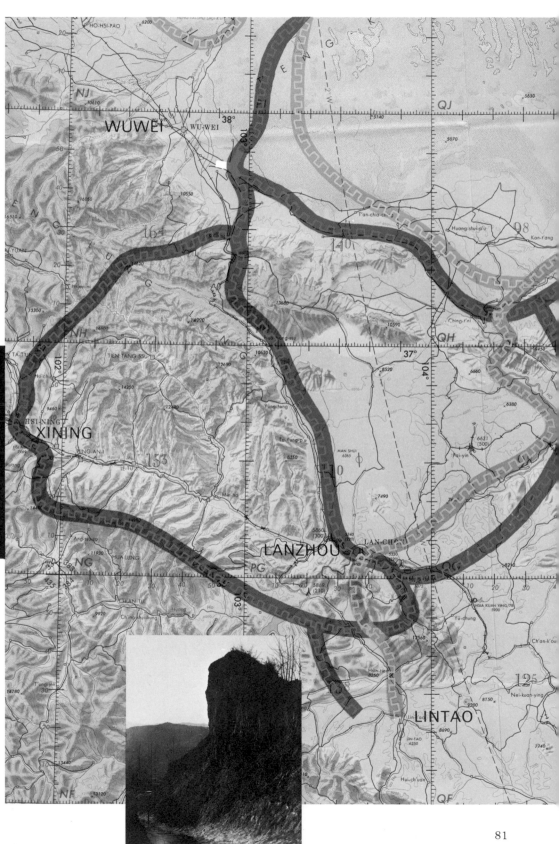

an attempt to superimpose this wall network upon a modern map: in yellow, the wall of Qin Shi huangdi; blue, the Han dynasty wall (206 B.C.–A.D. 220); red, the Ming wall (1368–1644). The course of the walls is in many places uncertain, and we have relied heavily on the travel descriptions of J. B. William Geil and the map sketches by Henry F. Ridley (early twentieth century). Additional details were derived from General Staff maps from the period 1900–1910, as well as the map reproduced at right, from the U.S. Defense Mapping Agency Aerospace Center, St. Louis (1974).

81

Although pandas mostly live in the more southerly province of Si-chuan, a few are to be found in the south of Gansu, in the area of the Bailong, a sub-tributary of the Blue River. These animals are often given in friendship to other countries by the Chinese authorities and have come to symbolize the opening of China to the modern world.

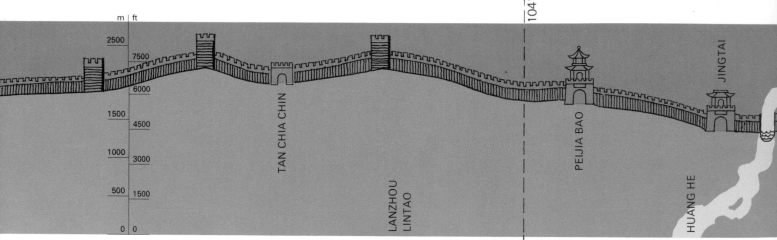

Maijishan sculpted as many as 194 caves and niches in the south of Gansu *(above)* and there are more than 1,000 Buddhas there *(right)*. This was a place of Buddhist worship from the sixth century onward, and since then has been decorated without a break in tradition, providing important artistic and historical material. Most of the sculptures, however, date from the Middle Ages.

ZHONGWEI

From Wuwei in central Gansu the Great Wall stretches to the southeast until it meets the Yellow River near Jintai in the same province. There it turns to the northeast and runs along the left bank of the river into the Hui Autonomous Region of Ningxia.

Zhongwei was once known by the name of Ningxia Zhongwei, which means literally "the central garrison under the Ningxia subcommand," a name pointing to its importance as a strategic point along the Great Wall. Some time during the mid-1300s or soon after the founding of the Ming dynasty in China, there was set up a wei or garrison in Ningxia which later was raised to a zhen or subcommand. Zhongwei commands the gap between the Tengger desert and the Helans which become lower abruptly as they extend into this district. And this was where the strategic significance of Zhongwei as a citadel lay.

Between Zhongwei and Zhongning situated across and down the Yellow River there lies a plain stretching like a belt as

An isolated fortress in the mountains looks on to the River Wei not far from its source in the Weiyuan region (to the south of Lanzhou, Gansu province).

Visitors to the town of Longxi, a few kilometers east of Weiyuan, may enjoy the sight of this imposing bell tower (below left).

Still further to the east of Weiyuan lies the town of Qin'an, where two three-colored ceramic bulls (of which this is one), typical examples of Tang pottery, were discovered.

GANSU ◄┼► NINGXIA

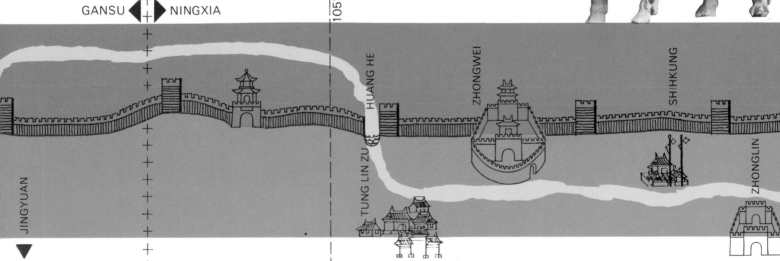

broad as 6 to 20 kilometers. This alluvial plain at so high an altitude was the product of the movement of the river which flows rather slowly here. The belt is the southern stretch of the Ningxia plain which is reputed as comparable in fertility to the vast areas south of the Yangzi River. Animal husbandry and agriculture are equally important sectors of the economy here and flocks of sheep are extensively raised.

Other products around Zhongwei include licorice root and Chinese wolfberry which are both used as medicines.

West of Zhongwei, Huanghe (the Yellow River) flows through the wall once again, as it has already done at Lanzhou and Jingtai. It crosses the wall twice more, in the north of Ningxia province, and again north of Fugu, where it forms the boundary between the provinces of Shaanxi and Shanxi. The detail from the eighteenth-century "Lateran Map" (left) shows one of the points at which wall and river cross.

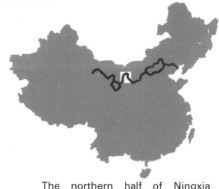

The northern half of Ningxia resembles more than anything its great western neighbor, Inner Mongolia: the common landscape (as opposite) consists of desert areas and grazing land for horses.

THE QINGTONGXIA GORGE

Proceeding from the strip of plain between Zhongwei and Zhongning, the Great Wall extends northward along the eastern foot of the Helan Mountains to reach the outskirts of Yinchuan, Ningxia. Sheltered by it is the northern stretch of the fertile Ningxia plain. There is a loop in the wall beginning at Yinchuan; crossing the Yellow River, it descends to Hengcheng and heads eastward for Yanchi through Lingwu county.

The Qingtongxia gorge was formed by the Yellow River cutting through a mountain range. In this region narrow valleys and small plains lie next to each other and thus there are enormous potentials for developing waterpower resources. A key water-control project has been completed at the Qingtongxia gorge, which is practically the door to the Yinwu plain or the northern part of the Ningxia plain. Covering an area roughly 150 kilometers (100 miles) long and about 50 kilometers (35 miles) broad, the plain is known as one of China's leading farming districts with reliable irrigation. It was more than

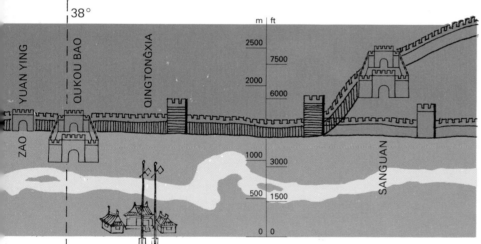

Unshaded wall = less well-defined stretches

The Huis (Muslims) are a not unimportant Chinese religious minority. They are mainly to be found in the north of the country, but above all in Ningxia province. Like all foreign religions, Islam has undergone strong Chinese influence, and its architecture retains few characteristics of Muslim art, as is demonstrated by the mosque at Tongxin (above), which lies about 250 kilometers (155 miles) south of Yinchuan.

two thousand years ago that the Hans and people of the other nationalities started large-scale projects here for irrigation, building the Qinqu, Hangu, Tanglaiqu canals and a number of other installations in this region. Here the tourist sees an extensive system of irrigation, vast areas of paddy rice fields, pools grown with reeds, and exuberant weeping willows looking down at their own reflection in the water. Waking up on a bright morning here, you will feel you are in one of the lush subtropical regions south of the Yangzi instead of a locality beyond the

HELAN SHAN

PING JI BAO

YINCHUAN

HELAN

106°

PINGLO

TA WU DI KOU

m	ft
2500	7500
2000	6000
1000	3000
500	1500
0	0

Unshaded wall = less well-defined stretches

Great Wall. The plain, so fertile and so beautiful, can well be compared to a piece of fine jasper inlaid between the Helan Mountains and the Ordos plateau.

The city of Yinchuan has long been an important site along the Great Wall. Marco Polo had a brief stay in one of his travels some time in late thirteenth century at a city called Arashai in Ningxia. Later he wrote about the camel hair cloth produced in that city, describing it as a fine weave which might well be called the best and the most beautiful sort of fabric ever known in the world of those times.

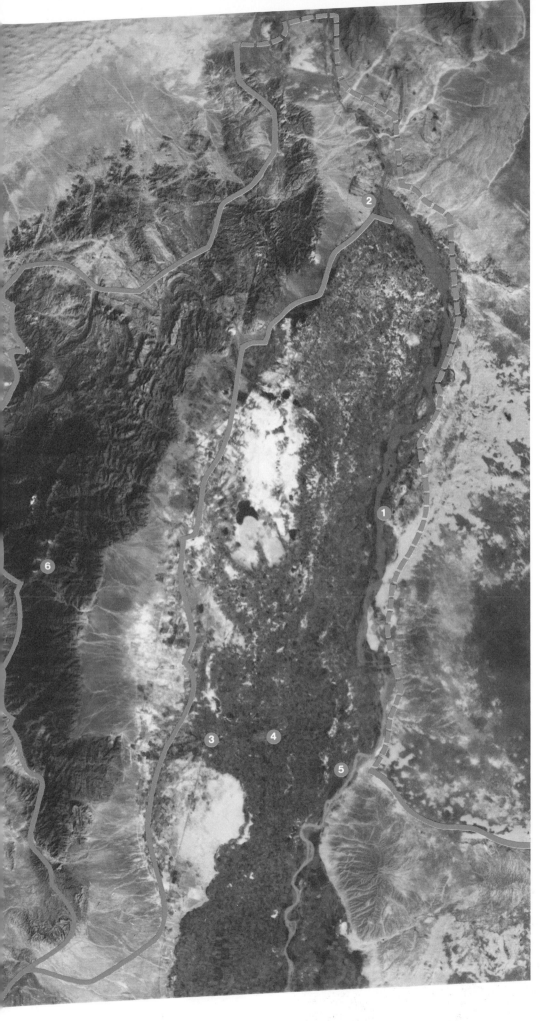

The Helan Mountains are girded to the west by a double wall, the traces of which are barely recognizable today. Following the line of peaks, they protect the urban area of Yinchuan on the right. The satellite photograph *(left)* shows details of the topography. The strategic importance of defending the town of Yinchuan on the banks of the Yellow River is evident: anyone who took possession of the town could then, by pushing south, go behind the fortifications built upstream on the left bank; this did in fact happen several times.

The photograph of the region (105 to 107 degrees east, 38 to 40 degrees north) includes the following sites: (1) Huanghe (Yellow River), (2) Shizuishan, (3) Xiucheng, (4) Yinchuan, (5) Yongjing, (6) Highest summit, 11,670 feet.

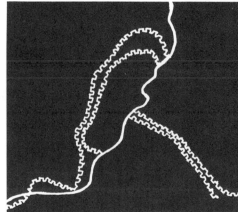

Opposite page:
The Helan Mountains, together with the Liupan range, which are divided by Gansu in the south, are the only high mountains (3,550 meters; 11,646 feet) in Ningxia province. The abundant vegetation of this region provides a strange contrast with the surrounding steppe areas. To their right flowing north, the Yellow River divides into numerous streams.

NINGXIA AND GUYUAN

Being the smallest among the provincial districts, the Ningxia Hui Autonomous Region occupies an area of less than 100,000 square meters, with a population close to 2 million, most of whom are of the Hui nationality. The Hui people is one of the principal minorities of China, totaling up to four million, with a wide distribution throughout the country. As good Muslims, they love tidiness, bathe often, and abstain from pork.

Ningxia is an area which saw a great deal of contact and exchange between peoples. It was inhabited successively or simultaneously by the Xiongnu, Xianbei, Qiang, Dangxiang, Mongol, Hui as well as Han since the first century before the Christian era. The condition was encouraging not only to a cultural exchange and national emergence, but to a struggle for hegemony.

Wars were carried on intermittently, and so were the constructing and repairing of barriers. In the region in question, one can meet the ruins of the barriers which were left from the periods of Chunqiu and Zhanguo, Qin-Han and Sui. The Ming dynasty, which expelled the Tartar Mongols, attached great importance to the defense here.

Yinchuan, capital of the Ningxia Autonomous Region, served then as headquarters for the Ningxia Zhen. The city and its neighboring land are skirted and fed by the Huanghe River which runs northward. The history of irrigation here goes back to the Qin-Han time. The pass of the Helan Mountain to the west of Yinchuan is joined by a pass of the Great Wall called Sanguankou or "Third Pass"; while at the foot of the mountain lie some hundred tombs of the Xixia kingdom which lasted nearly thirteen centuries, in oppositon to the Song and Liao dynasties. The cemetery, which includes nine imperial tombs, is massive in scale.

The Guyuan Zhen had its headquarter set up at what is now the county seat of Guyuan. With Mount Liupan on the south and Mount Quwu on the northwest, the city holds a strategic post and drew attention from the government of every dynasty. The wall of the Qin dynasty started from Lintao in the west, and turned eastward from Guyuan. The ruins of the wall and castles of the time can still be found in its vicinity. Not far away from the city is an old pass, Xiaoguan Pass, which saw the frequent rushing in and fleeing out of the Xiongnu invaders during the early years of the Han dynasty. The abovementioned Mount Liupan, 240 kilometers (160 miles) from north to south and 2,000 meters (6,600 ft.) above sea level, is full of steep and rugged scenery.

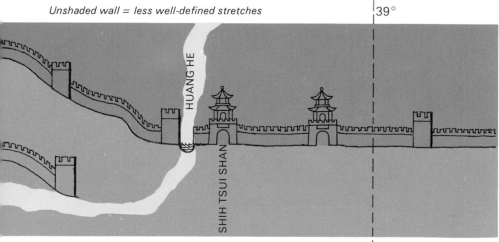

Unshaded wall = less well-defined stretches

39°

HUANG HE

SHIH TSUI SHAN

From its height of 50 meters (164 feet), the old Lingwu tower, built of bricks and tiles, looks on to the Yellow River to the west and to the north over the walls that adjoin the town of Yinchuan. Even higher, at 53.9 meters (173 feet), is its neighbor in Yinchuan, known as the White Tower. It is older as well, dating to the fifth century.

Between Yinchuan and the Helan Mountains slightly to the west lie the tombs of the Xixia sovereigns *(above)*. They ruled the area from about the eleventh to the thirteenth century.

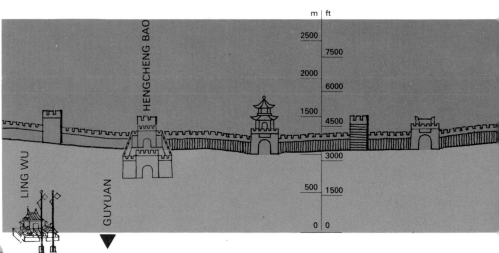

Opposite page: Like many other sites dating from the fifth century, under the impulse of the Weis from the north, who were devout Buddhists, Mount Xumi, near Guyuan (south Ningxia) was early adorned with enormous Buddhas, such as this one of the Tang period, and with other religious sculptures housed in caves.

Above left:
The lion with a ball—a kind of chimaera in fact—is an ancient mythological theme which became common beginning with the Ming dynasty. The one shown here is of iron, a fifteenth-century work located in Guyuan.

Opposite page: The Hui Muslims comprise 30 percent of the population of Ningxia and their community revolves largely round cultural centers: these worshippers belong to the Tongxin Mosque in south Ningxia.

Ningxia lambs are an important source of wealth for the province, as much for their wool as for their renowned leather.

This delicious fruit, the litchi *(left)*, is grown in the more fertile, wooded parts of the Ningxia region. The oval-shaped fruit has a hard, scaly shell, and a small hard pit surrounded by edible flesh. The flesh becomes firm and sweet when dried. Most of the litchi yield in this area is dried and exported to the rest of the country. It is appreciated as a delicacy. Altogether the northern regions of China offer considerable variety in vegetation: another important plant, grown farther east in the arid region of Inner Mongolia, is the sunflower, valued as a source of oil and cattle fodder.

Now a protected species, the Tragopan is a type of pheasant found in the wooded areas of north Shaanxi. The Tragopan is one of the short-tailed types of pheasant, and is intermediate between pheasants and partridges. Most pheasant species, now found around the world, originated in Asia. Many are raised in captivity; in the wild they have always been a popular target of hunters, who have decimated their ranks. Another threat to their existence is the destruction of woodlands.

A rare Ningxia variety to be found close to the line of the Great Wall, the red willow *(above)* is one of the only plants to grace these desert zones.

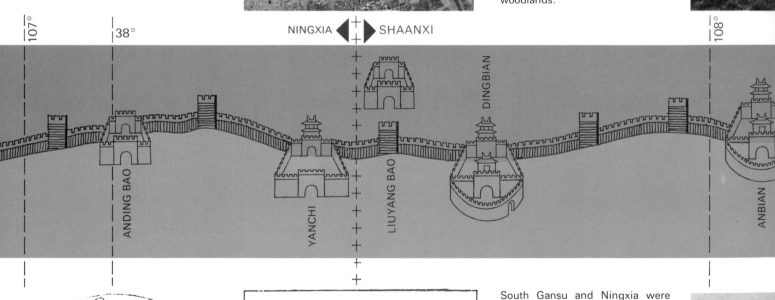

NINGXIA ◀▶ SHAANXI

107° 38° 108°

ANDING BAO
YANCHI
LIUYANG BAO
DINGBIAN
ANBIAN

South Gansu and Ningxia were early absorbed into the Chinese domain; but approaching the Wei valley, these country residences, withdrawn palaces, and other summer resorts of men of letters and state officials *(as left)*, which are miracles of luxury combined with simplicity, could be admired in former times.

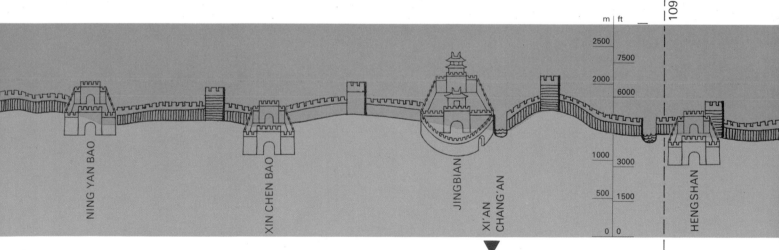

										m	ft			109°

NING YAN BAO

XIN CHEN BAO

JINGBIAN

XI'AN
CHANG'AN

HENG SHAN

2500 / 7500
2000 / 6000
1000 / 3000
500 / 1500
0 / 0

The Kazakhs of north Gansu and Ningxia are great sheep farmers *(above),* while the age-old tradition of the Mongolians is horse-breeding *(left):* it was this that led to the creation of the great steppe empires. Mongolian horses, which are rather small, are one of the earliest kinds known on earth. Indeed, this type of horse still shows some of the general traits of its prehistoric ancestors.

THREE NORTH SHAANXI TOWNS

The three towns in north Shaanxi bearing the names Dingbian, Anbian, and Jingbian, which mean literally "Stable Frontier," "Peaceful Frontier," and "Calm Frontier" respectively, express the hopes cherished by ancient inhabitants along the Great Wall.

Crossing the Ningxia-Shaanxi border at a town called Yanchangpu several miles to the east of Yanchi, the Great Wall extends all the way northeastward to Yulin, passing by these towns.

In the early eleventh century the border line between the North Song empire and the Xia kingdom ran through this region which was inhabited by both the Dangxiangs and the Hans. This time of peaceful coexistence and friendly transactions was frequently interrupted by armed clashes. During the reign of the Ming dynasty this part of the Great Wall was under the subcommand of Yulin which was to defend these frontiers against the invasion of the Mongol tribes. A command post was set up in Jingbian and there was an outpost in each of the other two towns. A project of tremendous scale was set going in 1466 for the reinforcement of the Great Wall. Besides general mending of the barrier itself, more watch towers were built, more camps were put into operation, moats were dug where necessary, and at some locations the crags were rendered steeper by removing the deposits at their foot. The year 1575 witnessed the commencement of another series of attempts at the further strengthening of the defenses under this subcommand, including the construction of another barrier running along the Great Wall itself. As the controlling center on the left wing of the Yulin zhen, the post at Anbian gave orders to twelve other outposts.

The region around these towns is a part of the Northern Shaanxi Plateau with an average altitude of 1,000 to 1,600 meters above sea level. Sand carried by the gales from the Inner Mongolian desert Mu Us drifts over the land. Rainfall, however, is enough to maintain sufficient moisture in the soil covered by the drifting sand. A flora of hundreds of plants acclimatized to this sandy region, including some species of willows, may well be very useful for any attempt at checking the expansion of the desert.

YULIN ZHEN

Yulin Zhen was one of the nine military zones the Ming dynasty established along the Great Wall. It was located between 109 and 110 degrees east longitude. Within this area there are other strategic cities including Hengshan, Yan'an, Xi'an, and Lintong, to the south of Yulin and closely related to the construction and defense of the Great Wall. The wall runs from a point northwest of Hengshan County through the southern edge of the Mu Us Desert to Yulin. Remains of

the Qin Great Wall can still be seen in Hengshan county.

Yan'an used to be a strategic point in the defense of the Great Wall. Yulin Zhen was formerly called Yansui Zhen, combining the name of two cities—Yan'an and Suide. Today in this loess highland region are tier upon tier of terraced fields, clusters of cave dwellings, grottoes at the foot of Qingliang hill, the pagoda atop Jialing hill, and many other cultural relics and historical sites.

Xi'an, in the center of the long Central Shaanxi Plain (i.e., the Wei River

A fort on the Great Wall in the city of Yulin in north Shaanxi *(below)* and *(far right)* an observation tower of more modest dimensions, the remnants of which stand not far from the Mongolian border.

Opposite page: Poyan, Kublai Khan's General, drastically reduced the ranks of the Chinese army entrenched in the south. He took Hangzou in around 1270, and it was due to him that the united empire of the Yuans was founded. Here, he can be seen taking one horseman away, having unseated another.

This pagoda, built during the Ming dynasty near Yulin, is a wise compromise between military defense and religious piety; it was used as an observation post.

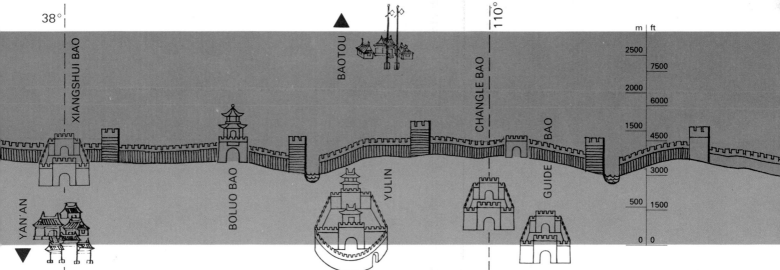

Entrance to the mausoleum of Emperor Gaozong (ruled 604–684) of the Tangs, lying about 50 kilometers (31 miles) west of the capital of Shaanxi province. It was Empress Wu, buried with him, who held the reins of power from 654, and it was she who deposed Gaozong's successor and ruled officially from 684 to 704.

The Sanniangzi Sanctuary, built in the fifteenth century, houses the tomb of a Mongolian lady who strove to bring Mongolians and Chinese together at that time. This sanctuary lies near the Yellow River, east of the town of Baotou in Inner Mongolia, and it is regarded today as the symbol of Chinese-Mongolian friendship.

Further south, about 150 kilometers (93 miles) from the Great Wall, not far from Huangling in Shaanxi province, stands a mausoleum built in memory of the Yellow Emperor. This legendary Emperor is dear to the heart of all Chinese, who consider him one of the fathers of their civilization.

Near the town of Suide, the pavilion of Fu Su, eldest son of the emperor Qin Shi huangdi, recalls that it was here in Shaanxi province, where he had been sent to supervise the building of the Great Wall, that he met his death at the end of the third century B.C.

The county of Lintong in Shaanxi province is steeped in history. The burial mound of Qin Shi huangdi is to be found here, as is the Huaqing pond, a hot spring where Yang Guifei, the famous royal concubine of one of the Tang emperors, came to bathe.

Plain), is the largest ancient city in China which served as the capital of eleven dynasties including that of Qin Shi huangdi, who built the magnificent Opang palace there.

The subsequent Han dynasty also had its capital in Xi'an, called Chang'an at that time. Its remains are in the vicinity of modern Xi'an city.

The Great Wall was built along the boundary of the desert to the north of Yulin city. Half the Great Wall in this part and part of the northern city wall of Yulin are now buried in sand owing to the southward encroachment of the desert over the centuries. A river flowing from the desert was vital to Yulin. It is mentioned in an ancient poem about the sorrows of married women: "Have pity on the skeletons by the Wuding River, they are the men in the dreams of young women."

FROM YULIN TO FUGU

The section of the Great Wall from Yulin to Fugu on the Yellow River has collapsed, but many forts and beacon towers still stand on the mountains or in the valleys along the line stretching all the way through the edge of the Mu Us Desert and Shenmu between 110 and 111 degrees east. It was also the route of the Great Wall built under Qin Shi huangdi. At Shenmu, a stronghold was set up in the Song dynasty, and a garrison was stationed here during the Yuan dynasty. In the Ming dynasty, Shenmu became a strategic point along the wall. The Kuye River flows from the Inner Mongolia Autonomous Region into the Yellow River via Shenmu. Several small temples atop a nearby mountain overlook the countytown of Shenmu and the Kuye River. It is said that the peaks of the mountain were moved here by Yang Jian, a legendary figure in Chinese mythology. To the south of Shenmu is Suide county, a strategic stronghold on the ancient Great Wall. The town lies in the convergence of two rivers—Wuding and Dali. Suide is said to be the place where a huge Qin dynasty army under General Meng Tian and Prince Fu Su was stationed and constructed the Great Wall after driving out the Xiongnu. The tombs of Meng Tian and Fu Su are still preserved in the county. Both fell victim to a frame-up more than two thousand years ago. When Qin Shi huangdi died on his inspection

This bronze masterpiece is one of the most beautiful pieces of the statue army buried near Qin Shi huangdi's grave near Lintong. The expression and posture of this chariot driver is evidence of a rare skill in plastic art.

This Han bas-relief, in which a horse tied to a tree is depicted, was dug up not far from the town of Suide.

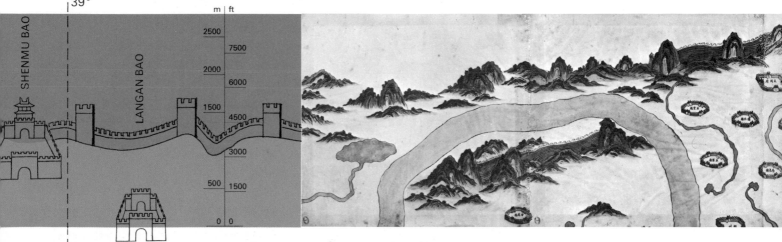

These bronze horses discovered, like the chariot driver, in March 1980 also bear witness to the artistic skill and high degree of technical expertise achieved in metalwork before the Christian era. They are among many works excavated at Qin Shi huangdi's tomb near Lintong which were covered up again with earth and left as they were found. Only photographs such as this one survive to give us an idea of their impressive quality.

tour, Eunuch Zhao Gao usurped the power and ordered Li Si to forge the emperor's edict on his death bed to the effect that the youngest prince Hu Hai was to be made emperor and Meng Tian and Fu Su were to hang themselves on account of conspiracy.

Between 110 and 111 degrees of east longitude, the Yellow River meanders from north to south and becomes the natural boundary line between today's Shaanxi and Shanxi provinces. Before the time of Qin Shi huangdi, the princes of the Wei, Han, and Qin states often crossed swords in these places. In the fourth century B.C. the state of Wei built a long wall from Huaying in the south up along the Yellow River. Now one section of the Wei Great Wall still remains in Hancheng county by the Yellow River. This area nurtured China's first great historian Si Maqian, whose Historical Records was the first general Chinese history.

The Yellow River makes an abrupt turn eastward by Mount Huashan, one of China's most famous heights. The Great Wall erected by Wei during the Warring Kingdoms period from the foot of the mountain to the north was obviously meant to resist offensives by the powerful Qin state in the west. But this hope was dashed when Qin Shi huangdi unified the six states in 221 B.C., thus rendering this section of the Great Wall a mere historical site. To reach the top of the steep Mount Huashan, climbers must enlist the help of iron chains at some points. The difficulty is well expressed in an old saying: "There's only one sheep trail up to the mountain."

Where the Yellow River turns eastward, there is also an ancient pass called Tongguan which protected the Central Plains and the capitals of the Qin and Han dynasties—Xianyang and Chang'an. Numerous battles were fought there, and a carved stone on the ancient battlefields reflects only a small bit of the history.

One of the great heroes in China's history was named Li Zicheng. From 1629 to 1644, this peasant-turned-soldier led troops and fought in Shaanxi, Henan, Hebei, and Hubei provinces, and overthrew the Ming dynasty. He grew up in Mizhi county by the Wuding River where Meng Tian and Fu Su had performed defense duty for the Great Wall. His country folk built a palace for him on a low hill near the county town. But he never spent a single day there for he died in battle in Hubei province.

In the pasturelands of Inner Mongolia, horse- and cattle-breeding is the traditional occupation and the markets consist of traveling stalls such as photographed here *(left)*.

Mount Hua *(right)*, near Huayin at the crossroads of Shaanxi, Shanxi, and Henan provinces, is one of China's holy peaks; at the "West Peak" a great number of these porches of honor can be seen. Over the centuries it has been visited by innumerable pilgrims and lovers of the countryside.

The plateaux of Shaanxi province have for a long time been terraced for cultivation. These terraces are not far from Suide, at Mizhi, the birth place of the war leader Li Zicheng, who lived at the end of the Ming period.

One of Emperor Taizong's six chargers *(right)*, which were sculpted in his tomb in 637 in memory of his battles at the frontiers. The depiction of horses became a flourishing art during the Tang dynasty; many painters and sculptors were masters of this art, and succeeded in representing the vigor and power of this animal to perfection, as can be seen here.

Yan'an *(right)*, an important commercial center of the northern half of Shannxi, made history in 1936 when it became the provisional headquarters of the Central Committee of the Chinese Communist Party. It was here that Mao Zedong proclaimed the principles of a revolutionary proletarian culture. The photographs shows the nine-story octagonal Baota Pagoda which became a symbol of the Communist revolutionary movement. It stands 44 meters or 145 feet high and dates to the Tang dynasty (618—906). The city, situated on the bank of the River Yanhe, was already an important site under the Tang and succeeding Song dynasties. Nearby are several major mountain peaks, and the town commands a view of the terraced mountain slopes as in the picture opposite.

FUGU AND HOHHOT (HUHEHOT)

Fugu, at the end of the Yansuizhen Great Wall of the Ming dynasty, between the Kuye and Yellow rivers, was below the eastern Ordos highlands in Inner Mongolia. When the northern nomadic horsemen came south to invade Shanxi, they had to pass the southern and northern ferries in the vicinity of Fugu. Therefore Fugu was in a very important position. In fact, in the Warring Kingdoms period (475–221 B.C.) and the Qin (221–207 B.C.) and early Han (206 B.C.–A.D. 24) dynasties, the place was already part of the interior. The Great Wall built by King Zhaoxiang of the Qin state started from Nixian county in Gansu and passed through Weiyuan, Guyuan and Huanxian county to Jingbian in Shaanxi province. Passing by the river north of Shenmu county, it went east into Inner Mongolia. Shierlian northeast of Jungar Banner was its eastern end.

Across the river is today's Togtoh.

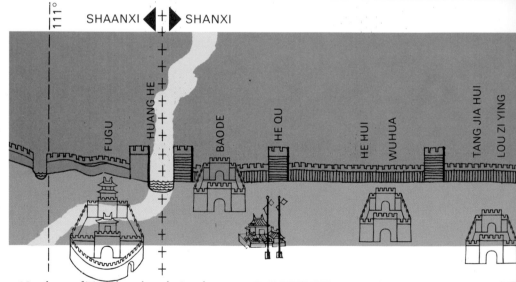

SHAANXI ◄► SHANXI

111°

FUGU HUANG HE BAODE HE QU HE HUI WUHUA TANG JIA HUI LOU ZI YING

Northeast of Togtoh and on the Southern bank of the Dahei River is the site of the Yunzhong prefecture of the Zhao state. The Great Walls of the Qin and Han dynasties lay near the line of Baotou and Hohhot. In the Eastern Han dynasty the southern Xiongnu (Hsiungnu) gave their allegiance to Han and moved to the area south of the bend of the Yellow River and what is now northern Shaanxi and Gansu provinces.

It was an important area for the activities of northern nomadic nationalities. Some nationalities which had been active on

Left: The Yellow River in Pianguan county. The Great Wall is visible at the right-hand side of the photograph.

This region was of enormous strategic importance, and therefore was equipped with a whole network of fortresses and garrisons. *Below:* A fortress and tower near Fugu.

EXTERIOR AND INTERIOR LINE

After the wall, on its eastward course, crosses the Yellow River (Huanghe), it follows the river northward for a certain distance, then turns to the east, climbs into the mountains, and reaches a point west of the 112th meridian where the Exterior Line of the wall separates itself from the Interior Line. The two segments join up again north of Beijing, to the east of the 116th meridian. From this point in the diagram of the Great Wall, we follow the course of the Exterior Line to the point of juncture (page 107); from there the reader returns to the point of division, to follow the course of the Interior Line (beginning on page 108) through the mountains of Shanxi and Hebei. The detail from a map *(bottom*

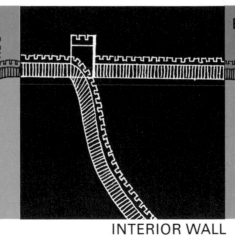

HUA LING BAO HOHHOT LAO NIN WAN PIAN GUAN SHUI QUAN YING LU PI YAO KOU

EXTERIOR WALL

112°

m | ft
2500
7500
1500
4500
1000
3000
500
1500
0 | 0

MI HU KOU

INTERIOR WALL

right)—a French General Staff map of 1901—shows the point where the wall divides into two lines.

Opposite page: Satellite photograph of the area between Fugu and Hohhot, including a segment of the Yellow River flowing from the north. The colored line shows the course of the Great Wall. (1) Huanghe, the Yellow River, (2) Hohhot, (3) Hovinger, (4) Qingshuhe, (5) Pianguan, (6) Fugu.

Left: General view of Fugu, from the other side of the Yellow River.

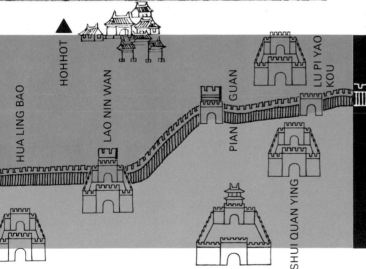

99

Mongolian grasslands, including the Xiongnu, Xianbei (Sienpi), Tujue (Turks), Khitans, Jürchens, and Mongolians, for a time lived in Hohhot. Ten kilometers (6 miles) northwest of Hohhot was the foot of Daqing hill (Big Blue Hill) near Wusutu Village, where there are remains of the Great Wall of the Zhao state, on which layers of rammed earth can still be clearly discerned.

Quite a number of ancient cities of the Han dynasty have been discovered in the area north and south of Yinshan Mountain and around the ferries of the Yellow River. This area was a battlefield in periods of tension in the relations between the nationalities and served as a staging

It was into these areas in the north of Shaanxi and Shanxi that lie on the border with Inner Mongolia, that the Mongolian soldiers, who can be seen in this late illustration, made frequent incursions. A watch tower, where fires of alarm were lit, still stands (left) near the Great Wall, at the side of the Shahukou Pass near Youyu in Shanxi province.

post for economic and cultural exchange in periods of harmonious relations. Even in times of war such exchange was not entirely interrupted. And thus the Great Wall did not break up such friendly relations between nationalities.

In the early sixteenth century Altan Khan (Dayan in Chinese), one of the chiefs of the Tumet tribe (the Tumeds), united various Mongolian tribes and the area south of the desert. The Tumet tribe settled down here. In the ninth year of the Wanli era of the Mings (1581) the city of Hohhot was officially built, called by the Ming rulers Guihua, but by the Mongolians the "Blue City."

Photo, opposite page: The blue tomb of Huhehot. The royal concubine Wang Zhaojun, who is the heroine of numerous romantic tales starting in the first century B.C., helped in the dealings between Emperor Yuandi of the Hans and the Khan. Her tomb is at Huhehot, the capital of Inner Mongolia, where—some say—she died. Legend has it that her funeral site remains green all year round.

Left: The brick pagoda at Feng-zhou, near Huhehot, was erected nearly 1,000 years ago. It reportedly housed the 1,000 volumes of Buddhist writings that form the basis of the Huayan school, founded in the eighth century.

These three buildings, which are highly representative of religious eclecticism, all date back about 300 years and can be seen from Huhehot and the surrounding area. From the top, they are: a Buddhist temple; a Lama sanctuary; and a Muslim mosque.
They bear witness to the religious fervor of the Mongolians, but also to a diversity of style and architecture that is found less in the southern regions that are properly Chinese.

101

THE EXTERIOR LINE

The interior-line and exterior-line Great Wall in Shanxi province extend from longitude 112°–113° eastward into longitude 113°–114°.

The exterior-line Great Wall, also called the northern-line Great Wall, meanders eastward along the border between the Inner Mongolia Autonomous Region and Shanxi province. Starting from the Yajiao Mountain in the west and reaching Zhenkoutai in the east, this section of the Great Wall has a total length of 324 kilometers (225 miles). It is under the administration of the Datong township. Datong was a place of strategic importance near the Great Wall for successive dynasties as well as a city of historic renown. In the fifth to the third century B.C., this place was under the jurisdiction of Yanmen county of Zhao state, one of the seven powerful kingdoms in the period of the Warring Kingdoms. After Emperor Qin Shi huangdi vanquished the other six states and unified China, Pingcheng county was set up here. Since the building of the Great Wall north of Yanmen county by King Wuling of Zhao state, significant wars had repeatedly taken place in the Datong area. In 200 B.C. Emperor Gaozu of the Han dynasty personally led a huge army to fight the Xiongnu but was surrounded by them at Baideng for seven days and nights and his army was almost completely wiped out. Later he succeeded in breaking through the siege by using the strategem of his adviser Chen Ping to bribe the wife of Mao Dun, leader of the Huns—an event known historically as the "siege of Baiden." Baiden is to the northeast of Datong city.

In the fourth century, the Northern Wei dynasty set up its capital in Pingcheng and ruled the northern part of China for over a hundred years. During the eleventh to thirteenth century, the Liao and Jin dynasties took Datong as their second capital for two hundred years. Emperor Taizu of the Ming dynasty crowned his thirteenth son, Zhu Gui, Prince Dai here. Later he set up the Datong garrison post, one of the nine in the country.

The Yungang Caves, located in the south of Wuzhou Mountain 16 kilometers (10 miles) west of Datong city, is a treasure house of art inherited from the Northern Wei dynasty. The stone caves were opened up between B.C. 460 and 525

in the Northern Wei dynasty. Preserved to this day are twenty-one large caves and hundreds of small caves and niches. Altogether there are more than 51,000 Buddha statues, the largest 17 meters high and the smallest a few centimeters. The Upper and Lower Huayan Monasteries on the southern side of Xidajie Street in Datong city are two neighboring old temples built in the Liao dynasty. The Upper Huayan Monastery was built in 1062 but was destroyed in the war between the kingdoms of Liao and Jin between 1121 and 1125. The existing hall was rebuilt in 1140 in the Jin dynasty. With a total floor space of 1,559 square meters (53.75 by 29 meters), it is one of the two largest existing Buddhist halls in China. In the Lower Huayan Monastery is preserved a Buddhist hall built in 1038 in the Liao dynasty. Under the roof beam is an inscription written at the time of the hall's construction for the storing of Buddhist scriptures. On the four sides are wooden scripture cabinets carved in the form of pavillions of excellent workmanship.

The Nine-Dragon Screen, located on the southern side of Dongdajie Street in

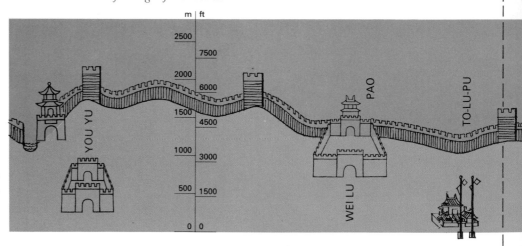

Datong city, was built between 1368 and 1398 in the Ming dynasty. Originally it was a shelter screen in front of Prince Dai's mansion. The mansion has long ceased to exist but the screen has remained intact. 45.5 meters long, 8 meters high, and 2.02 meters thick, it is the largest and earliest nine-dragon screen existing in China today.

The Shanhua Monastery, situated inside the south gate of Datong city, boasts a group of buildings constructed in the Liao and Jin dynasties comprising the Shanmen gate, the Sansheng hall, the Puxian pavilion, and the Daxiong hall.

YÜ LIN CHENG

Left: Section of the Great Wall in north Shanxi and Hebei. This map faces south, and the Chinese part is at the top. There are numerous fortresses and walled towns (some of which bear the same name today); in the lower part (Mongolia), they are contrastingly more widely dispersed.

Far left: Remnants of a line of defense built between Datong (in the extreme north of Shanxi) and the Great Wall.

The Bodhisattva is a being on the point of achieving the Awakening *(nirvana)* who devotes himself to the salvation of other men. This clay representation, dating from the Liao period (907—1125), has been preserved in the temple at Datong.

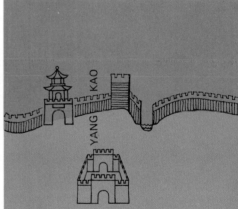

The "Wall of the Nine Dragons" at Datong has maximum votive scope: the dragon is an auspicious creature and the number nine (figure *yang*) is a good omen.

103

Li Shi (1413—1485), an important official of the Mings, conducted a good-will mission in Mongolian territory in 1450 to liberate Emperor Yingzong, who had been taken prisoner. Here he is seen negotiating with the barbarians; Emperor Yingzong was allowed to come back to China the same year, but was only reinstated as Emperor six years later.

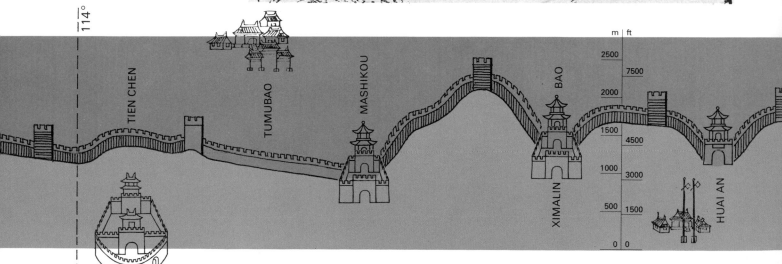

The Euphrates poplar (right) still grows today in the desert zones of northern China. Its wood was formerly used as construction material for the Great Wall. In various parts of China at various times, wood, even brushwood, was important as a building material and was relatively easy to obtain.

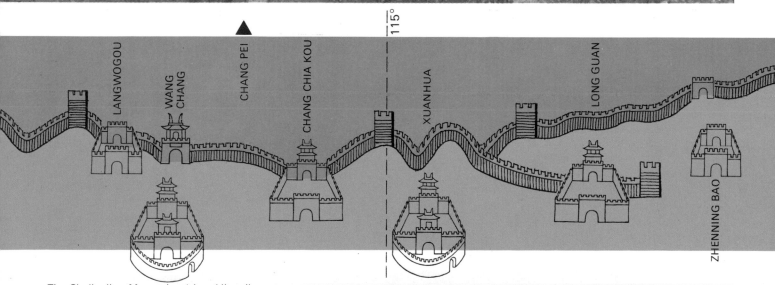

LANGWOGOU

WANG CHANG

CHANG PEI

CHANG CHIA KOU

115°

XUANHUA

LONG GUAN

ZHENNING BAO

The Chajianling Mountains *(above)* lie adjacent to the southern line of the walls in the Laiyuan region of Hebei Province. It was here that Yang Yanzhao, a Song general, held the Khitans at bay for a time at the end of the tenth century. In the end, however, they were victorious and established the Liao dynasty in China.

The surrounding walls and the gates of Zhangjiakou *(right)* have been admirably preserved. Zhangjiakou lies on the route to Beijing, halfway between the Chinese capital and the Mongolian capital of Huhehot: it has always been a point of strategic importance and its defenses had to be carefully maintained.

The brown lagopus is one of China's protected birds. It is to be found in the northern area of the Great Wall.

This variation of polo is played with an enormous ball and a team of eight horsemen. In contrast with standard polo, which originated before the seventh century, this game probably does not have a very long history in Mongolia.

An important city in the vicinity of the exterior wall is Zhangjiakou, a communications hub between Hebei province and Inner Mongolia and a market for the exchange of commodities between the Mongolian and Han nationalities. Zhangjiakou and its vicinity constitute a major stockbreeding area noted for its horses and lambskin. Guyuan, north of Zhangjiakou, is famous for its mushrooms, known as the "Zhangjiakou mushroom." This area has many ancient sites and remains including a pagoda in memory of Jing Ke in Yixian county. Jing Ke failed in his attempt to assassinate the king of Qin state who later became the First Emperor, of the Qin dynasty (221–207 B.C.). Jingxingguan Pass in Hulu was the ancient battlefield where in the early Han dynasty, Chief Marshal Han Xin defeated Chen Yu of the Zhao state. Among other ancient sites are the tombs of the kings of the Zhongshan state and the Han tombs in Wangdu discovered in recent years where rare historical relics were unearthed. There are also famous ancient buildings including "Liao Di Ta" ("See-enemy-through Pagoda") of

Unshaded wall = less well-defined stretches

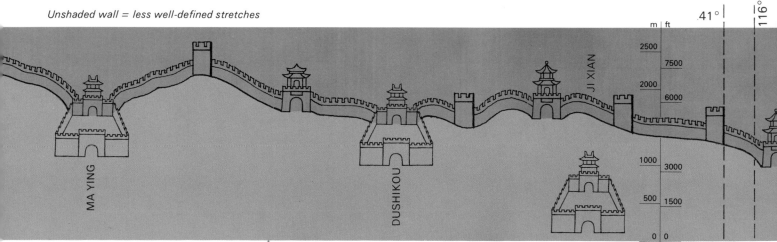

Wrestling is another very popular sport in Mongolia; great tournaments take place during the seasonal folk festivals. As in Japanese sumo, the winner is the one who succeeds in making his adversary touch the ground. The northernmost parts of the Great Wall traverse an area that offers rich cultural contrasts to the southern Chinese way of life (see pp. 158 ff.).

the Song dynasty (960–1279) in Dingxian county and Colossal Buddha Monastery of the Tang dynasty (618–907) in Zhengding. Quite a number of remains of the Liao (916–1125) and Jin (1115–1234) dynasties have survived. All these eloquently explain that the people of various nationalities in the north and south have pooled their efforts to create spiritual civilization and material wealth.

Women's ceremonial costumes have not changed much since old times, and the head-dresses are still made with pieces of silver decorated with semi-precious stones (amber, jade, etc.).

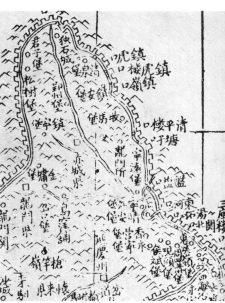

This map detail from the Jesuits' atlas from the Kangxi period (early eighteenth century) shows the northernmost buckle of the Great Wall, through which the important road from Beijing leads by way of Guyuan toward Inner Mongolia (Nei Monggol). The map gives a good idea of the course of the wall, which is indicated only in fragments on modern maps.

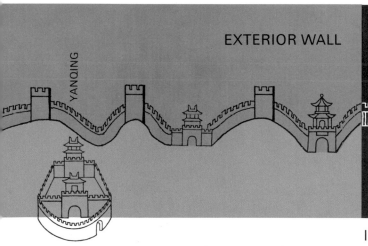

EXTERIOR WALL

YANQING

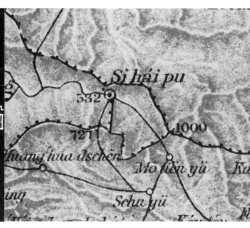

INTERIOR WALL

The doubling of the Wall undertaken during the Ming dynasty ends, in the east, in the Beijing area, not far from the small town of Xihai (Si hai pu on the old western map, *right*). The northern Great Wall juts out to the north, this pattern being visible on the Jesuit map *(top right)*. On the following page our diagram returns to the western "Y" and follows the course of the Interior Line.

The "horse-head" lute *(left)* is still the most popular instrument of the Mongolians and the inhabitants of the frontier regions today.

The eastern "Y," as the point of juncture north of Beijing is known—the point where the exterior and interior lines of the wall come together once more—is depicted here on a detail from a German General Staff map of 1902. According to this information, this nearly impenetrable mountain area contained an impressive system of fortifications, consisting of several walls which ran in part along mountain ridges, and elsewhere blocked off valleys.

107

THE INTERIOR LINE

The Yanmenguan Pass, on the southern line of the Great Wall, formed a gap in the line of peaks 1,500–2,000 meters (6,561 feet) —sometimes even 3,000 meters (9,842 feet)—in height, in the north of Shanxi. Anyone who could gain possession of the Pass had an open road to the rich plain of Hebei.

Under pressure from the Mongolians, the second line of defense was built around 1440 south of the first wall. It extends from northern Shanxi province, near the Yellow River, in the west, to the area north of Beijing, in the east. The west junction of the two wall segments

South of Datong city, the interior-line Great Wall extends from the Yanmen Pass to the foot of Mount Hengshan and then, winding its way across Mount Hengshan and the Wutai Mountain, it enters Hebei province along the Taihang Mountains. Yingxian county, situated in the loess plain close to the northern foot of Mount Hengshan, is an important old city by the side of the interior-line Great Wall. In the center of the county seat is a wooden pagoda 67 meters (221 ft) high with a base diameter of 30 meters (99 ft). It is the only remaining Buddhist pagoda in China built entirely of wood. Originally called Sakya Pagoda, it was built in 1056 in the Liao dynasty. At that time the rulers of the Liao and Song dynasties often fought in the north or south of Mount Hengshan. Yingxian county was a frontline defense position of the Liao army. The building of such a high wooden pagoda also served the purpose of observing the military movement of the Song army.

The main peak of Mount Hengshan, one

handed down from the Liao and Song dynasties. Since the Liao and Song rulers were in confrontation against each other and Hunyuan was in Liao domain, the emperor of the Song dynasty could not come to Mount Hengshan to offer sacrifices. As an alternative, he built a temple in what is today Quyang county of Hebei province east of the Taihang Mountains to offer sacrifices 200 kilometers (120 miles) away. Thus there are two North Mountain Temples, one on Mount Hengshan and the other a long way distant. There are scores of other ancient buildings on Mount Hengshan or in its foothills. There is a temple of unique design at the foot of the mountain called the "Temple in Mid-Air."

The Wutai (Five Platforms) Mountain to the south of Mount Hengshan is named for its five flat peaks. The main peak, 3,058 meters (10,032 ft) above sea level, is a noted summit in north China. The Wutai Mountain is a famous Buddhist holy land in China, devoted to Budhisattva Manjusri rites. Among the five peaks there is a small basin called Taihuai where there were once more than 100

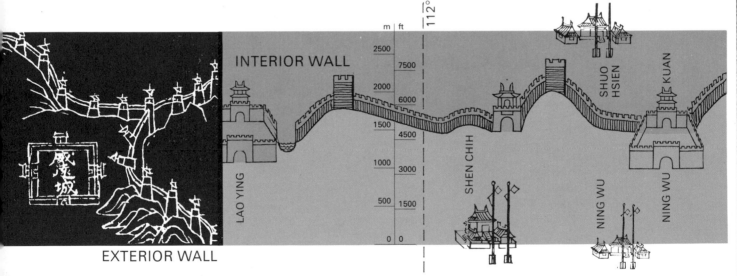

is illustrated on the map above, near the town of Weiyuan: the map looks to the south. The last several pages of the diagram have followed the course of the exterior wall (the northern wall) all the way to the region north of Beijing. We now return to the point, east of the Yellow River, where the double wall began, and we proceed to follow the inner defense line on its way through the wild mountainous regions of Shanxi and Hebei.

of the five well-known mountains in China, is by the side of Hunyuan county, northeast of the interior-line Great Wall in Shanxi province. The Great Wall turns southward here, passing through the eastern foot of the Wutai Mountains and going northward along the Taihang Mountains. From Hunyuan to Datong, beacontowers stand in a row, linking up the exterior-line and interior-line Great Wall.

Emperors in ancient China often offered sacrifices to Mount Hengshan. In this regard an interesting anecdote was

temples. Many interesting Buddha-worshiping activities are held in the temples. There is a kind of mechanism called "Buddha appears as flower blossoms." When the mechanism is turned on, the lotus flower petals automatically open and the Buddhist statue appears for the believers to worship.

Near the Wutai county seat about 80 kilometers (50 miles) from Taihuai are two of the earliest wooden structure buildings in China, built during the Tang dynasty: the Nanchan Temple built in 782, and the Foguang Temple (857).

The Great Wall in this longitude has scores of passes and castles, the Pingxing and Niangzi passes being the more renowned. The Pingxing Pass, located in the northeast of Fanchi county, Shanxi province, holds a strategic position and is in the shape of a bottle; hence in ancient time it was called the Bottle-Shape Pass. It is an important pass of the Great Wall. In the war of resistance against Japanese invasion, the Eighth Route Army ambushed the Itagaki division, a crack unit of the Japanese army, in September 1937 and won a resounding victory here.

The Niangzi Pass is located in the central part of the Taihang Mountains 200

enlisted at least 70,000 women and to have organized them into a women's army which was stationed at this pass, hence the name Niangzi (Young Women's) Pass. Xuanfu, located in present-day Xuanhua county, Hebei province, guarded the Juyongguan pass, gateway of the capital at Beijing. But as the Ming dynasty became gradually corrupt and militarily weaker, in the year 1449 the "Tumubao Incident" occurred on the important route leading from Juyongguan pass to Xuanfu.

Emperor Yingzong and his eunuch Wang Zhen concentrated the main forces at Tumubao, a mountainous site unsuitable for defense and for effective rest and reor-

The complete line of the inner Great Wall as it appears from east to west (from left to right) on Ming map. Many famous places are recognizable, including the Juyongguan Pass, already mentioned several times: this was the pass crossed by the Manchus when they came to take Beijing. The Yanmenguan Pass is the last one on the right (a photograph of this appears on page 109); the sanctuary of Yang Ye, the brave general who died fighting the Khitans not far from the Pass around 986, is to be found there. This sanctuary contains the painting (right) illustrating his greatest feats in arms.

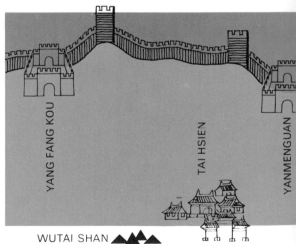

YANG FANG KOU — TAI HSIEN — YANMENGUAN

WUTAI SHAN ▲▲▲

kilometers (120 miles) south of the Pingxing Pass. It is a communications hub between Hebei and Shanxi provinces and an important pass to link up with the Great Wall. It is said that in A.D. 617 Princess Ping Yang, daughter of Emperor Gaozu of the Tang dynasty, recruited women fighters in today's Huxian county, Shaanxi province, to form an army to coordinate with her father in a rebellion against the ruler of the Sui dynasty. She is said to have

ganization. Returning toward the capital, the emperor's army was raided by two contingents of Oirat tribes and the emperor was taken prisoner.

Later, Yu Qian, minister of defense, and other high-ranking officials eager to resist the enemy aroused troops and civilians and successfully defended the capital. Defenses thereafter were strengthened, and peaceful relations with the Oirats were restored.

Mount Wutaishan, slightly to the south of the inner Great Wall, reaches its highest point in the north of Shanxi at 3,058 meters (10,032 feet). It is traditionally dedicated to the worship of the Bodhisattva Manjusri, and by reason of this is adorned with numerous porches of honor preceded by endless stone staircases; this one (above left) is at the summit.

Many mountain heights throughout China have been imbued with religious significance and are adorned with shrines, temples, inscriptions, and statuary. Another of these sites in the vicinity of the Great Wall is the hanging Buddhist temple at Mount Heng (page 113).

The Zhaogaoguan temple (below), built under the Northern Weis (386—534) into a cliff near the Yanmenguan Pass, was restored under the Mings and has many of the characteristic architectural features of the Great Wall.

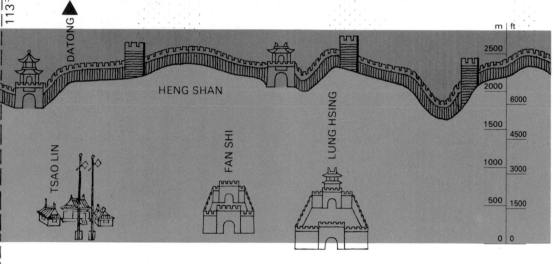

The monumental "Peaceful Frontier" gate of the Yanmenguan Pass is in proportion with its importance: as its sign indicates, it commands access to three other subsidiary passes. Like the other passes of the inner Great Wall, it was built in the middle of the fifteenth century and is a showpiece of typical Ming architecture.

111

Niangziguan, the "Young Women's Pass" *(below)* is a strategic point on the inner Great Wall in the north of Shanxi. It takes its name from a warrior princess who commanded a Chinese garrison here at the beginning of the seventh century.

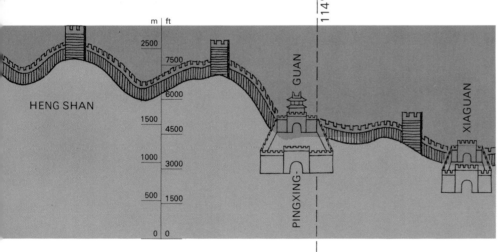

Pingxingguan, another important pass of the area, commands the route from Shanxi to Hebei—and was accordingly the scene of numerous battles; a view of the eastern postern is shown here. As we proceed westward along the wall toward the region of Beijing, the fortifications and passes are generally more substantial and, in order to defend the capital, were well maintained throughout the Ming dynasty and even earlier.

"Temple in Mid-Air" is the name of this Buddhist temple built on the slopes of Mount Heng in the fifth century. Its pagoda has the most unusual feature of resting on beams driven into the cliff. Mount Heng reaches its summit at a little more than 2,000 meters (6,561 feet) about 50 kilometers (31 miles) southeast of Datong in Shanxi. Its topography is particularly uneven; and it is one of China's holy peaks, the North Peak, overlooking the great watercourses of the Chinese empire.

Lotus flowers are often chosen as pedestals for Buddhas, and are often stylized into a form as impressive as that of the beings they support, as can be seen here in a temple near Mount Wutaishan in Shanxi province, not far from the inner Great Wall. The petals of the flower can be opened and closed.

An additional object of architectural interest in this region is the Sakyamuni Pagoda *(below left)*. It is the oldest wooden pagoda in China (A.D. 1056) and reaches a height of 70 meters (168 feet).

Right: One of the passes in the area of Jingxing (Hebei), to the west of Shijiazhuang. Narrow though it may be, it seems that this pass was of great strategic importance.

At the top of the arch of the Juyongguan Gate, near Beijing, the two divinities Fuxi and Nüwa, who had human bodies and the tails of snakes, encircle an auspicious spirit *(far right)*. This spirit may have been able to chase away evil influences but it was powerless against the Manchu invaders, who had a chance to admire this bas-relief in passing in about 1644.

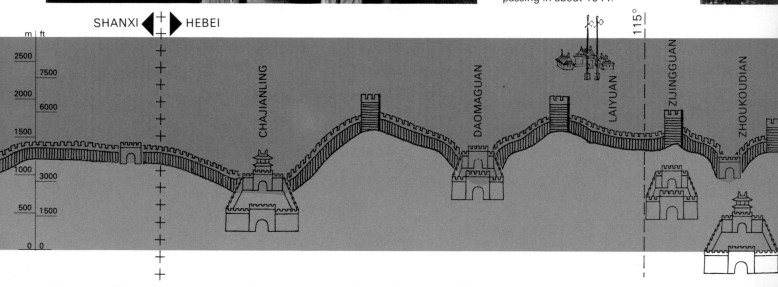

SHANXI ◀✛▶ HEBEI

m | ft

2500 | 7500
2000 | 6000
1500 |
1000 | 3000
500 | 1500
0 | 0

CHAJIANLING   DAOMAGUAN   LAIYUAN   ZIJINGGUAN   ZHOUKOUDIAN

115°

With their wealth of common and rare birds, the mountain regions of Hebei are an ornithologist's paradise.
The *Crossoptilon manchuricum (right)* is a protected species of pheasant found in Shanxi province. The beauty of its plumage, especially the characteristic whiskers at each side of its head, is much appreciated by the Chinese, who breed it for ornamental purposes. Another species altogether, the eagle-owl *(Bubo bubo)* is a familiar sight *(far right)* on the Great Wall —it is found all the way along from Gansu to Hebei.

THE JUYONGGUAN PASS AND MOUNT BADALING

It is in the proximity of the Juyongguan Pass and Mount Badaling that we can find what may well be called the best sample of the Great Wall, constructed by the Ming dynasty during the fifteenth century. A series of forts were built in a valley cutting through the Jundu Mountains forming a part of the Yanshan range. Peaks above peaks, clad in green, stand on both sides of the valley, the southern entrance of which is controlled by the town of Nankou. On the ridges flanking the town we can see the ruins of walls and beacon towers—they are all that is left of the forts built here.

Proceeding six kilometers (4 miles) to the northwest along the valley, we come to the Juyongguan Pass and the Cloud Terrace. Another nine-kilometer drive (6 miles) will bring us to the northern entrance of the valley under Mount Badaling. The fort erected here has been carefully preserved to this day. It has two gates. The one facing west bears an inscription which means "Lock of the North Entrance,"

mit of either of the mountains flanking the Juyongguan Pass. There they see the Great Wall wriggling among the peaks and extending beyond the horizon. This majestic view is reminiscent of the age-old saying: "The strategic significance of Juyongguan lies in Mount Badaling rather than the Pass itself." Two gates of this fort have been preserved to this day. The Cloud Terrace in this fort was constructed during the reign of the Mongol Yuan dynasty (1271–1368). It is a white marble arch over the road, richly decorated. Walking through this arch, which is in the shape of three sides of a hexagon, one beholds statues of the Four Invincibles in relief and inscriptions from Buddhist sacred writings, as well as an article recording the construction of the terrace in Sanskrit, Tibetan, Basban Mongolian, Uighur, Chinese, and Xixia characters. Researchers on ancient languages have shown deep interest in these inscriptions. Lying at the north of the Juyongguan Pass, a huge boulder is said to have served as a platform where Mu Guiying, a heroine of the tenth century, inspected her troops.

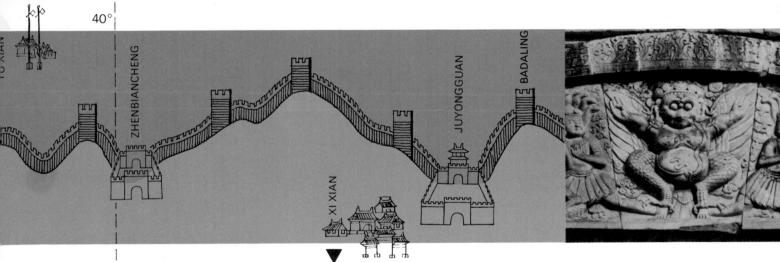

and the other facing east is inscribed with characters meaning "Frontline before Juyongguan."

Standing only 60 kilometers (40 miles) from Beijing, the Juyongguan Pass was valued high by the strategists for the Ming dynasty. This can be seen from the fact that forts were built so solidly and so close to each other, connected by walls forming more than two lines and surrounded by the beacon towers scattered here and there on the peaks.

Following the pavement on the top of the Great Wall, visitors will reach the sum-

As early as the beginning of the seventh century, a Buddhist monk known as Jingwan engraved stone tablets with inscriptions of the sacred writings to be stored in the once flourishing Yunju Monastery on Mount Tafanshan to the southwest of Beijing. His example was followed by later generations. Discovered in caves and the cellars under the ruins of the ancient monastery, these tablets total more than 1,500. And the numerous and exquisitely designed pagodas which have remained over the ruins are very good samples of Chinese architecture of

different periods from the seventh to the eleventh century.

The Juyongguan was known as one of the "Three Inner Passes," the other two being Zijingguan Pass and the Daomaguan Pass in Hebei province. Standing on Mount Zijingling, the pass named after it was another place of high strategic importance in north China because it controlled the entrance to the Hebei plain from the Taihong Mountains. In 1449, Mongol troops under the command of General Walayesian, who was holding Ming Emperor Yingzong as a hostage, broke through the Great Wall here to besiege Beijing. The Ming empire and her people owed a great deal to Defense Minister Yu Qian (1398–1457) for his efforts in concentrating powerful armies and organizing the inhabitants of the capital to repulse the Mongols.

After a ride of 30 kilometers (20 miles) to the east from the Zijingguan Pass we come to the Yishui River. In 227 B.C. Jing Ke, on his way to assassinate the king of Qin (who was later to become the First Emperor), parted on the bank of this river with the crown prince of the kingdom of Yan who had assigned him that risky task and who was seeing him off. Jing, to the music of his friend Gao Jianli, sang:
"A wind soughs over the icy Yishui River
Bidding eternal farewell to a gallant
   man!"

These lines have been recited through more than twenty centuries to this day.

Following the highway from Beijing to Laiyuan in western Hebei, we cross the Yishui River and come to the Qing dynasty's western tombs. The first emperor buried here was Yong Zheng who reigned from 1723 to 1735. While both his father and grandfather had been buried in the eastern tombs in Zunhua county, Hebei, this supreme ruler, chose to be buried here, because, according to a tradition, he who had usurped the throne by intrigues dreaded the prospect of being buried with his predecessors. Covering an area with a circuit of no less than 100 kilometers (60 miles), there are tombs of four emperors including Guangxu who had made futile attempts at reforms in 1898, three empresses, and four concubines. Guangxu's concubine Zhen Fei who was murdered by Empress Dowager Cixi who had been in control of the empire for nearly half a century, was also reburied here.

The north gate of the fortress of Juyongguan. Through this pass runs the important route from the capital of China to the north and west. It leads to important places in northern Hebei and Shanxi, such as Zhangjiakou and Datong and farther on to distant Baoton, Hohhot, and to Erenhot, of historical significance, in Inner Mongolia. Beneath, buried in a tunnel deep in the earth, runs the railway line, which makes a connection with the Transsiberian in Russia.

"It was here that Yang Liulang drove the enemy back." This stele was piously erected under the Mings in 1520 in memory of the defender of Yixian, which lies about 100 kilometers (60 miles) southwest of Beijing. This general's real name was Yang Yanlang and he owes his nickname ("the sixth") to the fact that he was the sixth son of General Yang Ye, who also won renown in this region fighting the Khitans in the tenth century. He is to be seen in the above illustration, grappling with an enemy, while bringing his troops to the aid of a Song emperor (probably Taizong) in danger.

Right: The wall running from the fortress to Mount Badaling, seen in the light of a winter's day. Faced with this fortification, with these impressive walls, even a warlord and conqueror like Genghis Khan was forced to turn back. This happened in 1211: the target of the Mongolian strike had been Yenching, capital of the Chinese empire.
Genghis Khan had very little respect for the wall as an obstacle. Events at the start of his campaign appeared to confirm his opinion; his hordes overran the Exterior Wall without significant loss. He was soon faced with the imposing fortress of Juyongguan, and its resolute defenders: this proved to be an insuperable obstacle.

The picture below gives a view over the fortress of Juyongguan. Together with Shanhaiguan and Jiayuguan, it forms part of the perfectly maintained stretch of the Great Wall, and is its finest ornament. Crowning glory of the fortress is the so-called "Cloud Terrace," built of white marble, with beautiful decorations and reliefs. A picture such as this, with the wall deserted, is rare. Every day, Juyongguan is the goal of thousands of tourists, Chinese and foreign (see p. 185). It is an obligatory stop for foreign visitors to Beijing, whether statesmen or package tourists. And no one turns away from the wall without a feeling of awareness of its powerful impact.

The inscription below, in Mongolian characters, is composed of a Buddhist citation incised on a stone tablet. Its erector had the text inscribed in six different languages.

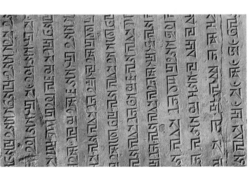

The King of Yan (Beijing area), feeling the growing threat of the future emperor of the Qin, sent a man to assassinate him in 227 B.C. This man, who was called Jing Ke, failed in his task, but this pagoda was built in his memory in the fourteenth century, not far from Beijing.

BEIJING CITY

Beijing was built in the early Ming dynasty (mid-fourteenth century). Part of its foundations, however, were left over from Dadu (Great Capital) of the Yuan dynasty. Dadu measured 30 kilometers (20 miles) around with eleven gates. (See illustrations.) The construction was started in 1267 and finished in 1292. The general plan was that palaces took up the northern part of the city, and markets the southern portion; temples were located in the west and ceremonial grounds in the east. Marco Polo (1254–1324) from Italy spoke of Dadu with "a circumference of twenty-four miles.... The streets are so wide and straight that it is possible to look along their entire length, and from one city gate you can see the gate on the opposite side. Besides magnificent palaces, there are many big hotels and sumptuous residences." "People crowded the city in and out...mostly having luxurious houses with palace walls and pavillions decorated with gold or silver hues, and images of dragons, unicorns, and cavaliers." What we call Yuan Tucheng

destroyed the city with fire. The Yuan dynasty (1279–1365) moved their capital here, rebuilt the city, and named it Dadu. Ming dynasty General Xu Da stormed Dadu in 1368, renaming it Beiping. The city walls were renovated and its north wall was moved southward some 2.5 kilometers (1.5 miles). When Chengzu ascended to the throne, he changed the name of Beiping to Beijing and made it the capital. Work on palaces started in 1406. The south wall moved southward about one kilometer in 1419 (fifteenth year of the Yongle era) because the newly built palaces had so expanded. The imperial palaces were tightly guarded. Toward the end of the Ming dynasty, insurgent peasants led by Li Zicheng took Beijing and broke into the imperial palaces. Emperor Zhuangliedi fled out of the palaces and hanged himself. Peasant uprings broke out in Hebei, Henan, and other provinces in the eighteenth year of the Jiaqing era of the Qing dynasty (1813). A peasant force in Beijing, in coordination with some palace eunuchs, entered the imperial palaces and fought a fierce battle in the Forbidden

The area where Beijing lies today has been inhabited for a very long time, for the *Sinanthropus pekinensis* lived there. It has been possible to reconstitute the skull of this hominid from fragments discovered at the paleolithic site of Zhoukoudian. "Beijing Man" has been traced back to the beginning of the Quaternary period.

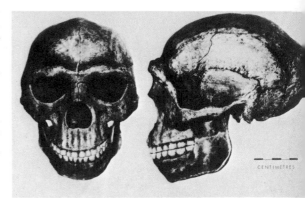

The diagram has once more reached the point (already mentioned on p. 107) where the north and south branches now join up as a single wall running all the way to Shanhaiguan.

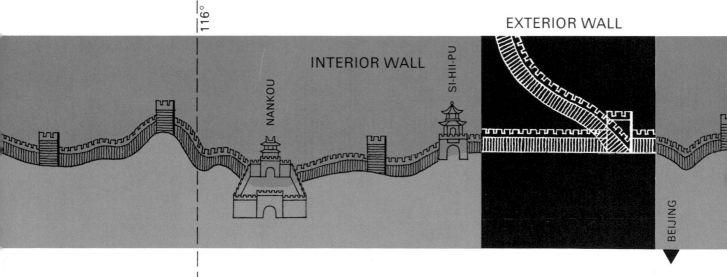

EXTERIOR WALL

INTERIOR WALL

NANKOU

SI-HII-PU

BEIJING

SHISANLING

116°

(Earth City) today is the site of the city wall of the once world-famous Dadu. Remains of this golden city can still be seen outside Deshengmen in today's Beijing conurbation.
Beijing was the secondary capital of the Liao dynasty (916–1125), under the name of Nanjing or Yanjing. The Jin Dynasty (1115–1234) made it their formal capital, expanding this Liao city and renaming it Zhongdu (Middle Capital). When Mongolian troops captured Zhongdu and overthrew the Jin dynasty, they

City. Arrow heads can still be seen on a plaque and a roof beam in the northeastern corner of the Longzong Gate in the inner palace.
The Qing dynasty also made Beijing its capital, but made virtually no changes to the Ming city walls. The walls were gradually demolished after the founding of New China in 1949. The moat circling the wall has formed the basis of the underground railway round the city, on top of which run boulevards that help improve the capital's communications.

On this aerial photograph of the Imperial Palace at Beijing, the three successive courtyards giving access to the palace proper are clearly visible. The elegance and harmony in the proportions of these buildings are again to be found in the Temple of the Sky *(below)*, an architectural miracle supported by 28 pillars without crossgirders.

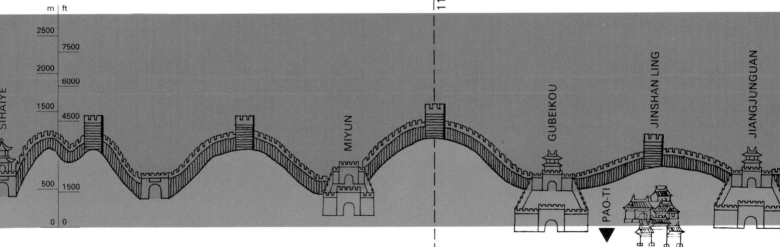

Far left: The postern of the Zheng-yang Gate was finished under the Mings in 1439, destroyed in 1900, and has since been restored. Its massive and imposing aspect is typical of a particular style of architecture in Beijing, many valuable examples of which were razed to the ground during and after the Cultural Revolution.

The Temple of the Reclining Buddha is in the western part of the Beijing district. It contains this immense bronze, weighing 54 tons, which was cast in 1321 during the Yuan dynasty.

The tomb of Emperor Shenzong is representative of the prosperity that China enjoyed at the beginning of his reign, the Wanli era (1573–1620). Its construction, begun in 1583 in the hills northwest of Beijing, led to the settlement of certain accounts between high officials; these palace intrigues were very much part of the climate of the time and were one factor that caused the state to become so weak at the end of the sixteenth century.

Opposite: Like its big sister in the north, the inner Great Wall crosses the mountains and rivers in a series of complex windings. This photograph shows the impressive pattern as it appears from a satellite (118°–119° E, 40°–41° N): (1) Luanhe (river), (2) Paohe (river), (3) Lulong, (4) Qiangxi, (5) Chang Ling Fang, (6) Gu Shanzu, (7) Qinglong, (8) Chengde Xian, (9) Sangu, (10) Chengde.

Below: The Great Wall in the Nankou region in the Badaling Mountains. This part of the wall, as we have seen, could not hold the Manchu armies back, although it was well maintained.

THE WALL IN EAST HEBEI

Between 117 and 118 degrees longitude, there are many Great Walls. In Weichang county are the Great Wall erected by the Yan state during the Warring States period, the Great Wall built in the reign of Qin Shi huangdi, and the Great Wall and forts of the Han dynasty. The Great Wall inside Luanping, Xinglong, and Zunhua counties is a magnificent section under the jurisdiction of Ji Zhen (Ji military zone). It is built on high and steep mountains and with lashings of ramparts.

Gubeikou, a gateway to Beijing in the northeast, is a key pass of the Great Wall as significant as Juyongguan and Badaling. During the Ming dynasty, a military unit called lu under the zhen was established here to control a dozen or so passes. A 30 kilometer (20 mile) section of the wall, which was once a pass under the command of Gubeikou, was found between June and July 1980 in Hebei province's Luanping county bordering on Miyun. Called "Second Badaling" because of its magnificent scenery, plans are being

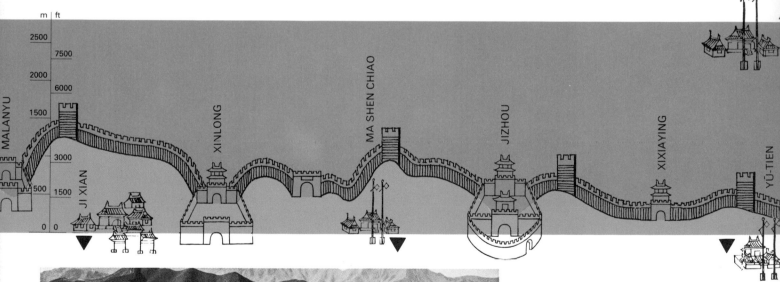

made to repair it and then open it to the public (see reconstruction, p. 137).

There are traces of the Great Wall in Weichang county, all built of earth by the state of Yan during the Warring Kingdoms period, the Qin dynasty, and the Han dynasty (a total period from 475 B.C. to A.D. 200). Many small castles have been found in this area, which lined the Great Wall at an interval of about ten kilometers (6 miles).

In Jilin province, northeastern China, at the city of Chengde, the impressive lamasery of Potala occupies a mountainous site. This region borders on Manchuria, from which the successors to the Ming rulers were to come. But the religion practiced here is Tibetan—the faith of the Lamas.

Panoramic view of the Great Wall making its way through the region of Xifengkou, halfway between Beijing and Shanhaiguan.

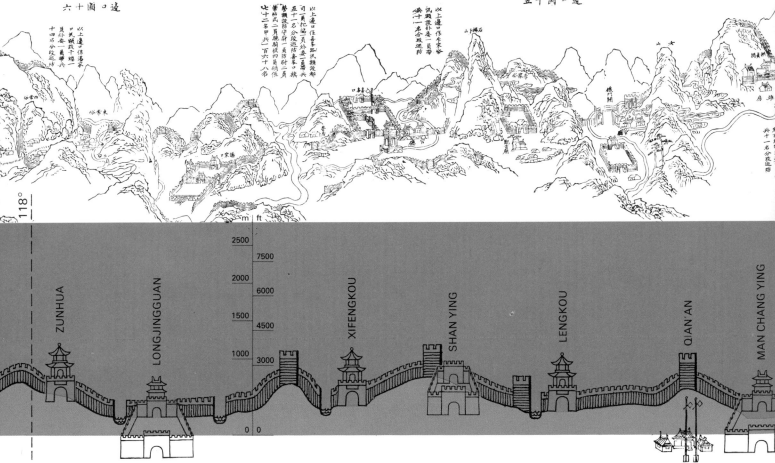

In Hebei province, at the midway point between Xifengkou and Beijing, the Great Wall forces its way up into the Wuling Mountains. This is the approximate point where the Chinese emperors, leaving the capital city, used to cross the wall on the way to their summer residence, the Palace of Chengde, about 150 kilometers (100 miles) away to the northeast.

THE SHANHAIGUAN PASS

The Shanhaiguan Pass, so important in the eastern section of the Great Wall in the Ming dynasty (1368–1644), is located northeast of Qinhuangdao city, Hebei province, and borders on Liaoning province. Qinhuangdao, nestling against hills, facing the sea and of strategical importance, was often visited by ancient Chinese emperors while inspecting border areas. According to records in Chinese history books, Qin Shi huangdi came to Jieshi during his travel in east China and had an inscription carved on the city gate called "Jieshi Menci." Hence Qinhuang-dao was named.

An earlier pass in the vicinity, the Yuguan, had been situated on a plain and had no strategic importance. Thus it was abandoned later and a new pass was built instead when Xu Da began building the Great Wall in the early Ming dynasty. The new pass, with the Yanshan Mountains to the north and the Bohai Bay to the east, was named the "Shanhaiguan Pass" because it lies between the mountains and the sea.

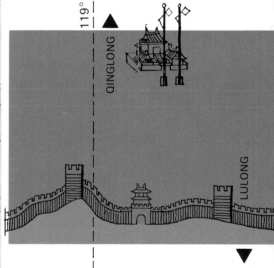

This stele was erected by the Qing emperor Gaozong (reigned 1736–1796) in a mountain pass situated near Chengde, over which he traveled on his way to his hunting grounds. It is a strategically important pass, since it serves to connect the Hebei plain with the Mongolian plateaux. Gaozong, fourth of the Qing or Manchu rulers and one of the ablest, governed at a time of significant change in China: acquisition of control over Tibet, establishment of trade with the United States, and links with Britain.

Another area of great strategic interest, the region of the northeast of Hebei as far as Shanhaiguan was the scene of frequent military maneuvers. The exercises illustrated in this print are taking place in this area. Proximity to Beijing gave the Shanhaiguan Pass its great importance. This is the point where the Great Wall as such came to its eastern end, though a crude extension was added at one time.

Climbing up to the tower of the pass and gazing at the mountain ranges in the north, one can see the Great Wall winding in its majesty over the hills. How marvelously wrought! Overlooking the sea in the east, one can see the sea joining with the sky, broadening the mind and cleansing one of cares. In the Ming dynasty, there was also a nearly 1,000 kilometer (600 mile) Great Wall east of the Shanhaiguan Pass, extending to the bank of the Yalu River. However, only remnants of this crudely built section of the Great Wall can be found today.

123

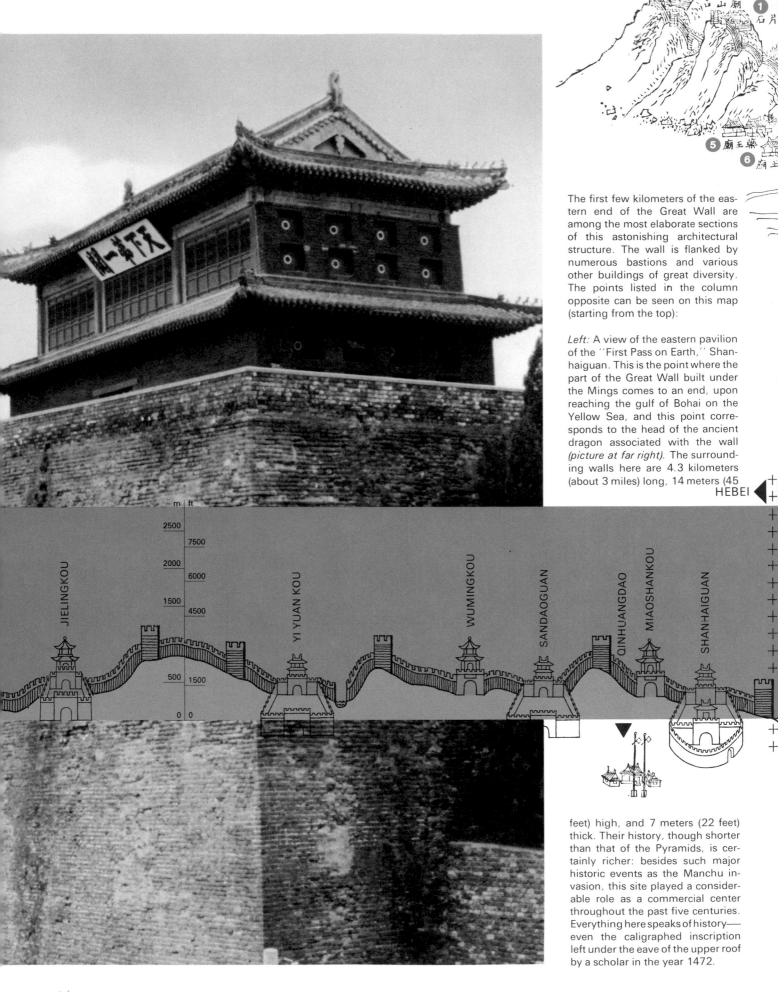

The first few kilometers of the eastern end of the Great Wall are among the most elaborate sections of this astonishing architectural structure. The wall is flanked by numerous bastions and various other buildings of great diversity. The points listed in the column opposite can be seen on this map (starting from the top):

Left: A view of the eastern pavilion of the "First Pass on Earth," Shanhaiguan. This is the point where the part of the Great Wall built under the Mings comes to an end, upon reaching the gulf of Bohai on the Yellow Sea, and this point corresponds to the head of the ancient dragon associated with the wall *(picture at far right).* The surrounding walls here are 4.3 kilometers (about 3 miles) long, 14 meters (45

HEBEI

feet) high, and 7 meters (22 feet) thick. Their history, though shorter than that of the Pyramids, is certainly richer: besides such major historic events as the Manchu invasion, this site played a considerable role as a commercial center throughout the past five centuries. Everything here speaks of history—even the caligraphed inscription left under the eave of the upper roof by a scholar in the year 1472.

124

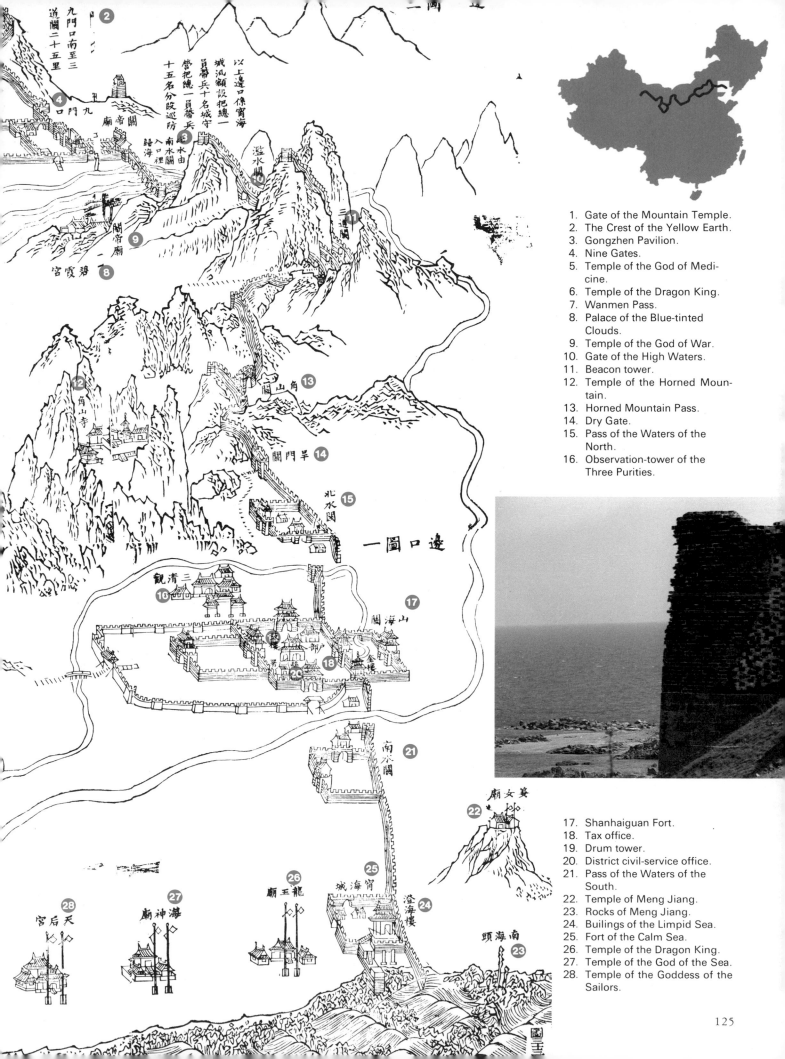

1. Gate of the Mountain Temple.
2. The Crest of the Yellow Earth.
3. Gongzhen Pavilion.
4. Nine Gates.
5. Temple of the God of Medicine.
6. Temple of the Dragon King.
7. Wanmen Pass.
8. Palace of the Blue-tinted Clouds.
9. Temple of the God of War.
10. Gate of the High Waters.
11. Beacon tower.
12. Temple of the Horned Mountain.
13. Horned Mountain Pass.
14. Dry Gate.
15. Pass of the Waters of the North.
16. Observation-tower of the Three Purities.

17. Shanhaiguan Fort.
18. Tax office.
19. Drum tower.
20. District civil-service office.
21. Pass of the Waters of the South.
22. Temple of Meng Jiang.
23. Rocks of Meng Jiang.
24. Buildings of the Limpid Sea.
25. Fort of the Calm Sea.
26. Temple of the Dragon King.
27. Temple of the God of the Sea.
28. Temple of the Goddess of the Sailors.

The fort of the Shanhaiguan Pass is square, about 4 kilometers (2.5 miles) in circumference, 14 meters high, and 7 meters thick. Its walls were built of earth inside and bricks outside. It has four gates, the east gate Zhendong, the west Ying'en, the south Wangyang, and the north gate Weiyuan. Outside the east gate there is the protruding fortress of Luocheng. On the east, south, and north of the fort is a moat 17 meters side. The southern and northern sides of the fort's east wall are linked with the Great Wall. On the southern wall there once stood the Kuiguang pavilion and Muying tower, and on the northern wall there used to be Weiyuan hall and Linlu tower. Inside the wall on the southern and northern sides of the fort, there are two fortresses, one in the south wing, the other in the north. They coordinate with the fort from a distance to strengthen the defense. On the four gates there are two-story towers, which have peepholes on three sides. On the east gate of the fort is a horizontal plaque inscribed with five powerfully written characters, "The First Pass On Earth," making the fort even more spectacular.

The name of Meng Jiang, who sits here in her temple between her son and daughter, will always remain inextricably linked with the Great Wall, synonymous with the misfortunes and ruptures experienced by the Chinese while it was being built. To understand the affection that the Chinese still feel for this woman today, her immense grief must be imagined, when she realized that her husband had died of exhaustion at his work.

Left: View from the entrance of the Temple of Meng Jiang, east of the Shanhaiguan Fort.

Right: Meng Jiang cried so bitterly when she learned of her husband's tragic end that part of the wall—the part where her husband died, according to the legend—collapsed.

Far left: This stele faces the sea at Shanhaiguan.

MENG JIANG

The Shanhaiguan Pass is a place which all strategists tried to seize because its terrain is strategically situated and difficult of access. The troops of the Qing dynasty (A.D. 1644–1911) entered the interior of China through the pass toward the end of the Ming dynasty. Prior to this, the Shanhaiguan was guarded by General Wu Sangui as head of the subcommand of the pass. While in Beijing, Wu Sangui took the young singer Chen Yuanyuan as his concubine. Because of her unrivaled beauty, she won great favor with Wu Sangui. She remained in Beijing when Wu left for the Shanhaiguan. Not long after, Li Zicheng captured Beijing, thus overthrowing the Ming dynasty. Since Wu Sangui guarded the important Shanhaiguan Pass, Li Zicheng sent envoys to persuade him to surrender. Hearing that his favorite concubine, Yuanyuan, had been seized by a general under Li Zicheng, Wu Sangui, in a rage, surrendered to the Qing dynasty at the expense of national interests. He guided the Qing troops inside the pass and made it possible for them to occupy Beijing with ease.

Another famous site of historical interest near the pass is the Jiangnu Temple. The temple, located in the Wangfushi ("searching for the husband") Rock Village 10 kilometers (6 miles) east of the pass, has a statue of the legendary Meng Jiang. According to records, the temple was called Zhennu ("chaste woman") shrine in the Song dynasty (A.D. 960–1279), but was abandoned later and *rebuilt in the Ming dynasty. Behind it there is the rock called Wangfu, from which vantage point people are able to enjoy the beautiful view of the mountains and the sea (see page 16).*

Legend has it that Meng Jiang lived in Shaanxi province in the reign of Emperor Qin Shi huangdi. Her husband being conscripted to built the Great Wall, she was always worried about his performing hard labor in a border region. Traveling thousands of miles across mountains and rivers, she carried winter clothing to him. Contrary to her expectations, on arriving at the destination, she found that her husband had died of back-breaking toil. Grief-stricken, she cried so bitterly that the sky turned dark and a section of the wall opened up, exposing to her the bones of her husband. She jumped into the sea with the bones. A temple was built later in memory of her.

Possibly, the legend of Meng Jiang comes down from the story of Qi Liang's wife in Zuo Zhuan *(Annals of Sir Zuo). In fact, of course there may have been no real Meng Jiang, and the legend might be a wrong conclusion drawn by false analogy.*

However, there were indeed thousands of people having the same fate as Meng Jiang. She has touched the hearts of later generations with her pure and sincere love and, what is more important, her spirit of opposition against persecution has always inspired people under oppression.

The folklore about how Meng Jiang wept for her husband and brought down the Great Wall has remained popular among people for over twenty centuries. This indicates that it had great vitality in the feudal society and reflected the Chinese people's ideals.

THE BALLAD OF MENG CHIANG NU WEEPING AT THE GREAT WALL

Then putting down the coffin: they started
   their labour
In a place of mountains and waters: true
   and fitting
The bier stood ready: the coffin by the
   tomb
And Mêng Chiang Nü waiting: by the
   cliff-temple

Finally she knelt: down on the ground
Prayed to her husband: Fan San-Lang
"Wait for me: in the other world
So we may come before: the King of the
   place together."

When Mêng Chiang Nü had finished:
   these prayers and orisons
Turning round she thanked: the tyrant
   Emperor
For burying her husband: by the Eastern
   Sea
And all the officials: for being present there

Having bowed to them all: she knelt down
   again
To her parents for having: nourished and
   raised her
Four prostrations and eight bows:
   solemnly she gave
Did obeisance to the parents-in-law: for
   their teachings

Mêng Chiang Nü was sorry: she could no
   more wait on them
So having thanked all: one by one
She turned to the Englightened One:
   speaking as follows
"Your maidservant Mêng Chiang Nü: is
   under a vow

How can I obey you: O evil King?"
Covering up her face: with her skirt of
   black silk
And lifting up her two feet: she leapt into
   the sea
As for the wicked Emperor: he could not
   stop her.

Excerpt from the English translation by Joseph Needham and Liao Hung-Ying, first published in *Sinologica*, 1948.

EAST OF SHANHAIGUAN

The Great Wall is commonly considered as beginning or ending (depending on the viewpoint) at the seacoast at Shanhaiguan, "the First Pass on Earth"—that is, at the border of Manchuria or, as it is now known, Liaoning province. And yet, beyond this point, as early as the year 1074, the Song rulers erected a 300-mile-long palisade "wall" or fence out of elm and willow trees, in the hope of presenting an effective obstacle to incursions by the wild horsemen called the Khitans.

This defense line was reinforced by the Ming emperors, though far less completely and perfectly than in the case of the Great Wall itself. The inscription shown here, which contains an account of military campaigns connected with this barrier, testifies to its existence in the area near Yinzhou.

This wall or fence, in a series of loops, traveled along the shores of the Gulf of Liaodong past Shenyang to the mouth of the Yalu River at Dandong, situated on the present-day border of North Korea.

LUO ZEWEN

It is said that when a dragon came to inspect this area of the Wall, where only foundations had been laid, the ground caved in. Out of respect for the dragon, this irregularity of the ground was taken into account when the wall was built. *Opposite:* Collective work has always been the rule in China, and the well-known danger of invaders from the north no doubt lent urgency to this esprit de corps.

HOW THE WALL WAS BUILT

Standing on Juyongguan, Badaling, Shanhaiguan, or Jiayuguan pass, one cannot help marveling at the Great Wall seen winding like a snake among the towering mountains. Since we today are invariably out of breath from climbing the wall empty-handed, it must have been strenuous indeed for the builders in ancient times to carry the bricks weighing more than ten kilograms apiece (or 22 pounds), and stone slabs weighing hundreds of kilograms, to the mountain tops and ridges. They paid dearly in sweat and blood for this project.

In this chapter we take a brief look at the actual work of building the Great Wall, both in ancient times and more recently under the Ming dynasty. The building, and continual rebuilding, of this structure is of course a technical subject—but when we consider the technical means available at the time of its construction, we realize that this is a human story after all, a testimony to human will and perseverance.

CONSTRUCTION HISTORY: THE MING WALL

The Great Wall built in the Ming dynasty was south of the earthen Great Wall built in the Qin dynasty along the Yinshan Mountains. From the Mongolian Plateau to the North China Plain and from the northwest to the southeast, the terrain lowers in a staircase manner. If the Yinshan Mountains are taken as the first stair, the Zhangjiakou area will be the second stair, and the Juyongguan area the third stair. The Great Wall built in the Qin dynasty is on the first stair. The outer wall of the Great Wall built in the ming dynasty lies on the second stair, while the inner wall occupies the third stair, most of these walls being built with bricks and stones.

Construction of the Ming dynasty Great Wall was started by General Xu Da and others during the reign of Emperor Taizu, first of the Ming emperors. Under Emperor Chengzu, the section of the Great Wall on Badaling was built with stones and the section between Xuanhua and Datong was also completed. The section of the Great Wall from Shanxi and Shaanxi to Gansu was built in the Zhengtong period of Emperor Yingzong (1436–1449) and the Chenghua period of Emperor Xianzong (1465–1486). The whole project took more than 170 years.

When Wong Wanda was in charge of the defenses of Xuanhua and Datong in the Jiaqing period (after 1544), he built over 500 kilometers of the Great Wall as well as 363 beacon towers. By then the scale of the Ming dynasty Great Wall had been roughly fixed. During the Longqing period (1567–1572), Tan Lun, Qi Jiguang, and others built the Jizhen section of the Great Wall in Hebei and constructed 472 watch towers. During the late Wanli period (around 1614), Xiong Jianbi built the Great Wall in eastern Liaoning. On the basis of the original earthern wall, he built the Great Wall which started from Shanhaiguan in the west and reached Kaiyuan in the north and then meandered southward to reach the estuary of the Yalu River, stretching for 1,000 kilometers (600 miles). The magnificent Great Wall of the Ming dynasty, built to serve military purposes, was completed through the painstaking work of several generations, using immense manpower and material resources.

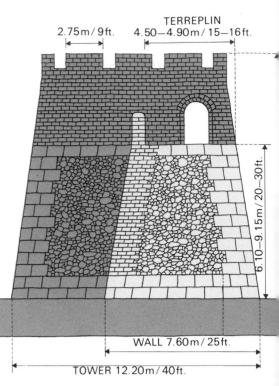

TERREPLIN

2.75m/9ft.   4.50—4.90m/15—16ft.

6.10—9.15m/20—30ft.

WALL 7.60m/25ft.

TOWER 12.20m/40ft.

Below: Bricks and tiles being made in the traditional way of the craftsman. Water poured into a hole at the top of the oven produced the glazing process. Ovens like these were probably used in certain areas of construction of the Great Wall where the topography made it impossible to bring in construction materials.

We now proceed to examine specific aspects of the construction of the wall throughout the ages.

ORGANIZATION AND DEPLOYMENT OF LABOR

Labor administration was of primary importance in undertaking such a gigantic project. According to historical records, the manpower came from the following sources.

1. Frontier guards. The *Historical Records* by Sima Qian inform us that the Great Wall of Qin Shi huangdi was completed in a dozen or so years (ca. 221—210 B.C.) by the 300,000-strong army under General Meng Tian, who remained at the frontier after repelling the harassments by the Xiongnu. The states before the Qin dynasty all used troops to construct their long walls. The *Zhushu Jinian*, a chronicle book written on bamboo slips, records that in the twelfth year (359 B.C.) of the reign of Prince Hui Cheng of the state of Liang, General Long Jia led his men to build the long wall west of the Wei Kingdom. Several dynasties later, Qin Shi huangdi followed suit.

2. Peasants. Qin Shi huangdi press-ganged about 500,000 peasants, besides the huge army, into building the Great Wall. This was also the case with the subsequent dynasties. In the seventh year (A.D. 446) of

Although the small forts flanking the wall generally resembled the one shown in section on the left, there were many architectural variations, as is shown by these observation towers *(below)*, which may or may not be part of the fortifications proper.

These illustrations form a part of the extensive stock of written and technically illlustrated instruction manuals compiled by both engineers and generals. They were concerned not only with where the various installations were to be built, but also gave very precise details of the method of construction; as such, they have proved to be of invaluable assistance to modern researchers.

Below: Yu Qian (1398—1457) won his greatest renown as the minister of war responsible for the construction of the Great Wall, notably in Zhejiang province. He was also to save the Ming Empire when, the ruler Yingzong having been taken prisoner in 1449, he succeeded in

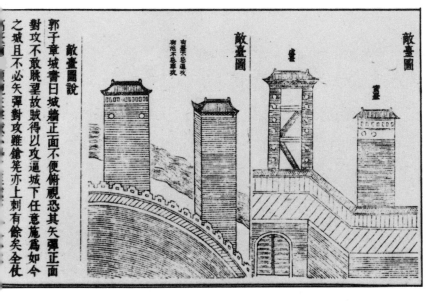

the reign of Taiping Zhenjun in the Northern Wei dynasty, 300,000 laborers from four prefectures were called up to construct the section of the Great Wall south of the capital, Pingcheng (present-day Datong). In the sixth year (555) of the reign of Tian Bao in the Northern Qi dynasty, the emperor ordered the recruitment of 1.8 million peasants for the reconstruction of the 900-*li* wall between Xiakou in Youzhou (present-day Juyongguan outside Nankou, Beijing) to Hengzhou (Datong area). In the third year (A.D. 583) of the reign of Kai Huang of the Sui dynasty, 30,000 male laborers were recruited to work on the wall at Shuofang and Lingwu. The following year saw the calling up of another 150,000 male laborers to construct fortresses along the Great Wall. In the third and the fourth year (A.D. 607 and 608) of the reign of Da Ye, over a million males, and then another 200,000, were press-ganged into this work respectively.

3. Convicts. There existed a special penalty during the Qin and Han dynasties, under which convicted criminals were made to work on the wall as a way of atoning for their crimes.

CONSTRUCTION MANAGEMENT

The Great Wall stretched over 10,000 *li*. It would be inconceivable to accomplish such a gigantic project but for a set of scientific methods for overseeing and organizing the construction.

Construction tasks were divided up and assigned to garrison areas; in other cases large forces were concentrated to tackle certain sections.

When the section of the Great Wall in the Gansu Corridor was built at the time of Emperor Wu Di of the Han dynasty, the military governors of the four prefectures (Wuwei, Zhangye, Jiuquan, and Dunhuang) were made responsible for the reconstruction of the wall within their respective areas. The governors in turn divided the tasks among their subordinates.

The Ming dynasty put the wall construction in the hands of the commanding generals in the nine strategic towns. The section at Liaodong outside the Shanhaiguan Pass was built under the supervision of Wang Ao, Bi Gong, and others during their terms of office as military commanders there. The several thousand watch towers and beacon towers along the Great Wall from Shanhaiguan to Juyongguan

beating off the invaders and placed a substitute, Daizong, on the imperial throne. His presence of mind in the face of these dramatic circumstances was ill rewarded, for he was condemned to death in 1457, when the former Emperor was reinstated, for treason.

No other construction project in the history of the world can boast the participation of a whole race, building, changing, improving, and renovating their handiwork over a period of some two thousand years. And probably no other has had such a constant history of dispute over the ultimate usefulness of the end product.

This brick comes from a wall at Dongluocheng near the western end of the Great Wall. "Made in the twelfth year of the era of Wanli (1585) at Luanzhou," it had to be transported about 80 kilometers (50 miles). Its weight may be guessed from its size: 38.2 × 18 cm, and 9.5 cm thick (15 × 7 × 3¾ inches).

were constructed under the supervision of the well-known General Qi Jiguang when he was the military commander at the strategic town of Ji. The work was similarly divided among the garrison officers and soldiers.

A stone tablet found on the top of the wall at Badaling is inscribed with a record of how thousands of soldiers and large numbers of civilians undertook to repair a 200-meter portion of the Great Wall in the tenth year (1582) of the reign of Wan Li during the Ming dynasty.

PROCUREMENT OF BUILDING MATERIALS

Earth, stone, timber, and tiles were the chief materials for building the Great Wall before the Ming dynasty, and bricks were used only in the later periods. Use of local materials was the rule followed by the wall builders throughout the centuries. Stones were quarried to build walls in the high mountains; tamped earthen walls were erected on flat or loess areas; walls in the Gobi Desert were raised with alternating layers of sand and pebbles and tamarisk twigs and reeds; walls at Liaodong in the northeast were built of locally available boards of oak, pine, and china fir trees.

Apart from earth, stones, and timber, large quantities of bricks and lime were used during the Ming dynasty. Bricks and tiles were mainly produced by the kilns erected on the spot, as was the lime. Trees were felled in the vicinity to construct forts and watch towers. If bricks and tiles could not be made on the spot, they were fired in nearby prefectures and counties. Markings on the bricks at Shanhaiguan Pass show

that they were made in nearby counties. If there were no forests near the construction site, timber had to be brought on from afar. Since procurement of materials was a vital link in this large-scale project, special sections were set up for this purpose as well as offices in charge of kilns and quarries.

TRANSPORT OF BUILDING MATERIALS

Building materials for the Great Wall were transported by the following methods:

1. By man. Rocks, bricks, lime, timber, and other building materials were carried on human backs or with carrying poles. Sometimes they were passed on from hand to hand: builders stood in line from the foot of the mountain or from a completed section of the wall to the hilltop or mountain ridge, and then building materials

The wheelbarrow, with or without the addition of mules or even sails as for a boat, is a Chinese invention dating back to the beginning of the Christian era. In contrast with the western wheelbarrow, the wheel is placed at the center of gravity permitting heavy loads to be transported.

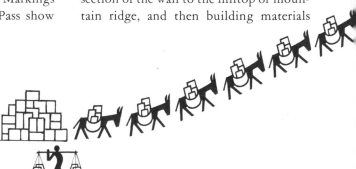

132

Among the means of transport that use only human energy, the two baskets attached to a rod, familiar throughout Asia, probably far outnumbered other methods in the construction of the Great Wall. The simple wheelbarrow was also used extensively.

were passed along. This method spared the builders the trouble of long walks on narrow mountain trails, thus avoiding collisions.

2. By simple tools. Handcarts were the common means of transportation, which could be used on flat ground or gentle slopes. Rocks weighing up to 500 kilograms (110 pounds) were carried by using wooden rods, levers, and also windlasses. Ropes were also slung across deep ravines and valleys, to convey basketfuls of bricks, tiles, lime, and other building materials.

3. By animals. It is said that sure-footed animals such as goats and donkeys were used to carry bricks and lime when the wall was being built at Badaling. The donkeys were made to carry on their backs baskets filled with bricks and lime; as for the goats, bricks were tied onto their horns. The animals were then driven up the mountain. It was no easy task to build the Great Wall at any time. It involved untold sorrows of many families and the blood and sweat of countless laborers. However, the Great Wall stands as an immortal witness to the wisdom and indomitable will of the Chinese people. Even today people can still draw on the experience of its construction.

walls were built of stone slabs and bricks. Builders had to level the ground before laying bricks in a systematic way. The wall at Juyongguan and Badaling near Beijing snakes its way through the mountains. A closer look shows that stone slabs which serve as the bedrock of each layer of bricks

This is approximately how materials were transported to places difficult of access, not including river transport, which certainly played a large part. Donkeys, which were brought in from the West by the Xiongnus from the time of the Hans onward, must have been particularly useful on the mountain routes.

CONSTRUCTION TECHNIQUE

It was indeed an extremely hard job to build the Great Wall at a time when no advanced construction machines or means of transportation were available. The Ming

are parallel. The brick battlements on the wall were also built layer upon layer. Flights of stairway were used to compensate for the variation in elevation.

The outer and inner sides of the thick wall were faced with stone slabs, and then stones, cobbles, lime, and earth were stuffed in between. When the slabs and land-fill reached the prescribed height, bricks were laid on top, complete with battlements and parapets. Two methods were employed for the brick work. Wall

For thousands of years horses, donkeys, and mules have been used to transport goods of every kind in many parts of the world. This Chinese illustration of a caravan of donkeys in the Liupan Mountains emphasizes the point that in the inaccessible regions through which the Great Wall coils, four-legged transportation was essential.

Mud walls in wooden shutters were the traditional housewalls in China. Numerous clay regions lend themselves particularly well to this form of construction.

The construction of the wall was based on the idea of the mud house walls: two stone walls were used as a shutter and were simply filled with earth and pebbles. The construction of the Great Wall here provides the setting for a historical scene *(above)*: Fu Su, the eldest son of Emperor Qin Shi huangdi, receives the death sentence for rebellion (in fact, he was assassinated), together with General Meng Tian, another suspect in the eyes of the despot.

When there was no stone to be had, a brick shutter was built, as can be seen here in the land of Wei (Shanxi-Henan).

tops with a gentle gradient were covered with bricks laid slantways. If the gradient exceeded 45 degrees, bricks were lined in the form of a staircase. A steep portion of stone wall outside Shanhaiguan was built in a double-staircase fashion. The gradient was minimized by interposing small steps with large ones, one to three meters each. The wall near Dunhuang was built of sand and pebbles sandwiched with layers of tamarisk twigs and reeds to a height of six meters. Each layer of twigs and reeds measured five centimeters (2 inches) thick, and that of sand and pebbles, 20 cm (8 inches). It stands to this day after two thousand years.

Earthen wall was built by ramming down the earth, a traditional Chinese technique. Posts or boards were fixed on both sides of the wall, and yellow earth was dumped between, to be rammed solid layer after layer with wooden hammers. Each layer of rammed earth was 7 to 10 cm thick (3 to 4 in.) in the Qin and Han dynasties, and about 20 cm (8 in.) in the Ming dynasty.

PLANNING AND DESIGN

The Great Wall was to be a massive system of defense works across mountains, plains, deserts, grasslands, rivers, and gullies. In view of such complex geographical conditions, the ancient soldiers and builders acquired a stock of experience. First and foremost was taking advantage of the terrain to build walls, forts, beacon towers, and other defense works at crucial points for the purpose of intercepting the invading enemy.

All the fortifications along the Great Wall were located either in a narrow passage between two mountains, or in a sharp bend of the river, or at a road junction on the flat land. These strategically important points also permitted economy of labor and building materials.

It was all the more important to follow the terrain in building beacon towers, signal platforms, and strongholds. The *Tong Dian*, an encyclopedia written by Du You of the Tang dynasty, says: "Beacon towers must be built at crucial points of high mountains or at turning points on flat land." Only in this way could the signal be seen from afar. The *Wujing Zongyao*, a book

Under one Ming emperor, there was an outstanding development of techniques. This endless chain of earthenware baskets, inspired by the bucket-conveyor shown in a catalog of 1627, was an improvement on the traditional bamboo pole with two baskets used in the construction of the Ming Wall.

On this fairly recent illustration of the building of the walls of a town *(left)*, the process of construction can be examined in greater detail: large stones at the bottom, flat bricks and earth filling.

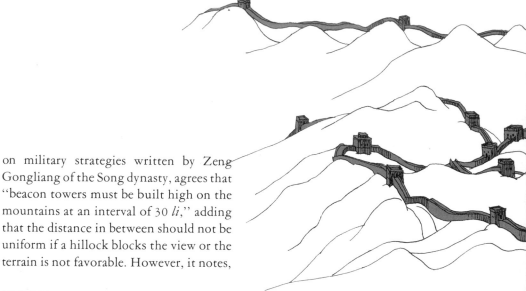

This reconstruction is an attempt to provide an idea of what the Ming Great Wall looked like in the area along the Helan Mountains in the Yinchuan municipality of the

on military strategies written by Zeng Gongliang of the Song dynasty, agrees that "beacon towers must be built high on the mountains at an interval of 30 *li*," adding that the distance in between should not be uniform if a hillock blocks the view or the terrain is not favorable. However, it notes,

Autonomous Province of Ningxia. At right in the picture is the fortress of Shanyuan as it has been possible to make an impression from the foundations and few ruins remaining. In this area the wall commanded a great number of passes, calling our attention to the very active relationships existing between the peoples on both sides of the wall.

the smoke or fire must be visible to the next two towers, otherwise the information or alarm would be delayed.

The rule of "following the terrain" was most essential for the construction of the walls. The walls at Badaling or Juyongguan pass were built along the mountain ridges. The ridge itself was a natural barrier, and when lined with a length of wall, could serve much better as a defense work. Besides, steep cliffs and huge boulders on the ridges were used to save on bricks and stone slabs. Certain sections of the wall look precipitous from the outside, but gentle from the inside.

The dragon whom legend has it designed the course of the wall had "colleagues" of flesh and blood—the engineers and architects. Their first drafts were of course totally dictated by military requirements;

that is to say, defense and communication. And yet the wall owes its beauty to these very people. For they created the most diverse styles of towers and gates, in beautiful architectural proportions, and often furnished with artistic decoration that from the military viewpoint could only be said to have been superfluous. Such, for instance, is the case with Jiayuguan Fort, which lies far out in the wilderness, and its magnificent East Gate, where the tower is decorated with rich wood carvings on its columns and rafters, and the roof is worthy of a temple. The same may be said of Shanhaiguan at the other end of the wall, and of many garrisons, castles, and passes which lie in between.

The pride of the builders themselves is testified by the inscriptions they made on certain stones, noting the date of completion

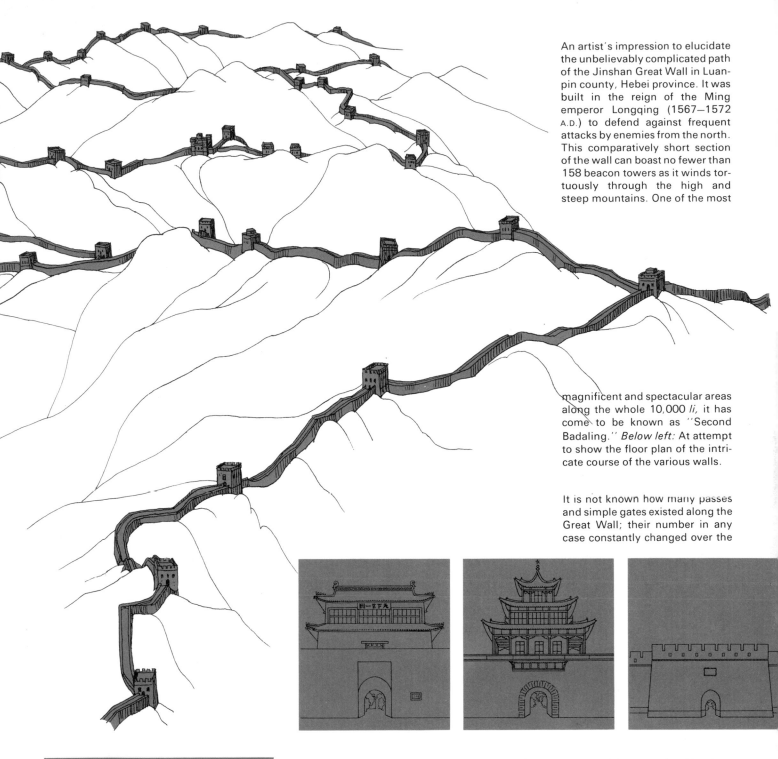

An artist's impression to elucidate the unbelievably complicated path of the Jinshan Great Wall in Luan-pin county, Hebei province. It was built in the reign of the Ming emperor Longqing (1567–1572 A.D.) to defend against frequent attacks by enemies from the north. This comparatively short section of the wall can boast no fewer than 158 beacon towers as it winds tortuously through the high and steep mountains. One of the most magnificent and spectacular areas along the whole 10,000 *li,* it has come to be known as "Second Badaling." *Below left:* At attempt to show the floor plan of the intricate course of the various walls.

It is not known how many passes and simple gates existed along the Great Wall; their number in any case constantly changed over the

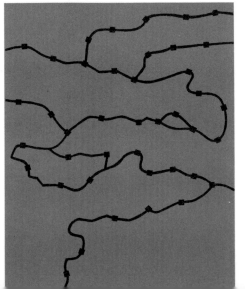

of each particular section of the wall and perpetuating their own names; as for example in the following case (the translation is according to Geil):

"General of the Light Brigade, Tsui Ching, Commanding the Yeomanry under the jurisdiction of the Governor by Imperial Appointment at Paoting. Ensign Shen Tzu-hsien of the above Department, Ensign Sun Erh-kuo, Superintendent of Works, Liu Ching, Military Contractor, and others to the number of 130 names cooperated in building this extension of

course of the centuries. But there must have been literally thousands. And not only their number, but their names have changed, a factor which often presents the student of the wall's history with considerable difficulty. A tremendous diversity of architectural styles was evolved for the different types of fortified gates. They range from the simple "mountain gate" to those with richly decorated superstructures whose bright colors lit up the surrounding countryside.

137

Stele in commemoration of the restoration work undertaken at Jiayuguan during the reign of the Ming Emperor Xuanzong, who is known to have continued the work of reinforcing the northern defenses begun by Chengzu at the beginning of the fifteenth century. This stele dates from the spring of 1428, but the exact date is difficult to ascertain due to the presence of taboo characters (names of the Emperor and of his reign).

Interior of the small fort on Mount Badaling, northwest of Beijing, already seen on page 68. Built at the beginning of the fifteenth century, it was subsequently restored partly during the Manchu dynasty. This turned out to be a wasted effort: the foreign barbarians who brought about the fall of the Qings arrived by sea this time...

591 ft. 6 in. of Third Class Wall, beginning in the north at the end of the Military Graduate Lung Kuang-hsien's portion of Tower No. 55 of the Black Letter 'Wu' series. The completion of the construction was reported by the Autumn Guard on the 16th day of the 9th moon of the 4th Year of Wan Li.

"Master Stonemason Chao Yen-mei and others. Master Border Artisan Lu Huan and others."

These reports give no information about the personal sacrifices and sorrows of the men—although an ample supply of such stories is to be found in folk songs and legends. Nevertheless, the designers did not only think about purely military necessities: they also enhanced the garrisons and castles with sacred buildings, temples, and shrines. Innumerable temples were thus

From the high command posts, which were responsible for planning and construction, very detailed guidelines were released concerning the erection of the small forts which strengthened the wall at short intervals and protected the garrison barracks. Although these instructions set out uniform building methods, variations did evolve, mostly due to differences in the immediate surroundings of each location.

erected for the worship of the war god Guandi even in the vicinity of only small forts. Jianchang Fort, for example, has several tea-houses and other establishments such as drum or clock towers, and temples for a whole army of deities.

The most overwhelming beauty of the wall, however, resulted from the premise that its path had to follow the course of the crests of the mountains. By this process a notably alien element made its appearance on the already dramatic mountain landscape; a unique and romantic adornment.

LUO ZEWEN

Still carefully maintained today, the Sanctuary of Yang Ye, who sits here with his wife, reminds visitors to the Yanmenguan Pass in the north of Shanxi of his great feats in arms. He victoriously fought the Khitans in this area during the reign of Emperor Taizong of the Songs at the end of the tenth century, and starved himself to death when he fell into their hands.

THE GREAT DEFENSE LINE

As seen on the map, the Great Wall seems to follow an unplotted, meandering course. But this appearance is deceptive, for there is throughout its length neither a wasted line nor an isolated stretch of wall, and the whole embodies a comprehensive military defense system. In times past the wall served as a protective girdle around the northern reaches of successive dynasties, providing security to the towns and cities and the countryside as a whole. As well as being the mainstay of the local defense forces, each major station on the wall was in close contact, through complex military and administrative organizations, with the central government in the capital.

The function of the Great Wall remained basically the same throughout the various dynasties, though its defense system might have been given different names. Let us take the Ming Great Wall as our example. As a means of rapid military deployment, the wall's administration under the Mings gives us a typical picture.

The Shahukou Pass, the fortress of which is shown on page 67, was an important point of the defense line that depended on the military area of Datong (Shanxi). Not far from there lies the tomb of Wang Zhaojun and a stele in memory of the brave Han General Li Ling.

The Ministry of War was a body of officials responsible for all military administrative affairs, appointed by, and under the direct instructions of, the Ming emperors. In times of war the Ministry of War assumed the post of commander-in-chief, or else

another minister was appointed to the post by the emperor. At times the emperor even led the troops himself. The military organ of the central government was set up in the capital city.

The *zhen* were military zones along the Great Wall. According to the *Book on Military Affairs, History of the Ming Dynasty*, the defense system of the Great Wall throughout the Ming period "stretched 10,000 *li* in an unbroken chain from the Yalu River in the east to Jiayuguan in the west, with the garrison duty parceled out among the various regions. At first, four *zhen* were established, namely Liaodong, Xuanfu, Datong, and Yansui. Later three were added: Ningxia, Gansu, and Jizhou. Then the commanding general of Taiyuan established headquarters in Piantou, while a subcommand was created in Guyuan. They were considered two additional *zhen*." This made a total of nine military zones, each commanded by a general. In the event of enemy attack, all *zhen* came under the command of the minister of war, as appointed by the emperor, to resist the invader or to support other military zones. The *zhen* headquarters were usually stationed in the cities along the wall, or in forts of strategic importance.

Lu is a term applied to a subdivision of the *zhen* created out of expediency. The officer in charge of a *lu* was the equivalent of a modern garrison commander. The *lu* were mostly stationed in vital fortresses; for instance, the command posts of Shanhai Lu and Juyong Lu were at Shanhaiguan and Juyongguan, each of which had control over a dozen passes *(guan* is the Chinese word for "pass").

Above the commander of the individual *zhen* and *lu* stood a further officer whose rank was equivalent to the chairman of a province or a minister of the central government; he was responsible for the *zhen* of Yansui, Ningxia, and Gansu. In

Xu Ta is among those who greatly aided Zhu Yuanzhang to become the first Ming emperor. He achieved many victories over the Mongolian occupiers, especially the taking of Beijing in 1368.

The expression "The Great Defense Line" encapsulates a breadth and variety of events and occasions that is difficult to picture. Along this line have occured historical events of immense importance, and decisive events have

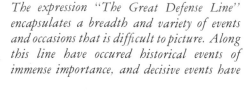

the northwest, a governor general was appointed over the subcommands of Xuanfu and Datong, and there were similar posts for the eastern *zhen*. This administration, by virtue of its decentralization, necessitated the existence of efficient communication and close cooperation between the military and civil officials under the emperor.

One of many illustrations celebrating the military prowess of Yang Liulang, the sixth son of Yang Ye, who lived during the tenth century. Here, he is seen on horseback, pursuing Ye Long, the Khitan chief, whom he killed.

The insignia of command are the pledges of dignity and an important element in the organization of the Chinese army. One such tradition is that the general is always accompanied by the standard indicating his rank *(at right).* The same is true of the round insignia of command *(above right),* which pertains to a lower rank and was used during the Ming dynasty. This one was found near Jiayuguan.

As an example of the system working at its best, consider the history of General Qi Jiguang, who was the governor general of Ji for sixteen years. He made a great contribution toward the construction of the wall and the training of troops, and because of his understanding and knowledge of the customs of the people on both sides of the wall, established many trade links across it. He is mentioned in the *History of the Ming Dynasty* as follows: "After sixteen years of Qi Jiguang's administration in Ji Men as governor general, he was loved by everyone, from the high officials down to the common people of Ji Men. No enemy dared to invade Ji Men, the best-administered and most strongly defended section of the Great Wall. By following in his

affected the survival or disappearance of whole peoples. In addition to the historical aspect, there is the fascination of the military organization, and its component parts, which made up the imposing machinery of imperial power.

If the general is to be feared, thought the Chinese, he is to be compared to a tiger. Generals were indeed often given an effigy of half a tiger by the emperor (who kept the other half) when they were sent on a mission. The half statuette secured him the aid of the local officials.

footsteps, Qi Jiguang's successors protected the Ji Men section against any invasion for decades. Qi Jiguang was helped in his achievements by the ministers Xu Kai, Gao Hong, and especially Zhang Gucheng...."

As for the more military as opposed to cultural or administrative aspects of the Great Wall, the basic defense units along and beside it were the castles (which also contained civilians), each under the command of petty officers at the head of several companies of up to one hundred men each. All castles were equipped with beacon towers which created an efficient means of communication. Provisions came from the nearby towns.

The various forts and passes along the wall were important strongholds guarding the immediate terrain or supporting the defense of other centers. The number of troops in a garrison was not fixed. According to documentary records, the garrison troops at the Shanhaiguan, Juyongguan,

Alarm! Enemy in sight! This reconstruction fire was lit by a Chinese photographic team to give a particularly realistic impression of how the beacon-fires looked. But there are no more soldiers along the Great Wall, and so, hopefully, no one was alarmed this time.

143

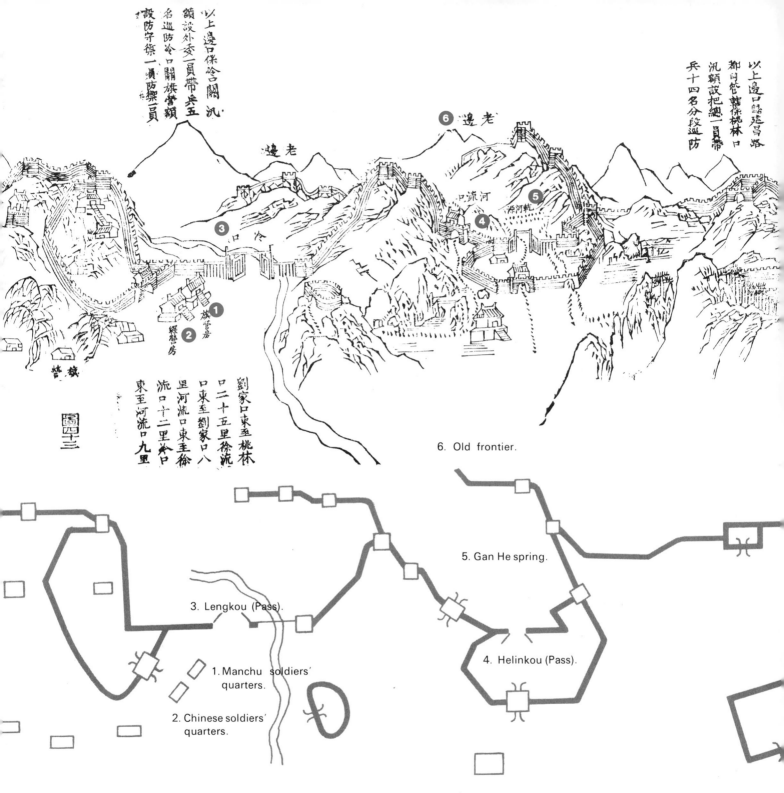

6. Old frontier.

5. Gan He spring.

3. Lengkou (Pass).

4. Helinkou (Pass).

1. Manchu soldiers' quarters.

2. Chinese soldiers' quarters.

A section of the Great Wall in Hebei Province about 100 kilometers (62 miles) from Shanhaiguan can be seen on this fairly late map (which points north). On the left, the Lengkou Pass is shown, with its nearby town, which today has a population of less than 10,000; on the right, the river Qinglong, a tributary of the Luan, drains the whole northeast of Hebei. Several secondary passes interpose in the twenty or so kilometers (about 12 miles) that lie between the two places.

Jiayuguan, and other passes ranged from a few hundred to one thousand. Contingents were smaller at less crucial points. Watchtowers, beacons, buttresses, and ramparts were of great tactical importance in the wall's defense system. The beacons flashed messages and were guarded by only a small number of troops, who could resist minor attacks, if any. They were built on both sides of the wall. Buttresses and ramparts were built astride the wall to serve as shelters for patrols and watchmen or to

help repulse attackers. The number of troops guarding each beacon, buttress, or rampart varied from only a few up to a hundred; they were commanded by a petty officer.

Altogether, this was a comprehensive system offering easy accessibility and communication between the military installations and the civil administration, and effective coordination between various forces stationed along the wall's entire length of 10,000 *li* (6,000 km or 4,000 miles).

144

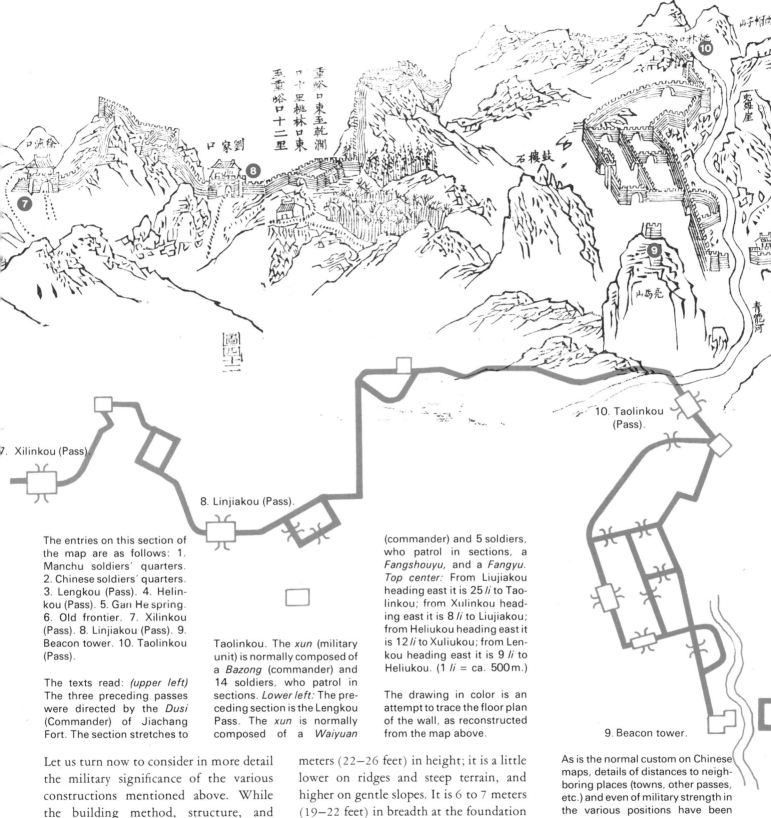

重嶺口東至乾澗
口十里桃林口東
玉重嶺口十二里

口流條　　口家劉　　石欀鼓　　山子帽尚利

⑦　　⑧　　⑨　　⑩

圖四二

宽雞崖

青龍河

亮蛎山

7. Xilinkou (Pass).

8. Linjiakou (Pass).

10. Taolinkou
(Pass).

The entries on this section of the map are as follows: 1. Manchu soldiers' quarters. 2. Chinese soldiers' quarters. 3. Lengkou (Pass). 4. Helinkou (Pass). 5. Gan He spring. 6. Old frontier. 7. Xilinkou (Pass). 8. Linjiakou (Pass). 9. Beacon tower. 10. Taolinkou (Pass).

The texts read: *(upper left)* The three preceding passes were directed by the *Dusi* (Commander) of Jiachang Fort. The section stretches to

Taolinkou. The *xun* (military unit) is normally composed of a *Bazong* (commander) and 14 soldiers, who patrol in sections. *Lower left:* The preceding section is the Lengkou Pass. The *xun* is normally composed of a *Waiyuan*

(commander) and 5 soldiers, who patrol in sections, a *Fangshouyu*, and a *Fangyu*. *Top center:* From Liujiakou heading east it is 25 *li* to Taolinkou; from Xulinkou heading east it is 8 *li* to Liujiakou; from Heliukou heading east it is 12 *li* to Xuliukou; from Lenkou heading east it is 9 *li* to Heliukou. (1 *li* = ca. 500 m.)

The drawing in color is an attempt to trace the floor plan of the wall, as reconstructed from the map above.

9. Beacon tower.

As is the normal custom on Chinese maps, details of distances to neighboring places (towns, other passes, etc.) and even of military strength in the various positions have been given. As one may expect, the map reveals that the garrisons on the passes have a preventive rather than a defensive role, since even the Lengkou Pass is guarded by no more than ten men.

Let us turn now to consider in more detail the military significance of the various constructions mentioned above. While the building method, structure, and architectural appearance varied greatly between dynasties, a fairly adequate conception of the general plan may be gained by examining, say, the walls at Juyongguan and Badaling, near Beijing, which were built in the Ming dynasty.

The Badaling section is well preserved. The wall in this area averages about 7 to 8 meters (22–26 feet) in height; it is a little lower on ridges and steep terrain, and higher on gentle slopes. It is 6 to 7 meters (19–22 feet) in breadth at the foundation and 5 meters (16 feet) or so on top. Its cross-section is trapezoidal. An archway opens on the inside of the wall at intervals of 100 or 200 meters (yards), from which a brick or stone stairway leads to the top of the wall, which was a path for garrison troops. The top is 4 to 5 meters (13–16 feet) wide, allowing five horses or ten men

Shortly before reaching the Yellow River, the inner line of defense joins the Great Wall in the mountain

plateaux of north Shanxi. This section can be seen on the right half of the large map here (which points south). Between the two lines of walls, the main fortified towns can be seen, as well as numerous secondary forts; the large town in the top left-hand corner is Beijing. A great number of horse markets flank the inner (northern) line of the walls on the Mongolian side. The photograph (inset) is of the area shown on the main map, of which the Chinese more modern version is shown at right.

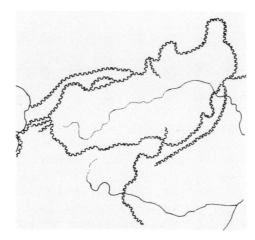

to walk abreast. There are 1 meter (3.2 feet) high parapets along the inner edge of the pavement to prevent patrols from falling off the wall in bad weather. Battlements about 1.5 to 2 meters (4½ to 6½ feet) high are raised along the outer edge. There is a peephole in the upper part of each merlon and an embrasure lower down. Besides this there are drainage ditches running along the top; long stone waterspouts guide the culvert far out from the wall to protect against waterlogging and erosion.

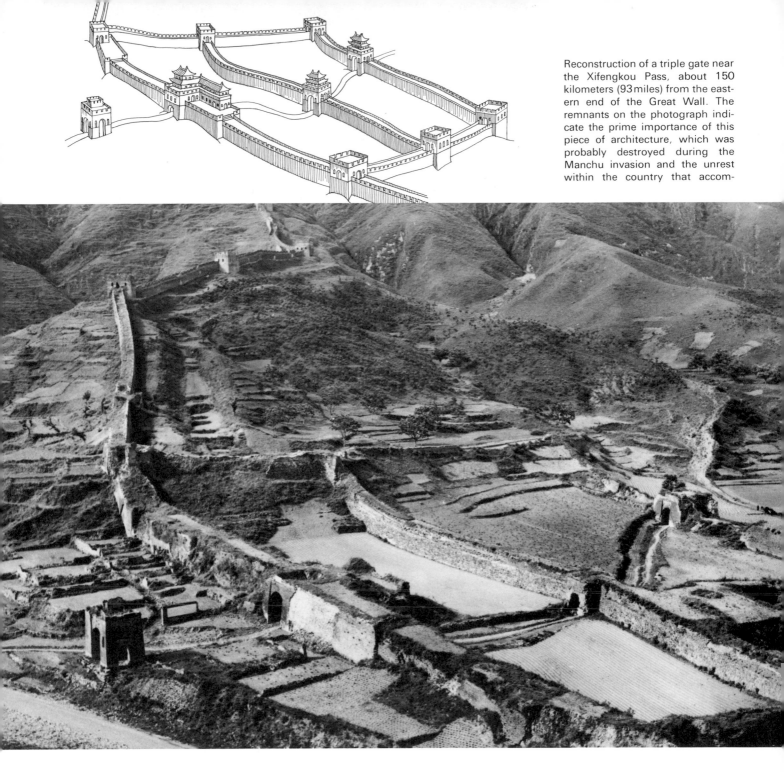

Reconstruction of a triple gate near the Xifengkou Pass, about 150 kilometers (93 miles) from the eastern end of the Great Wall. The remnants on the photograph indicate the prime importance of this piece of architecture, which was probably destroyed during the Manchu invasion and the unrest within the country that accom-

Not only at Badaling, or in the time of the Ming dynasty, do the style and structure of the walls vary; they change from one area to another. According to a recent investigation the Great Wall in Liaodong Zhen, in the northeast, was very different. Some sections of it were built of hard-packed earth or stones, others erected against high mountains; some sections were made by cutting into steep cliffs, and some were built of oak.

Buttresses and ramparts were important everywhere. At regular intervals, every 100 or 200 meters (yards), a platform protrudes from the wall, either to strengthen it or to provide a rampart. The surface of the buttresses is as high as the top of the wall, the difference being that part of the buttress projects from the wall and crenels dot its outer sides. The buttress was also called a "horse face" because it looks like the head of a horse. And like the horse, indeed, it played an important role in warfare. If there had been no such buttresses, the soldiers on the wall would have been unable to look downward or shoot at panied it. For military aid, this position was dependent on the town of Jixian, halfway to Beijing, which lies only about 200 kilometers (124 miles) away.

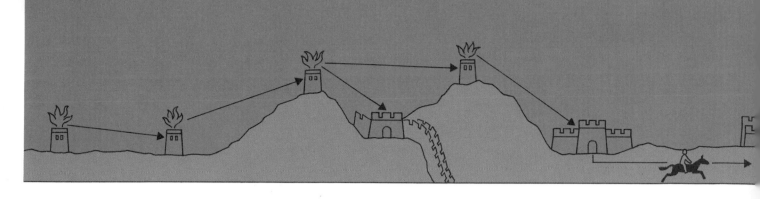

A whole relay system, developed by the successive dynasties from the Hans onward, runs between the watch tower and the imperial palace via the forts and command areas. Even in times of peace, couriers and military gazettes informed the authorities of the state of the borders. The four towns shown here are in fact at some distance from each other. They give an idea of the growing importance of halting-places and local authorities on the way to the capital. The local officials could, at their own level, while waiting for imperial orders, take the appropriate defense steps: alert the neighboring towns, prepare for siege, raise an army, etc.

The entries on these maps are as follows: *Prefecture capital town Yongping, Lulong district.* 1. North Gate. 2. Temple of the God of War, Guandi. 3. Jiaochang River. 4. Qinglong River. 5. Military training headquarters. 6. Offices of the local government. 7. Prefecture civil-service school (Yongping). 8. Prefecture local government. 9. Temple of the Earth Spirit. 10. Temple of the Art of War. 11. Drum tower. 12. Clock tower. 13. Meng Tian Fountain. 14. Military watch tower. 15. "Palace of the Sky-blue Clouds." A temple to the daughter of the god Taishan. 16. East Gate. 17. District government. 18. District civil-service school (Lulong). 19. A watch tower, named after the constellation Kui. 20. Headquarters of the Qianzong (a military official). 21 and 22. Two military outposts, responsible for the frontier fortresses on the Great Wall.

District capital town Qian'an. 1. Temple of the God of War, Guandi. 2. Temple of the God of Riches. 3. School for newly recruited officials. 4. Temple of Erlang. Erlang is a popular mythical figure, a fighter of demons. 5. Temple of the Honorable Women. 6. An observation tower. 7. Temple of the Fire Spirit. 8. Temple of the Earth Spirit. 9. Seat of the district government. 10. Stabling for horses.

Jianchang Fort. 1. Temple of the God of Wind. 2. Temple of the Three Officials. 3. Wolong Ridge. 4. Temple of the Jade Emperor (the highest Taoist divinity). 5. Military barracks. 6. Headquarters of the deputy fort commander (Qianzong). 7. Name of a granary. 8. Headquarters of the fort commander (Dusi). 9. Temple of the Town God. 10. Temple of the Spirit of Horses.

Fort. 1. Local command post. 2. North Gate. 3. East Gate. 4. South Gate. 5. West Gate.

the approaching foe with ease. With the buttress, however, they could shoot from the flank and prevent the enemy from climbing the wall. In times of peace, the buttress also served as a place of rest for soldiers on duty. Remains of such encampments found at Badaling show that they were also used as shelter from wind or rain. The rampart, or two- or three-storied structure, rises high above the top of the wall. It served as living quarters for the soldiers and as a depository for weapons and gunpowder. The rampart was designed by General Qi Jiguang, whom we have mentioned above. It provided the troops with a resting place and shelter and strengthened the defense capability of the wall. In his book *Records of Military Training*, Qi Jiguang gave a clear description of the structure of the rampart and the defense methods in use. He wrote that the rampart was 10 to 13 meters (30—40 feet) high and 40 to 60 meters (yards) square. They were built every 100 meters (109 yards) at key points, or every 200 to 300 meters (yards) on gentle slopes, so that any two neighboring ramparts were in easy reach of one another. The foundations were level with the wall, but projected about 5 meters

FORT

JIANCHANG

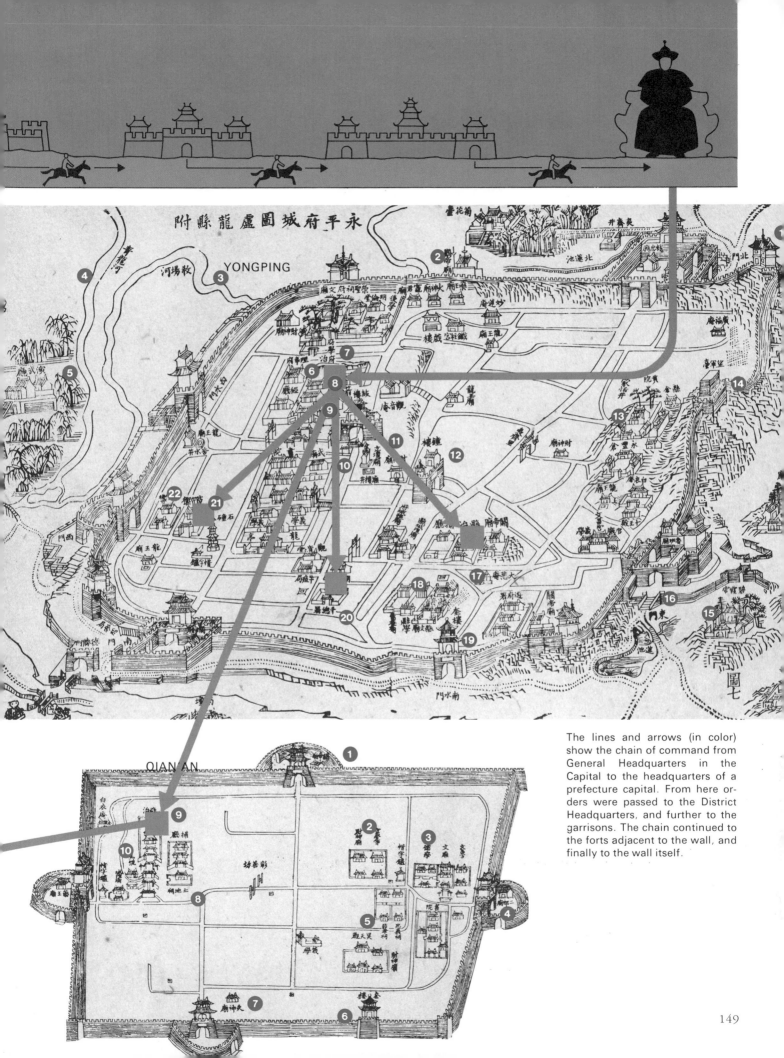

附縣龍盧圖城府平永

YONGPING

The lines and arrows (in color) show the chain of command from General Headquarters in the Capital to the headquarters of a prefecture capital. From here orders were passed to the District Headquarters, and further to the garrisons. The chain continued to the forts adjacent to the wall, and finally to the wall itself.

QIAN AN

Not everywhere does the wall have the classic aspect it obtained during the Ming dynasty, as demonstrated by the photograph shown here *(left)*. In certain mountainous regions, as here in Jinshan, the architecture was adapted for important military reasons, and holes were pierced in the wall for the archers.

Below is shown a reconstruction drawing of part of the wall in Hebei province, after a photograph by William Edgar Geil. There are many places where a branch leaves the main line of the wall, but comes to an end at a particular point, without entirely enclosing an area. These bits of wall served to bar important crossings, and were provided with battlements on both sides, since an attack could take place from either.

Architecturally, the inner Great Wall, built by the Ming emperors, has no need to envy its big sister in the north, as witness this very well-preserved section at Chachienkou, near Laiyuan in Hebei Province, not far from the neighboring province of Shanxi. Emperor Shenzong (1575–1620) ordered its construction.

(16½ feet) on the outside and 2 meters (6½ feet) on the inside. The tower was hollow in the middle, with embrasures on all four sides. On the top was a structure encircled by crenels to protect the garrison soldiers, from where the cannons could be fired. This was beyond the range of enemy arrows, and the enemy cavalrymen dared not move close. Each rampart housed 30 to 50 soldiers under the command of a petty officer. The several thousand ramparts on the 600 kilometer (400 mile) long section of the Great Wall from Shanhaiguan to Juyongguan are mostly of this type.

Also of importance were the beacon towers, otherwise called smoking towers and a variety of other names, which used fire or smoke to pass on information. The slightest enemy movement would be signaled either by raising smoke in daylight or by lighting a fire at night.

The tower, as found throughout the whole length of the Great Wall, is a separate high terrace built of earth with a stone or brick face. The apparatus for raising smoke and setting fires is normally on top, but in some cases this could also be done at the foot of the tower. Each is surrounded by the soldiers' quarters, stables, storerooms, and other buildings, These towers were erected either on or near either side of the wall, at key points leading to the capital, or at other sites as necessary to maintain contact with the neighboring prefectures, counties, forts, and passes, and the *zhen* headquarters. Coordination between the towers

This reconstruction demonstrates how a valley could be blockaded to shut off access to an important pass. The fortification is built at the narrowest part of the valley, thus enabling it to be defended with a relatively small number of men.

Interior of one of the small forts on the Great Wall in the Badaling Mountains near Beijing.

When the Manchus rushed to attack China in the 1640s, the Great Wall provided a formidable obstacle for them. With no real artillery

was facilitated by their proximity; they were generally between 2.5 and 5 kilometers (1½–3 miles) apart. They were also built on mountains and hills so that their signals could be seen from afar.

Guard troops were billeted in buildings adjoining or near some of the towers. Buried under these buildings not far from Dunhuang in Gansu and also in Mongolia near Juyan a great number of archival documents were discovered which have shed considerable light on the organization of the defense system and garrison life. These documents, typically for those times, were written on slats of wood. Signals, once received, had to be transmitted and noted down. Patrol and reconnaissance missions had to be organized. Elaborate arrangements were made for registering patrols: when two patrols met, they would make notes on both sides of a wooden board or slat, saw this "card" in half, and then each party would bring its half back to the garrison. To avoid losing contact on distant reconnaissance missions, patrols would carry drums and portable

signal devices. Traps were set at the base of the forts or towers, where the ground would be cleared and smoothed out so that enemy intruders at night would leave footprints. The forts also provided postal service way-stations.

such as that which brought about the destruction of the fortified castles in the West, the Manchus had to work at sapping and demolishing the Wall, the only way of opening a passage for the soldiers and cavalry.

The insignia of command, generals' banners and various flags played a determinative role in Chinese military organization. Their characteristics and usage were codified in ancient times in the *Zhou Ritval,* probably written in the third century B.C.

In battle illustrations, standards are sometimes a precious source of information. It is from them that we know that the characters *liu* and *du* are the names of two generals who were victorious—for a time—over Nurhaci, the founder of the Qing dynasty.

An individual identification card like this one, which demonstrates the thorough organization of the Chinese army, had to be worn by all soldiers.

The beacon fire system was set up in the Qin and Han dynasties (third to second century B.C.), when a fixed number of beacon fires was used as a code to report the strength of the enemy forces so as ro prepare adequately for a counterattack. As it had lasted already for more than a thousand years, the system reached its perfection by the time of the Mings, when not only the number of beacon fires but also a number of gunshots was used. A decree issued in the second year of the reign of Cheng Hua (1446) during the Ming dynasty read: "The frontier troops are hereby ordered to set beacon fires. If one or two or up to 100 enemies are found, light one beacon fire and fire one salvo. If the enemy numbers 500, light two beacon fires and fire two salvos. Three beacons fires and three salvos indicate more than 1,000 enemy forces. Four fires and four salvos are for upwards of 5,000 troops. Five fires and five salvos correspond to more than 10,000 enemies." By night a fire of dry wood was lighted, but during the day the sentries would burn a mixture of wolves' dung with sulfur and niter to raise smoke; a message could be transmitted as far as 500 kilometers (300 miles) within a matter of hours.

As accurate communication was of vital importance, the beacon towers were kept under tight control. Absence from duty without leave, or delay in transferring information, was strictly forbidden. The decree issued under Cheng Hua (1446), cited above, also stipulated: "The beacon towers, together with their guards, must be inspected regularly. Stocks must be stored in quantity, and lookouts placed around the clock. In case of emergency, raise smoke in the daytime, or light a fire by night, to pass on the alert. See to it that no damage is done to the towers, so as to ensure prompt communication. Those who convey the information quickly and help defeat the enemy will be rewarded. Violators shall be punished according to military law."

Besides flashing the alarm, occupants of the beacon towers guarded the towers themselves, kept a watch on enemy movement and reconnoitered the terrain, safeguarded the nearby land reclaimed by the garrison troops, checked and protected the passing merchants or trade caravans, supported neighboring troops in defense, worked on agricultural and other kinds of production so to as be self-supporting, and maintained nearby sections of the wall.

There were many other important, though less well studied, interrelated defense works inside and outside the Great Wall: the *cheng* (fort), *bao* (castle), *zhang* (walled encampment), and *hou* (outpost).

The *cheng* was used especially to station troops along the wall. *Cheng* were set up at intervals of 5 to 20 kilometers (3–12 miles). Smaller forts were erected on lower ground to house reinforcements from the interior. Traces of such forts can be seen beside the remains of the wall of the Yan and Qin in the province of Hebei.

The purpose of the flags and music was to galvanize the troops into action and to frighten the enemy before and during the battle. There was even a command shouted at the soldiers as they joined battle: "Look frightening now!"

A good knowledge of the land was one of the keys to victory, according

to the ancient Sunzi strategy, and numerous surveys of the land were made during military expeditions; shown here are a leveling staff and a measuring pole, which are among the oldest geodetic instruments.

Among the innumerable kinds of shield used by the Chinese soldiers, these "swallows' tails" are probably some of the most original.

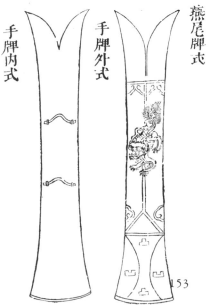

The *zhang* or walled encampment, a small fort as well, was used by troops to block the enemy. *Zhang* differed from *cheng* in that they had no civilians.

The *hou,* or outpost, was for lookout. *Hou* were used in coordination with beacon towers.

Bao (castles) had a function similar to that of the *cheng* or *zhang.* These castles were erected in large number on both sides of

the wall during the Ming dynasty. They were inhabited by both soldiers and civilians. They also contained beacon towers and were placed approximately 5 kilometers (3 miles) apart.

All these structures, seemingly complete in themselves, were skillfully knitted together to make the Great Wall not only unique, but perhaps the greatest military system known to mankind.

A fortification or defense line is only as strong as the men who defend it, as their weapons and the courage with which they use them. The Ming dynasty developed an extensive arsenal of weapons, armor, and machines of war. They discovered the military application of gunpowder, itself long known in China, and even used animals as "fireships" against the enemy.

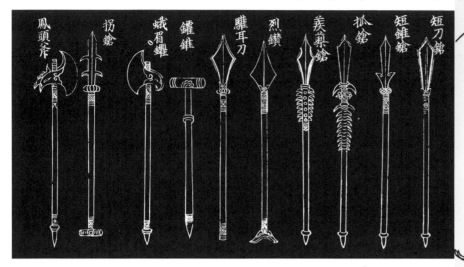

Chinese weapons have always been much more diversified than those of the West, and their use required rigorous training—so much so that a simple cudgel became a dangerous weapon in the hands of an expert.

Gunpowder, a Chinese invention, was used for a long time only in fireworks. However, before the Portugese showed them, in the eighteenth century, the advantages of a well-organized artillery, the Chinese made extensive use of grenades of all kinds, which made a great deal of noise and smoke more than anything else.

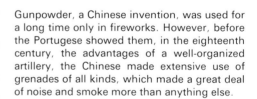

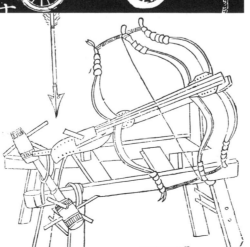

The "Ladder to the Clouds" and the siege crossbow, known long before our time, were some of the innumerable discoveries resulting from Chinese ingenuity. The crossbow could shoot large bolts to a distance of "200 long paces."
The use of horses and, above all, of stirrups, which probably originated in the steppe, radically altered the conception of art and war, and one wonders whether the Hans would have spread so far without them.

Overleaf: The Great Defense Line itself. A view of the wall in the region of Luanping, about 100 kilometers (62 miles) northeast of Beijing.

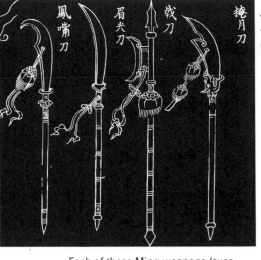

Each of these Ming weapons (axes, sledge hammers, lances, halberds) required particular handling according to its individual features.

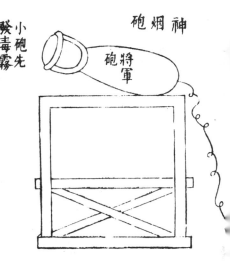

Below: Fairly typical of the Chinese use of gunpowder for warfare, this canon did not fire canonballs but smoke bombs.

Armor was developed very early on. Traditionally made of wicker and above all leather, it had to be light but solid and also to arouse fear in the enemy.

Apart from units of incendiary cavalry, animals who were terrified by fire created a great deal of havoc among the infantry.

DAI WENBAO

Overleaf: Chinese Turkestan, an area of high plateaux and nomadic farming. Scenery like this stretches for hundreds of kilometers.
In such places the emperors made their hunting grounds (Kublai Khan's hunt is shown at right) and traders led their weary animals in caravans.

Left: Children from Inner Mongolia.

THE NEIGHBORS OF THE WALL

Hunting is by far the best training for archery, and the barbarians (such as the Uighur below), who were nomads and hunters, were always formidable archers.

Wars bring about destruction, it is true, but at the same time they are great catalysts of economic and cultural exchange. The Great Wall of China was once an extensive system of warlike fortifications preventing the free interchange of ideas or materials, yet even so it has contributed a great deal toward bringing together the vastly different ethnic groups which form the Chinese nation. The peoples on either side of the Great Wall bear witness to this wonderful pageant of history in which the wall stands both as a sign of division and conflict and as symbol of strategy and strength. China has been a multi-national country since very ancient times. The Han Chinese, who are generally credited with establishing Chinese civilization, are actually just one group forming the majority among a number of nationalities. Although ethnically each group is distinguishable from the others and preserves its specific character, this by no means diminishes its pride in being Chinese. This is a key point in considering the peoples inhabiting the regions bordering the Great Wall.

The ethnic roots go back far into the past. Until the founding of a centralized Chinese empire, the Yellow River Valley was populated by very differing tribes, some settled and farming, some living as nomads. During the Spring and Autumn Period (770–476 B.C.), those who had formed states within the relatively more advanced economy of the Central Plains,

or the middle and lower reaches of the Yellow River, called themselves Huaxia; the tribes living elsewhere were the Rong and the Di. The Rong and Northern Di tribes came into contact with the Huaxias very early in their history, and in many cases lived together with them. Later, in the Warring States Period (ca. 500–221 B.C.), the Rong and the Di came to share the common name of "the Hu," and occupied the territories beyond the northern Great Wall—at this time separately controlled by the kingdoms of Yan, Zhao, and Qin. In the third century B.C. the powerful Xiongnu defeated the eastern tribes of the Hu, who soon realigned themselves with the Wuhuan and the Xianbei and settled in what is now northeast China, on the "other" side of the Great Wall of those times. As a new tribal hegemony, the Xiongnu kingdom later extended its control from the Yinshan Mountains (in the west of modern Inner Mongolia) to the Liaohe River in the east and Lake Baikal in the north, as well as areas on both sides of the Tianshan Range in the west and the Great Wall in the south. Some Xiongnu tribes also crossed over the Great Wall to reclaim the uncultivated land and settled in coexistence with the Hans, while large numbers of Han farmers moved beyond the Great Wall to set up new homes. As the system of fortifications had failed to keep out ambitious outsiders, so did frequent economic transactions between the Xiongnu nomads and Han peasants begin to prove a mutual political viability.

The Xiongnu, also referred to as the Huns, played an important role not only in the history of China but of the world. When first encountered, they were nomads who had learned how to make bronze and iron tools and vessels. Those tribes that settled near the Great Wall started tilling and, adopting a more advanced system of slavery, evolved into a civilized society. As fre-

158

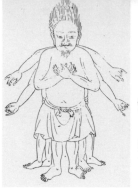

The image that the Chinese had of foreigners was the subject of many travelers' tales, old or new, with varying degrees of accuracy. A single anecdote could give rise to the most incredible ideas: countries of men covered with long hair, countries inhabited by bird-men, by men with three bodies, etc.

A Xiongnu (Hun) soldier killing a brown bear with his lance.

quent battles were anticipated by both nomadic and feudal tribes alike, Ying Zheng, founder of the powerful Qin dynasty (221–207 B.C.), stationed a huge army along the Great Wall to ward off possible Hun invasions; history records the names of the commanders as General Meng Tian and the crown prince Fu Su. Later the Western Han dynasty (206 B.C.–A.D. 8) waged prolonged wars against the nomadic tribes. In one of these bloody campaigns the Huns are believed to have mobilized as many as 100,000 men and extended their operations even to the outskirts of Chang'an, the Han capital. However, there were also peaceful intervals of trade and friendly relations—often created by the establishment of nuptial ties between the ruling clans. Modu, the war-like *Shanyu* or supreme ruler of the Huns, was the first to marry a Han princess and his example was followed by many a *Shanyu* in the succeeding generations.

Around 32 B.C. a new *Shanyu,* whose name was generally known to the Hans as Huahxie, married Princess Wang Qiang from the opposite camp, a marriage remembered to this day as a happy symbol of friendship among diverse ethnic groups. Huahxie's sons also took Han wives.

After a series of wars lasting for several decades, the Huns broke up into two factions in A.D. 48. One group, the Northern Huns, emigrated west to conquer the vast areas stretching from central Asia to the Caspian Sea—the first migration to shock Eurasia. The Southern Huns, on the other hand, preferred living under the rule of the Han dynasty and farmed peaceably south of the Great Wall.

Next the Turks were to become masters. They had risen as a united force and annexed all the tribes living on the Mongolian prairies, in central Asia, and in (modern) Xinjiang, to form a mighty khanate. With this khanate emerged the first consumer economy for the nomads, which melded the local nationalities enough to give the whole area the strong stamp of Turkish culture. Xuan Zang, the famous Buddhist chronicler who gave a detailed account of the luxury in which the Turkish ruler lived, was granted an audience by the khan somewhere in central Asia in 628. Later the eastern Turkish khanate collapsed because of intertribal contentions. The establishment of a Turkish empire had far-reaching effects on mobility and migration patterns. Through the long period beginning in the middle of the third century and ending at the close of the tenth century, an endless flow of Han migrants moved toward Xinjiang by way of the Gansu Corridor, and this led to much exchange in the fields of economy and culture between the Central Plains and the vast regions beyond the western end of the Great Wall. The Uighur tribes, which had previously been known to the Hans as Yuanhe or Weihe, also resettled in the regions around Zhangye, Gansu, Urumchi, and Xinjiang and maintained friendly relations with the neighboring Hans. By this time the Great Wall had become a reliable shelter protecting the Silk Road.

The reign of the Song dynasty (950–1279) saw the exploitation of vast territories in north China by the Khitans, Diangxiang,

months later his army reached the Great Wall at the Juyongguan Pass, the door to Beijing. The Mongol expedition of autumn 1213 completely routed the local kingdoms. Before the invasion ended in the following spring, the Mongol cavalry had ridden over practically all the territories north of the Yellow River, and the Great Wall had been left far behind in the dust.

The Mongol Yuan dynasty had reigned over China for less than a century before the subjected peoples rose in unity and drove the forces of the Mongol nobles out of the territories south of the Great Wall. Grazing lands and vast areas of wasteland were reclaimed and recultivated. But the threat of war never subsided, and the Mongol horsemen frequently broke through the wall to kill and loot. The danger from the north compelled the newly established Ming dynasty in the south to launch a

The barbarians, living far from the civilizing influence of China, were generally considered close to animals: they did not know the "five cereals," eating only meat, and clothing themselves with skins; like animals they had a great deal of hair. The northern barbarians *(above)* being closer, however, escaped a certain number of such foolish conceptions.

Left: General Huo Qubing (140–117 B.C.), a hero of the wars against the Xiongnus at the time of the Western Hans, holding a halberd and conversing with an enemy leader.

Jürchen, and Han. As a result of the harmonious coexistence and admixture of the various nationalities in this period, the Great Wall lost its military significance. Armed rivalry was not infrequent, though particularly between the Liao dynasty of the Khitans, the Western Xia dynasty of the Diangxiang, or the Jin dynasty of the Jürchen on the one hand, and the Northern or Southern Song dynasty on the other. However, once these minority groups came into regions predominantly inhabited by the Hans, they adopted feudalism, abolished the slave system, and gradually became identified with the majority nationality, thus becoming part of the larger polity. Special mention should be made of the Jürchen Jin dynasty which was marked by general prosperity and technical progress in many fields, such as the skills of making porcelain and paper, and of printing. The literature and the arts of this period broadened considerably in scope and show the high level of cultural attainment brought about by the assimilative, inclusive nature of Han society.

The year 1206 saw the founding of the Mongol Yuan empire by Genghis Khan. Within five years the emperor embarked on his policy of expansion, and only a few

This famous stone statue of a horse trampling an enemy underfoot comes from the funeral site of General Huo Qubing. It shows, more than twenty centuries after it was made, the calm and irresistible strength that he displayed—a work of homage of a rare emotional and artistic quality.

Among the neighbors of the Great Wall are not only the peoples themselves. Rich archaeological discoveries, as well as splendid works of art in wood, metal, and stone should also be included, together with works of architecture, in the guise of pagodas, temples, and monasteries.

Buddhist statuary of the Northern Weis is easily recognizable, its most typical feature being the eternal fixed smile on the lips of the Buddhas and Bodhisattvas. This Buddha was sculpted in 470 at the famous site of Yungang, near Datong in Shanxi, about 30 kilometers (18 miles) from the Great Wall. It is 13.7 meters (45 feet) high.

large-scale project to repair and rebuild these fortifications. Once again the Great Wall was of prime importance to the Chinese civilization.

Like all defenses, though, this one too was broken through in the end. The Manchus, earlier known as the Jürchen, who had lived in Manchuria, marched in through the Shanhaignan Pass in 1644 to found the rule of the Qing dynasty in Beijing. The Manchu emperor Kang Xi, however, who reigned from 1662 to 1722, adopted a radically new but lasting policy toward the different nationalities inhabiting the northern and western frontiers of the

Steppe art has always been essentially animal art, a fact that is connected with the economic conditions of the area, and is illustrated on this gilt bronze plaque dating from the third to second century B.C.

empire; a policy of bringing them into peaceful unity with the center through political and religious channels, instead of reinforcing the defenses against them. Thus the Great Wall once again ceased to be a military barricade.

Nowadays, besides the Hans, the regions along the Great Wall are inhabited by such minority groups as the Mongols (chiefly in Inner Mongolia), the Huis (chiefly in Shaanxi, Gansu, and Ningxia), and the

Peoples of the national minorities whose homelands lie in the areas adjacent to the wall. They are descendants of the barbarians with whom China has maintained a long and ever-changing relationship.
1. Dungxiang nationality.
2. Yuku nationality.
3. Mongolian children.

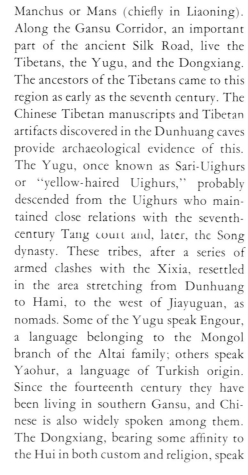

Manchus or Mans (chiefly in Liaoning). Along the Gansu Corridor, an important part of the ancient Silk Road, live the Tibetans, the Yugu, and the Dongxiang. The ancestors of the Tibetans came to this region as early as the seventh century. The Chinese Tibetan manuscripts and Tibetan artifacts discovered in the Dunhuang caves provide archaeological evidence of this. The Yugu, once known as Sari-Uighurs or "yellow-haired Uighurs," probably descended from the Uighurs who maintained close relations with the seventh-century Tang court and, later, the Song dynasty. These tribes, after a series of armed clashes with the Xixia, resettled in the area stretching from Dunhuang to Hami, to the west of Jiayuguan, as nomads. Some of the Yugu speak Engour, a language belonging to the Mongol branch of the Altai family; others speak Yaohur, a language of Turkish origin. Since the fourteenth century they have been living in southern Gansu, and Chinese is also widely spoken among them. The Dongxiang, bearing some affinity to the Hui in both custom and religion, speak

7

8

4. Mongolian nationality.
5. Ximeng nationality.
6. Owenke nationality.
7. Tibetan nationality.
8. Tu nationality.
9. Manchu nationality.
10. Yugu nationality.

9

10

a language closely related to Mongolian, with some words borrowed from Turkish or Chinese. Also some Yugu, especially the Islamic clergymen, use Arabic. This should demonstrate that China wears its coat of many colors with pride.

Any history of the neighbors of the Great Wall must include a mention of the scores of envoys, scholars, and artisans who traveled along the Silk Road during the time of the Tang dynasty (618–907). There was an endless flow of ambassadors of goodwill from various Asian and European countries into Chang'an, then capital of China. Some of them returned with information or goods; others decided to settle in China and share with the Chinese whatever goodwill or knowledge they had brought with them, yet few of their names survive in historical records.

DAI WENBAO

In addition to the most important trade routes which cross the Great Wall (see map) and to the most important trading centers, there were, and still are, countless smaller connecting routes and market places where men met to exchange their wares.

TRADE ACROSS THE WALL

To the grain-eating barbarians in the north, rice *(below)* was an image of the richness that China could provide.

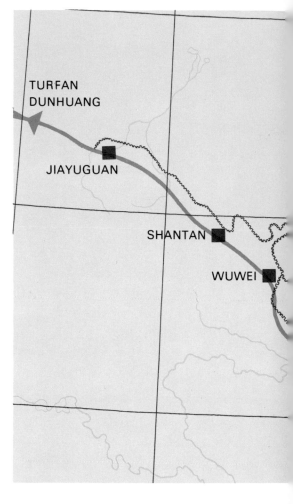

Along this barrier trade was conducted between the Han and the Xiongnu in early days. The Xiongnu, then, were basically herdsmen and hunters, traveling about on horses, oxen, and camels. Nomadism is often supplemented with commercial activities, and this is true in the case of the Xiongnu people, most of whom found it difficult to settle down to live a farmer's life and to have their own handicraft. So they had constantly to import grain, tools and articles of daily use from the areas inhabited by the Han people. Silk and woolen wear, gold and bronze or iron objects as well as exquisite luxuries were also sought—though of course their consumption was limited to the Xiongnu noblesse. The objects brought to light from some of the Xiongnu aristocratic tombs were largely products of the Han areas and the western region, except those made by their own workers, but even these still show a Han influence. Most of them reached there as commercial goods, though some were gifts from the Han emperors and some came as loot. By 200 B.C., China became united under a new dynasty, Han, of which Liu Bang was the first emperor. Bingzhou (in modern Shanxi) on the northern frontier was then a horse-producing area, and a horse market was opened at Mayi, a city in its territory. This same city was surrounded one day and later captured by the Xiongnu cavalry. Soon, the city of Taiyuan in the south was threatened. In the face of this crisis, Emperor Liu Bang personally led an army to beat the enemy back. They drove their way to Pingcheng, the present-day Datong, but fell into the trap there. Later, the belligerent sides came to an agreement whereby the Xiongnu could receive an annual offering of silk, cotton, grains, yeasts, and gold from the Han dynasty. We also read in historic annals that the Xiongnu envoys came to the Han court to present their horses and fur clothes and to ask for the music of the Han Chinese people. A relative peace was kept between the two nations from the reign of Emperor Jing (from 156 B.C.) through the early days of Emperor Wu's rule, during which trade was allowed go on the border areas. A historian of the dynasty thus outlined the then Han-Xiongnu relation: "The will of cementing two royal families by marriage

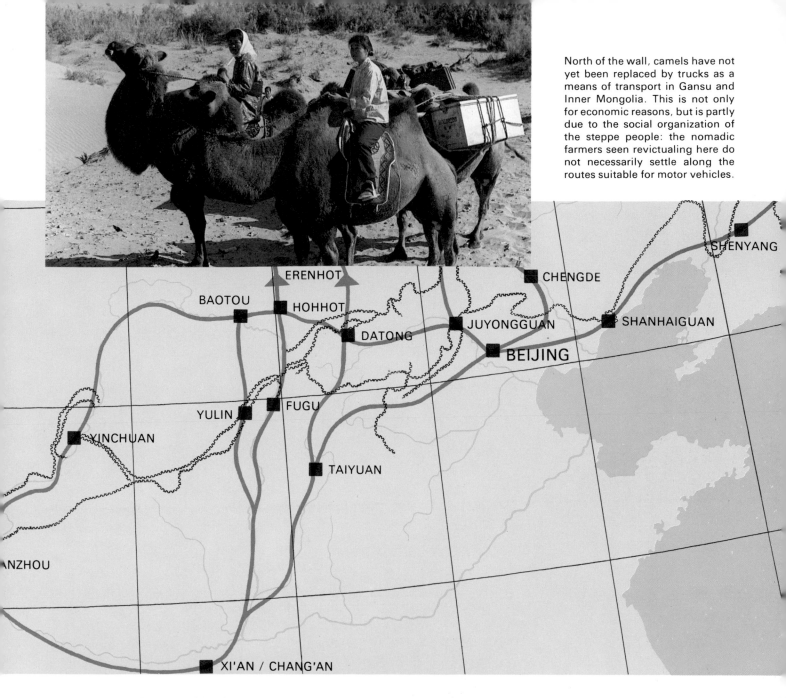

North of the wall, camels have not yet been replaced by trucks as a means of transport in Gansu and Inner Mongolia. This is not only for economic reasons, but is partly due to the social organization of the steppe people: the nomadic farmers seen revictualing here do not necessarily settle along the routes suitable for motor vehicles.

ERENHOT

SHENYANG

CHENGDE

BAOTOU

HOHHOT

JUYONGGUAN

SHANHAIGUAN

DATONG

BEIJING

YULIN

FUGU

YINCHUAN

TAIYUAN

ANZHOU

XI'AN / CHANG'AN

South of the wall, one of the local products of the western province of Ningxia is the lychee, seen here drying on trays. For economic reasons (such as slow transport) but also dietetic ones, fruit drying is common in China. The vast difference between the products of the north and south has been the main cause of China's history of invasions and trade.

169

Dunhuang was the obligatory halting place for pilgrims and monks bringing texts of *The Great Vehicle* into China. This fresco from a cave there, which mixes Indian religious tradition with historical reality, shows Buddhist texts being brought in on the back of a white elephant, the most sacred animal in the Buddhist religion. The composition of the fresco shows a great mastery of the art of scenery for the time. Not only for the virtuous pilgrim was Dunhuang a source of rest and refreshment. This place in the oasis was also a fortress marking the termination of the Han Wall and a very important stage on the Silk Road.

Beyond Gansu, to the west, in the arid regions of Xinjiang, the camel is still the ideal means of transport in the desert.

was affirmed anew; markets were opened on the frontier; and traders from the other side were promised greater gains than they had been accustomed to. Therefore, all the Xiongnu, from emperor to rank and file, remained kindly disposed toward the Han. And men of the two peoples came to and fro across the Great Wall.''

The subsequent years, though never quite putting an end to hostilities between the two, saw an enlarging of their economic intercourse and increasingly frequent visits on both sides. In 51 B.C., 34,000 *hu* of grain were sent to the Xiongnu, and three years later, 20,000 *hu* were on the way to Xiongnu, upon the requisition of its emperor, to save the people from starvation. When Zhao Jun, a lady of the imperial court, was married to the Xiongnu emperor, 18,000 bolts of silk and 16,000 *jin* of cotton went with her. Around 25 B.C., the Xiongnu emperor, who had succeeded his late father, came to the court at Chang'an and the gifts he received there include 20,000 bolts of silk and 20,000 *jin* of cotton, along with a large quantity of grain, yeasts, artifacts of gold or jade, and musical instruments. Trading activities not only flourished in the border area but took place occasionally in the capital. At the close of the second century

B.C., for example, one of the Xiongnu chiefs led his men to the Han region for shelter, and on arriving in Chang'an, they met its citizens and traders who lost no time in bartering with them. The scale of the trading was fairly and tragically indicated by the fact that five hundred persons were punished for violating the law which prohibits weapon and iron trading with the Xiongnu. Products of private craftsmen flowed to Xiongnu, as did those made at the imperial workshops.

The northern frontier area, since the Han dynasty, has been a racial mosaic. The Great Wall could not bar the peoples from trading with each other. And moreover, its western section, with a long chain of watch towers, provided a defense to the Silk Road, along which Chinese caravans traveled far westward, across the vast sands. The Chinese silk fabrics thus made their way to Parthia, then to Syria, and from Syria spread over the Mediterranean world. It is interesting to note that ladies in Rome clothed themselves with Chinese silks. On the other hand, badger furs of the Ural Mountains and woolen mattresses of the Western Region appeared in the markets of Chinese metropolises.

Ancient China, on entering the Tang Dynasty, entered her golden age. The unprec-

The Chinese products that aroused the envy of neighbors in the north and were used as exchange payment were principally manufactured goods: foremost among these products was silk *(as far right)*, which provides the theme of this painting by the Song emperor Huizong (ruled 1101–1125).

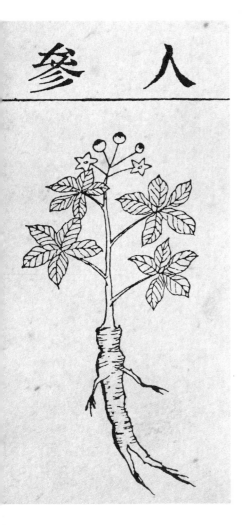

參 人

The ginseng, a plant of high energy value, accredited by some as a panacea, has often been state monopolized. Its cost has made it a valuable market commodity, especially in the northwest provinces.

edented flowering was evidently shared by the old Silk Road. It was in this period that China came directly into commercial and official contact with Byzantium, and that Chinese knowledge about sericulture first found its way to Europe, through Constantinople, a bridge linking the West and the East. Every year, Uighurs in the Western Region exchanged 100,000 of their horses for Chinese silk and tea (each horse fetching forty bolts of silk). Some Uighur merchants even stayed for years in Chang'an and other interior cities, dealing in livestock, woolens, jade, spice, and drugs. This close relationship between the Western Region and the interior survived the following dynasties of Wudai, Liao, and Song. Afterward, Mongols established the Yuan dynasty, and placed the region under its direct rule. Some trays of the blue-and-white porcelain of the time discovered in the ruined city of Gaochang have been identified as imports from the interior region. Pointed literary references

to flourishing Sino-Western exchanges can be found in the writings of Qiu Chuji, a Taoist priest, and the famous account by the Italian traveler Marco Polo.

During the Ming dynasty, the Mongols to the north of the Great Wall often drove their horses, in a "tribute" agreement, to the south of the barrier and there bartered them for a variety of products such as grain, tea, cloth, and gold. Three horse markets were thus opened in Liaodong on the northeastern frontier in the year 1414—two at Kaiyuan and one at Guangning. The government set four prices upon the horses to be bartered there: the first class for eight bolts of silk or twelve bolts of cloth, and the second for half of the first, while the other two decreased in like manner. Later, only one market at Kaiyuan remained active, but the other two reopened in 1478. The markets at Kaiyuan was held once a month and the market at Guangning twice monthly. In 1478 a horse market was opened at

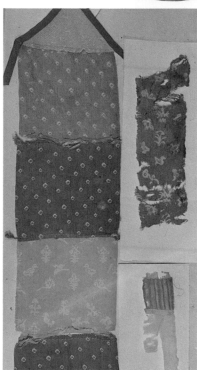

Not only silk, but also items of pottery were used as forms of payment, and Chinese ceramics (which were highly valued) for a long time served as models throughout much of the Far East. Some very beautiful examples, like this Tang vase, were sold along the length of the Great Wall *(below)*.

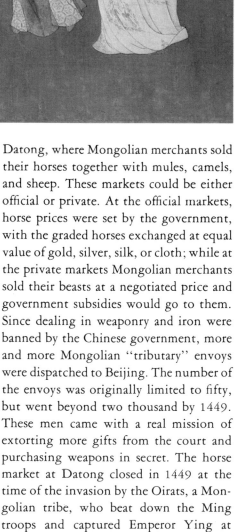

Datong, where Mongolian merchants sold their horses together with mules, camels, and sheep. These markets could be either official or private. At the official markets, horse prices were set by the government, with the graded horses exchanged at equal value of gold, silver, silk, or cloth; while at the private markets Mongolian merchants sold their beasts at a negotiated price and government subsidies would go to them. Since dealing in weaponry and iron were banned by the Chinese government, more and more Mongolian "tributary" envoys were dispatched to Beijing. The number of the envoys was originally limited to fifty, but went beyond two thousand by 1449. These men came with a real mission of extorting more gifts from the court and purchasing weapons in secret. The horse market at Datong closed in 1449 at the time of the invasion by the Oirats, a Mongolian tribe, who beat down the Ming troops and captured Emperor Ying at Tumu near Datong. In 1551 the market

Much of the beautiful pottery was produced in workshops like this one *(right)*. In this and other fields such as cereal production *(above)* the Chinese had considerable technical superiority.

173

What did the barbarians bring in exchange for Chinese products? Horses, mainly: they were a "commodity" highly appreciated by the Chinese—more so than camels, which were principally used in western regions. Moreover, it was the horse which contributed to the creation of the powerful dynasties in China: the Hans and the Tangs owed their strength and longevity to the horse.

This nineteenth-century engraving shows a scene on the Great Wall which was repeated many times throughout the centuries: herds of horses being traded on the way to their final destination in the Manchu empire.

was opened again, accompanied by a new one at Xuanhua, and in 1595 a "wood market" was opened at Yizhou in Liaodong.

The later Ming dynasty watched with anxiety the rise of the Jürchen to the northeast. In those days, some markets were opened at Liaodong. The Jürchen merchants came to these markets monthly or fortnightly, with their horses, furs, wood, and ginseng, and returned with Chinese grain, seeds, silk, satin, cloth, farm tools of iron, and handicraft articles. This kind of trade, to be sure, profited both sides and usually helped to maintain a peaceful coexistence. But this was not always the case. Some markets had to be closed when a commercial brush led to a military clash.

From the Qing dynasty on, the Great Wall lost its partitioning function, perhaps, forever. Three trading centers appeared in

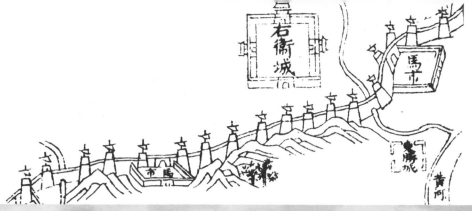

In numerous areas along the Great Wall, there were enclosures reserved especially for the selling of horses from the Steppe *(left and below)*. These markets provided mounts for the Chinese army and the upper classes of society.

Today, horses are still a source of wealth for nomadic farmers and horse fairs are the opportunity for

the area to the north of the wall and south of Mongolia. They were Zhangjiakou in the east, Baotou in the west, and Guihua (the old city of modern Huhehot) lying between, which was built by Third Sister, wife of a Mongolian prince, and served as a transfer post for goods. Along the Great Wall in Shanxi, one can still hear of place names such as "horse market" though no actual market is now to be found anywhere about. They are but a memory of the role these places had played in the past.

The region through which the Great Wall traverses is by no means a barren land. It is blessed with a variety of natural resources and is being turned into farm, ranch, and orchard lands by diligent people. The recent decades have seen, moreover, the implantation of modern industry. The Great Wall, to be sure, takes on an entirely new character when seen in this new setting.

great gatherings, like this one in a small town in Inner Mongolia *(above)*. The horse is indispensable to buffalo or sheep farmers in the immense steppe; it was used for hunting *(left)* until the introduction of fire arms which had a greater range than bows and arrows. *Below:* A hunter in the area today.

THE WALL IN RECENT TIMES

If you choose the right alleyway twisting north from London's busy Fleet Street, you will come, behind the palaces of the great British newspapers, to a small building marked: "Dr. Johnson's House." This is the original residence of the famous eighteenth-century man of letters. And if you should climb the stairs to the second floor, the first thing you would see would be a grey brick in a glass case—"Presented to the Johnson Club by Alfred Charles, 1st Viscount Northcliffe, June 1922."

This, it is claimed, is an actual piece of the Great Wall of China. Northcliffe, the newspaper proprietor, presented it because of a famous remark made by Dr. Johnson in 1788.

Dr. Johnson had become specially interested

The Chinese Wall after an English mid-nineteenth-century engraving. At this time there was enormous Western interest in China and its wall which grew to a legend even greater (if possible) than its original.

in China. He was a friend of Lord Macartney, the first ambassador to be sent from Britain to the Chinese court. Johnson would dearly have loved to visit China to see for himself the Great Wall, which he regarded as a wonder of the world. But the opportunity never came.

His companion and biographer, James Boswell, talked to him about this one day, commenting that he, Boswell, would himself like to go and see the Wall of China if he did not have a duty to look after his children. This elicited the scornful response from Johnson: "Sir, by doing so, you would do what would be of importance in raising your children to eminence. There would be a luster reflected on them from your spirit and curiosity. They would at all times be regarded as the children of a man who had gone to view the Wall of China. I am serious, Sir."

This was a time, at the end of the eighteenth century, when the Western world's admiration for China knew no bounds. Johnson expressed that feeling most strongly, though whether he would have approved a veritable stone from the wall arriving to grace his second-floor landing is to be doubted. The 1920s, when the stone was donated, was a time when people of means did not think twice about acquiring works of art or of historical importance from around the world. It is said that another piece of the Great Wall was inserted at the same time into the façade of the Chicago Tribune building in the United States, and a third in one of the newspaper buildings not far from Johnson's house. Where these bricks came from, by whose hand, and for what consideration is not recorded. Nor is there any evidence of a mark or inscription showing the brick's provenance. But there it is; genuine or imposter, it shows the lengths to which men go to acquire even a tiny piece of tangible history.

No doubt the Chinese themselves have long been using stones from the decrepit parts of the Great Wall for constructive purposes. When Edgar Snow, the American journalist, went to see in 1960 a new dam floating below the long serpentine of the Great Wall, the same thought came into his mind.

"The stones that went into the Great Wall," he philosophized, "would have made hundreds of Miyun Dams." "Maybe they will yet," the local engineer replied. "Farther west, dozens of smaller dams are being built with those stones where the wall is disintegrating."

And so the Great Wall of China represents a kind of perpetual resource for Chinese construction. I think Johnson would have approved of that, on the understanding that the better parts of the wall are preserved, as is the case.

Johnson represented perhaps the peak of foreign appreciation of this Chinese monument. It took a long time for the Western world to come to terms with it.

In the eighteenth century the Russians had become frequent crossers of the Great Wall, on their way to and from a China newly accessible because of the czarist expansion across northern Asia. One of them, Spathary, described how the Chinese used to boast of the wall that "when it was built there remained no stone in the mountains, no sand in the desert, in the rivers no water, in the forests no trees." He also described their complex security arrangements. He was met at the outer wall by a Chinese escort who accompanied him to the first gate, at which officials checked his documents and those of his fellow passengers, writing down their particulars, especially about their weapons, in great detail. "All those gates and towers," he noted, "are very strong, the third wall thicker than the others and all three are built across the stony ravine about 56 feet wide, with a high and rocky cliff on either side. The doors themselves in the gate towers are sheathed in iron."

A Scottish doctor crossed the wall by the same route in 1720 with a Russian delegation. They entered the Great Wall, he recorded, "at a great gate which is shut every night, and always guarded by a thousand men, under the command of two officers of distinction, one a Chinese and the other a Mantzur Tartar; for it is an established custom in China, and has prevailed ever since the conquest of the Tartars, that, in all places of public trust, there must be a Chinese and a Tartar invested with equal power.... The Chinese pretend that two in an office are sort of spies upon one another's actions, and thereby many fraudulent practices are either prevented or detected." These two officers offered the Russian party tea, fruit, and sweets before their onward march toward Beijing.

This Scots doctor, John Bell, commented on the wall itself that it had been "begun and completely finished in the space of five years; every sixth man in China being obliged to work himself, or find another in his stead. It is reported, the laborers stood so close for

many miles distance as to hand the materials one to another. This I am inclined to believe, as the rugged rocks would prevent all use of carriages; nor could clay, for making bricks or cement of any kind, be found among them.... I am of opinion, that no nation in the world was able for such an undertaking, except the Chinese. For, though some other kingdoms might have furnished a sufficient number of workmen for such an enterprise, none but the ingenious, sober, and parsimonious Chinese could have preserved order amidst such multitudes, or patiently submitted to the hardships attending such a labor. This surprising piece of work, if not the greatest, may justly be reckoned among the wonders of the world. And the Emperor, who planned and completed it, deserves fame, as much superior to his who built the famous Egyptian pyramids as a performance of real use excells a work of vanity."

With all these reports coming back with increasing frequency, including a perfect representation of the entire wall, exquisitely drawn on satin, brought back by French missionaries in the eighteenth century, it was small wonder that the image of the wall became solid in the European consciousness. There were probably many men of means like the eighteenth-century English Sir William Beckford who, after building a six-mile wall around the garden of his Fonthill House and Abbey, proudly declared it "not quite so long or so high as that of China, but better built I dare say."

Johnson's friend, Lord Macartney, went to Beijing as King George III's ambassador a few years later. He and his companions had the best chance so far of making a detailed inspection. On the way to see the Chinese emperor Qianlong at his Summer Palace in Jehol in September 1793, Macartney crossed the Great Wall in an English post-chaise at the Gubeikou entrance. This was the one favored by the emperor himself when traveling to and from the Summer Palace, and it is the one made famous throughout Europe by Thomas Allom in his famous engravings. Macartney found the ascent a steep one, crossing the summit of hills "inaccessible almost in every part," before running through a narrow pass to a military post where Chinese soldiers came to see the British party through, to the beating of

a drum at the top of the tower and a salute of three cannon placed vertically on the ground.

Macartney then passed another gate to the residence of the garrison, whose concentric works, united with the main wall, enclosed the fortress. This was the northern border of China proper, and the ambassador received military honors. From then onwards, whenever one of the Tartar attendants was ordered to be punished by a Chinese officer, the man would loudly protest that "no Chinese had the right to inflict punishment on a Tartar after having passed the Great Wall"—though in fact this complaint would usually lead to a double punishment for insolence.

Macartney described the wall itself in his diary of 5 September 1793. It was built, he noted, "of bluish-colored brick, not burnt but dried in the sun, and raised on a stone foundation and...about 26 feet high in the perpendicular." He then gives detailed measurements of the various sections of the wall and towers. He notes that the parapet of the wall was cut with embrasures 9 feet apart, with loopholes between the embrasures 12 inches long and 10 inches wide, "much better calculated for musketry than for arrows. This circumstance, together with that of the holes of the embrasures of the towers being pierced with small holes, similar to those used in Europe for receiving the swivels of wall pieces, would seem to countenance the conjecture that the Chinese had the use of some sort of fire arms in very ancient times: all their writings agree that this wall was built about 200 years before the Christian era.... If the other parts of it be similar to those which I have seen, it is certainly the most stupendous work of human hands, for I imagine that if the outline of all the masonry of all the forts and fortified places in the whole world besides were to be calculated, it would fall considerably short of that of the Great Wall of China. At the remote period of its building China must have been not only a very powerful empire, but a very wise and virtuous nation, or at least to have had such foresight and such regard for posterity as to establish at once what was then thought of as perpetual security for them against future invasion, choosing to load herself with an enormous expense of immediate labor and treasure, rather than leave succeeding generations to a precarious dependence upon contingent resources."

This was the age of the new science, and Macartney's secretary on this expedition, John Barrow, made some celebrated calculations regarding the Great Wall. He began his description with a characteristic outburst of irritation over the fact that, "there is not a watercloset nor a decent place of retirement in all China." But the wall itself called out all the admiration of which this British observer was capable. It had no parallel anywhere in the world, he declared, "not even in the pyramids of Egypt, the magnitude of the largest of these containing only a very small portion of the quantity of matter comprehended in the Great Wall of China."

Then came his famous mathematical computation, which has been repeated over and over again in books throughout the Western world. If, he said, one assumed the Great Wall to be fifteen hundred miles long , then its bulk or solid contents would be greater than "the materials of all the dwelling houses of England and Scotland." This would not take account of the projecting towers, which would contain "as much masonry and brickwork as all London."

To give another idea of the mass of the Great Wall, Barrow further calculated that its "stupendous fabric" was "more than sufficient to surround the circumference of the earth on two of its great circles with two walls each six feet high and two feet thick."

These sums were based on the false assumption that the wall continued throughout its length in the same fine state which the British visitors had observed at its eastern parts. They nevertheless reinforced the general high opinion of Chinese civilization.

By the nineteenth century the descriptions were becoming slightly more cautious. Pauthier, the French writer, said in 1837: "This monument, the most colossal and perhaps the craziest which has ever been conceived by the human mind . . . appears to have been built at almost every point with so much care and skill that after more than two thousand years it exists in its entirety without ever having had to be repaired." Other observers were more skeptical.

An extremely influential commentary on the Great Wall in the nineteenth century was the note written in 1843 by the Reverend G. N. Wright to accompany the engraved drawing of the wall by Thomas Allom in his series of Views of China published by Fisher in London and Paris simultaneously.

Allom's picture, of the gate used by the emperors and by Lord Macartney earlier, does justice to the wall, meandering mightily over the tops of the mountains, with a nice contrast in front of two traveling officials borne in their palanquins with a retinue of soldiers and a few local peasants gazing on. But the wall was demeaned even in Wright's preface to the book, where he noted that it was styled "in the exaggerated manner of the East . . . . The Wall of Ten Thousand Li, although it extends only half that length. . . ." He cannot resist the analogy of earlier walls—Alexander's, Tamburlaine's, and even Egyptian and Mede monuments. Yet China's Great Wall is relegated as "perhaps one of the most senseless conceptions that ever occupied the human intellect," and all because of the emperor Qin's over-arching ambition. "There was a time when a million scimitars glittered along its length from east to west, but all fear of invasion having subsided, the government is now content with guarding the chief passes that communicate with foreign countries."

Monsignor Huc, as Papal Envoy in central Asia, saw the Great Wall in 1845 and also found it disappointing. "This work of the Chinese nation," he wrote severely, "of which so much is said and so little known, merits brief mention here." Earlier writers had "preposterously exaggerated" its importance. Barrow, for instance, half a century earlier had based his views on the section of the wall which remained grand and imposing.

But Huc himself had crossed and recrossed it at fifteen different points, often traveling for days at a time parallel with it and without leaving sight of it, and in some places he found the wall, "a mere low wall of brickwork, or even earthwork." He found not the slightest trace of any foundation wall of free stones cemented with mortar, as other writers had claimed.

The general lay opinion continued to be enthusiastic. Tytler in his Universal History described the Great Wall as "among the most remarkable of the works of architecture in China" and as "a most singular monument both of human industry and human folly." This was because the Tartars were easily able to attack China by going round the end of the wall.

Western visitors were now so numerous that they became blase. One booklet for travelers described going to the wall in 1885 with the comment: "I do not think at first that we viewed it in any other light than as a place to tiffin at."

It was about that time that the spoof was perpetrated in a newspaper story about American engineers coming from Denver having been hired to demolish the Great Wall, purportedly as a piece of Chinese reassurance that foreigners were welcome. This joke fed into the negative and hostile material which China was receiving from the outside world and which eventually overflowed in the Boxer Rising.

So far every foreign visitor had seen only a small part of the wall, and had confidently generalized from that. Only in 1909 did an eccentric American writer-dilettante attempt to traverse the wall from end to end. He succeeded in all but one small spur, and his book, The Great Wall of China, became a classic. Unfortunately William Edgar Geil was as idiosyncratic as he was adventurous, though at least he was able to satisfy the rest of the world about the physical relationship between the various parts of the Great Wall.

The fascination with the Great Wall went deeper in him than perhaps anyone. Sailing across the Pacific to undertake his project, Geil wrote: "We ate with the Wall, slept with the Wall, thought Wall. Its bricky length would twist itself into peculiar contortions, into indescribable shapes. We fancied an immense arch from sea to desert, and under it the great events that have shaped and reshaped this planet earth.

"The Wall danced before us in ever-varying shapes, now rolling itself together like a scroll, now stretching itself out to its full length, again resolving itself into all sorts of geometrical figures, triangles, parallelograms, circles, until we could almost fancy the Wall to be some agile imp, playing hide-and-seek in our imagination, instead of the great structure that some lunar inhabitants see like a black welt across the face of the earth."

Geil described the wall as an ancient fossil, the largest on our planet. But fossils are useful and truthful, and this Wall furnished a dividing line between the herdsmen of the east Asian north and the tillers of the south, as well as between two areas, the China of misty legend and the modern China of history.

Its builders two thousand years ago had been "ahead of the senseless militarism of Europe." A wall to protect the living was better than a ditch to cover the dead, and Geil praised the "greatest wall in the world, which has for ages stood for peace, and which has for ages diffused delay."

So varied did the American find the various sections of the Wall that he invites us to conclude that "the Chinese people have built, during the last twenty-two centuries, more than a dozen Great Walls!" And that "the masonry exhibited almost as many varieties of construction." Rather than flowing out over all Asia, the emperor Qin had decided to go only so far and then stop the others coming in, hence the wall. He had "defined a clear and explicit Monroe doctrine for eastern Asia," and marked the boundaries with "a wall across half a continent! A wall from Philadelphia to Kansas City! A wall from Constantinople to Marseilles!"

Geil's enthusiasm could not be restrained. "Behold it by starlight or moonlight, gaze on it in twilight or in sunlight; view it through the haze of a dustfog or the spindrift of a rain shower or between the flakes of a snowstorm; ever is the Wall one great grey, gaunt, still spectre of the past...."

It was also a "Wall of blood!" Remembering the sweat, tears, and blood that were exacted from countless thousands of anonymous workmen, "we are prepared to hear that after two millennia the name of Ch'in (Qin) is cursed all along the Wall by the descendants of those who were driven to the hateful task, who labored in deathly fear lest when flesh and blood failed to respond to the taskmaster's scourge, that flesh and blood should be hurled into the mass of concrete to provide more material for the all-devouring monster."

Geil extracted from the course of the Great Wall a speculatory lesson in twentieth-century politics. The Great Wall ran from the Yellow Sea, past the Yellow River to the Yellow Sand, to peter out at the Big White North River near Suchow. It thus ran, he noted, "from the deep sea to the desert, from animation to stagnation." But the progression from the Yellow to the White raised other questions. "Will the yellows go to the whites and submerge them? Will it be from yellow to white; or will it be that the white will become yellow, and that these people ultimately predominate?"

Geil's imaginative adventure was the herald of half a dozen serious investigations by foreigners in the ensuing decade or so. In 1912 R. S. Clark and A. de C. Sowerby went through the desolate Ordos section of the wall, and five years later Frederick Clapp surveyed in the same area. He described coming to the ruins of a desert wall in the Ordos which the map said was the Great Wall, but the local inhabitants said was something else: "This is the First Frontier Wall, built only four hundred years ago; the Great Wall is farther north."

Emile Hoveluque was there in 1919 with an eloquent description: "During fourteen centuries they protected China and isolated her from the whole world; they are one of the forces which have made and preserved her civilization. They have fulfilled their task. They can crumble away. The race they have so long defended has built up, little by little, immaterial inner defences, has crystallized morally into forms harder than their granite, into traditions and a life that no invasion from outside will be able, for many a long year, to disintegrate." This was the first sound political scientist's view of the wall.

The battlements which centuries ago had been bright with all the pomp and fantastic armor of the imperial legions, were today deserted, "to defend nothing but empty space." The life of China had ebbed away from them. "Like a dead dragon, the wall undulates over the barren ridges. In its ruin and indescribable desolation it keeps its majesty. No human monument moves the human imagination more than this barrier on which the tides of barbarians have so often beaten, and which enabled this strange realm of China to gradually shape itself and to endure."

Meanwhile in 1907 the great archaeologist Sir Aurel Stein first saw the Great Wall in July 1907 as a faint white line lit up by the setting sun. He was twenty miles away, "yet I thought I could make out towers reflecting the slanting rays and beyond them a great expanse of dark ground, the fertile district of Suchow."

The Swedish traveler and art dealer, Orvar Karlbeck, toured the western part of the Great Wall in the 1920s and found much of it crumbled. Adam Warwick, who wrote about his visit for the National Geographic Magazine, described the difficult Ordos area: "There is little if any interest in following this crumbling mound, hastily thrown together, of materials collected on the spot by the builders, who made scarcely any effort to encase it in granite or protect it or embellish it with parapets."

A little travel book written for Europeans in China in the 1930s predicted that the Great Wall, at least the section near Beijing, would "send a thrill of romance through the most prosaic Briton, a quickening of the imagination akin to that inspired by the Sphinx and the Pyramids, by the wonderful ruins of Rhodesia, or the decaying glories of Rome and Greece."

"But for the Chinaman," it added reproachfully, "the Great Wall seems to have no kindling fire. He regards it with placid indifference, to be venerated, indeed, as ancient, but more especially as handsome proof" that former generations had enough money to pay for the building of that kind of thing.

Then came a period when the wall was difficult for foreigners to see. The ravaging warfare of the 1930s and 1940s set Chinese against Chinese as well as against the Japanese aggressor, and that was followed by a long period of isolation under the new People's Republic.

To André Malraux, the French writer, the Great Wall in the summer of 1965 was a tangled dragon which "stretches out across the hills as it did of old. Here are the same hollyhocks, the same willowy paths: but the stone roadway built for the war chariots is today as clean as a Dutch dresser. Are these waste paper bins set out like milestones to be found along the entire length of the Great Wall? Here, as before, are the herds of little Manchu ponies, the dragonflies, the russet-coloured Mongolian birds of prey, and large butterflies of a warm brown...."

In 1972 the latest in a long line of fashions for scaling the Great Wall was set, improbably, by President Richard Milhouse Nixon of the United States. His historic walk along the section nearest to Beijing brought thirty years of hostility between the United States and Communist China to an end. President Nixon's reaction to the wall itself was to remark, "What a great wall this is...."

Had not American astronauts flown through space to prove empirically what everyone below had been saying, namely that the Great Wall of China is the only man-made monument visible from the moon?

Nixon and Kissinger were the foreign pathfinders of our own day. Hundreds of other statesmen and world dignatories have now trodden in their footsteps. The Great Wall has become an expected item on the foreigners' itinerary while visiting the People's Republic of China, a routine stop in tight tourist schedules.

What thoughts occur in their minds as foreigners climb those ancient stones? Do they huff and puff up the steep slope with a sense of duty done? Are they enchanted by the physical delights of the view, the aura of history and the handiwork of earlier generations? Do they sense the ancient power of China, and wonder about its possible return in the future? How Dr. Johnson would have longed to be there—and to have replaced in its original setting, if possible, the brick which now adorns his house.

IN THE TWENTIETH CENTURY

In China herself, the fortunes of the wall in the twentieth century have been waning rather than waxing. No Chinese government since 1900 has been able to indulge in the luxury of renovating it, except for a small showpiece section for tourists near Beijing, because the country has been embroiled in so many wars or rebellions.

The wall was a witness to the bowing out of the nineteenth century, and with it a whole era of decadence and inefficiency; in 1900 Emperor Guangxu and the formidable dowager empress Cixi, in flight from the upheavals of the Boxer Rebellion, followed a route across it. In the past such an imperial crossing would have been an occasion of color and protocol, with graceful palanquins and exquisite silk brocade costumes.

But now, in the new century, the emperor's impromptu party had to spend the night just beyond the wall without advance preparation, stranded without proper bedding or food. A local magistrate brought a blue sedan chair for the empress, and the Chief Eunuch managed to find some tea cups, but otherwise they were reduced from the self-delusions of their customary imperial style to the realities of ordinary life in China. There also appeared at the beginning of this century a portent of doom for the wall in the shape of railways. William Geil, its self-appointed American defender, hearing rumors of a railway project at Shanhaiguan, warned that it would be "a cruel sacrilege to pierce the Great Wall with an iron track." Only a year later, in 1909, the first railway was driven through, further west at the Nankou Pass—the opening which legend attributed to the weeping Meng Jiang.

The wall, China's defense and boundary, was now threatened by modern technology, and yet her citizens were still too poor to visit this supreme monument to their civilization. A historian, Professor Ku Chikang of the National University of Beijing, described in the 1910s how the high cost of travel prevented him from seeing the famous site at first hand.

A silent witness to the collapse of the empire and to the rise and fall of such Republican hopefuls as Sun Yat-sen, the wall also lay helpless under the critical view of the growing number of conquering foreigners, such as the eccentric Mrs. Alec-Tweedie, who was able to see it in 1925 using the new technology of the train. She saw grafitti written by Chinese in English to express their contempt for foreign visitors like herself:

"British here are worse than dogs"

"You uncivilized Japs and British, go to your mangers and meditate"

"Britishers and dogs are not allowed to visit..."

The wall here anticipated the "Democracy Wall" in Beijing at the end of the 1970s and showed itself a place as good as any to advertise your opinions on.

Alas, for the next quarter-century conditions were too dangerous for many foreigners to visit the wall. Only in the 1950s did it become possible for the new Communist government to restore part of it near Shanhaiguan, convenient for visitors from Beijing. I saw this section in 1962; it looked in fine order, although the ancient stones seemed to be crumbling where it stretched away to the horizon. A sign had been put up: "Foreigners not allowed beyond this point without special permission."

And where Mrs. Alec-Tweedie had observed a few modest anti-foreign grafitti, in 1962 there were not only thousands of scribbled signatures by Chinese and foreign visitors, but also slogans of a more contemporary interest, such as "Viva Castro" and "Cuba Si, Yanqui No."

In one 450-year-old section of the Great Wall north of the Helan mountain range in Ningxia, displacements of between 1.45 and 0.95 meters were discovered in 1965 by a scientific expedition investigating the effects of the big 1739 earthquake in Ningxia.

There are also some active faults in the locality, and those near the Great Wall are now being monitored. Chinese scientists are not yet agreed whether the movements of the Great Wall should be attributed to a geological fault or to an old earthquake.

Though the wall itself remained relatively intact in the earlier part of the twentieth century, crumbling with a weathering slowness, much of traditional China had crashed into oblivion, as the ominous cracks in the fabric of government worsened. Mao Zedong, leader of the Chinese Communists, fought Sun Yat-sen's heirs for the inheritance which the effete emperors had left. Some of their earliest clashes in the 1920s were in the vicinity of the wall, in Shanxi province.

Mao then chose the Great Wall directly as his goal, in the famous episode of the Long March (1934–1936) where he led the Red Army across China to a new Communist base in its shadow. His poem reflected this:

> If we fail to reach the Great Wall we are not men,
> We who have already marched six thousand miles.

Then another foreign horde breached the wall, as the Japanese swept southward in the 1930s in their capture of northern China. The Japanese struck again in 1937 at central and southern China, often fighting near the wall. Having captured Beijing itself, for example, one Japanese force marched to the wall up Mrs. Alec-Tweedie's railway and fought bitterly with the Chinese army at the Nankou Pass. We

hear the voice of one Chinese soldier who "fought one whole day and one whole night without rest or food.... I fought in that position for twenty days and twenty nights. Often we were without food except for sweet potatoes which the peasants brought us. ... After twenty days we fought hand-to-hand battles with the enemy.... We had no doctors, no nurses, no first-aid workers on the battlefield...."

It was a commentary which might have been made many times within earshot of the Great Wall during those many centuries of its history. Thousands of men died within echoing distance of its mute stones.

The wall's passes, in particular, saw the changing life of the centuries.

This pass at Nankou where the Chinese soldier fought his Japanese foes had once been the great commercial highway to Mongolia. In earlier times it had been laid out with blocks of granite so that carts could navigate it with comfort. But neglect had led it by the end of the nineteenth century to become, in the description of Romyn Hitchcock, "a rough and almost dangerous path, where carts do not attempt to pass; the merchandise is still transported on pack animals—ponies, mules, donkeys, and camels—and of these there is an endless succession of caravans from dawn to sunset." Clapp found the same pass in the early 1920s "wild and gloomy, bounded by towering crags, scarcely leaving room for... the railroad." The arrival of trains had swept away the caravan traffic at one stroke.

In another battle of the Sino-Japanese War, General Lin Biao of the Communist Red Army achieved a spectacular victory in this Pingxing Pass. He secretly worked round the rear of an advancing Japanese division under the feared General Itagaki and ambushed it from the higher ground on both sides of the pass. A Chinese officer described the scene:

"The distant drone of motors was heard from the canyon. A fleet of vehicles carrying Japanese troops and military supplies was moving up towards Pingxing Pass....

"Following the lorries were more than 200 animal-drawn carts, and mules and horses were drawing large-caliber guns. Behind them was the cavalry. Vehicles and animals were stretched in an unbroken line...."

Opposite page: Empress Cixi, coregent from 1861 to 1881 and sole regent from 1881 to 1889, exerted a great deal of influence over Emperor Guangxu, her nephew and adopted son, until the beginning of this century. This influence concluded the downfall of the declining regime of the Manchu emperors.

Emperor Xundi, the last of the Qings, was placed on the throne in 1908 at the age of two. He ruled until February 1912, a month after the proclamation of the Republic, over an agitated China. The Japanese used him as a puppet ruler of their Manchu-kuo colony from 1932 to 1945. He spent the rest of his life (he died in 1967) as a botanist and archivist in Beijing.

"The Japanese troops riding on horseback or sitting in lorries wore leather boots, steel helmets and woollen overcoats. They had rifles slung diagonally across their shoulders. They were quite at ease, talking and laughing."

When the Chinese opened fire, the Japanese at first calmly stood their ground, but were soon forced to take shelter under their lorries. Finally, Itagaki retreated in disorder with big losses, and the Chinese celebrated a great victory. They were not to score many more in the eight years that were to remain of the bloodiest war ever to be fought in China.

The Great Wall was not the hero in the war against Japan because, like the guns at Singapore in 1940, it faced the wrong way. It was as obsolete as the English Channel in the days of airplanes. China's enemies in the twentieth century did not come from the northwest, but from across the sea, to strike China by ship.

Only in symbolism and with poetic license could China continue to see the wall as a defense.

> The Wall of China today
> Likewise stands as a guard...
> Few countries have walls
> More magnificent than ours.

Thus Liu Hou-tze (Liu Houzi), in a 1942 poem called The Tattooed Wall. Kuo Mojo, the most famous poet of the Communist regime, wrote more conventionally in 1937, when the Japanese were pouring into China:

> We are no cowards, nor are we arrogant.
> But we do believe that we must defeat our
>   enemies.
> We must build a new Great Wall with
>   our very flesh and blood.

Japan was defeated, but no sooner was the ink dry on the ceasefire than the civil war within China broke out again. The wall was an immediate battleground as right-wing forces on one side attacked General Lin Biao and his men encamped on the other. The Communist armies won, against all the odds. And then, almost at the end of that final orgy of Chinese fratricide, a participant recalled the maneuver in which the huge Northeast Field Army of the Chinese Communists, again under the leadership of General Lin, passed through the Great Wall to victory.

"This mighty army of 800,000... entered the passes along a vast stretch of the Great Wall extending from Shanhaiguan in the east to Kupehkou" (Gupeikou, where the silk-clad emperors and Ambassador Macartney had passed, and which Allom had drawn) "and Hsifengkou (Xifengkou) in the West....

"The mighty Great Wall winds its way rising and falling over an unbroken chain of mountains. With its ancient battlements, high massive walls, and mighty ponderous gates, it stands on the north guarding the country to the south. During the ages, the smoke of beacon fires on countless occasions rose from its heights to signal the approach of the enemy! The Great Wall has seen much of the history of China, and now it was to witness the victory of the unbeatable armed forces of the Chinese proletariat."

The Great Wall had long ago lost its major intended function of keeping the "barbarians" out of China. Arnold Toynbee in A Study of History was able to cite it as a great example of how rulers' efforts to create permanent protection against invasion never succeed. The wall shares the same military fate as the Siegfried Line and the Maginot Line. But if it faced the wrong way in all of China's recent wars, it does in several important respects act as a frontier.

It was certainly an irony of the twentieth century that the wall which had been intended to keep China united and safe from foreign foes instead actually divided her. Once the Manchurians had conquered China in the sixteenth century, to form the Manchu dynasty, the wall cut through what they regarded as their new unified realm.

Even when the dynasty fell in 1911–1912, and the Japanese slowly annexed Manchuria in the following years, the wall once again performed the function of a frontier, this time between Chinese China and Japanese China. When Henry Puyi, the last boy-emperor in Beijing, became the puppet "Emperor of Manchu-kuo" under Japanese sponsorship in the 1930s, his recollections often referred to the visit of relatives "from south of the Great Wall," or to events of one kind or another "south of the Great Wall." The perpetuation of a frontier role within China became an actual possibility in the 1940s, when Stalin agreed with some American military leaders that the civil war between China's Communists and Nationalists could be resolved by separating Manchuria again from China. Manchuria would have become a Soviet-influenced Communist state, while China proper south of the wall would have remained a Nationalist stronghold, along

the pattern eventually followed in Vietnam, Germany, and Korea.

But the most important sense in which the Great Wall stands as a frontier is by embodying China's isolationism. This has been expressed most convincingly by the American scholar Owen Lattimore, who knew more about the "other" side of the Great Wall than perhaps any other twentieth-century Western expert. "It was necessary to restrict Chinese enterprise beyond the Great Wall... because Chinese who ventured too far beyond the Great Wall became a liability to the state; the business in which they were engaged, whether farming or trade, contributed more to the barbarian communities than it did to the Chinese community. They passed out of the social orbit... and accommodated themselves to an un-Chinese social and economic order...." Inevitably they then acquired an allegiance to barbarian rulers or else took up barbarian forms of government themselves.

Even into this century the symbolism of home for Chinese has persisted. Chinese traders and merchants who worked beyond the Great Wall in central Asia did so with reluctance. If they died "beyond the Mouth," as the old phrase put it, they would try to have their body brought back for burial inside the wall, inside the homeland.

And yet one is tempted to speculate what might have happened to Russia, to the Soviet Union, and even to Europe, if that barrier had not been there. More Chinese entrepreneurs, professionals, intellectuals, and workers might have come to Europe much sooner and helped to establish a more realistic image of China much earlier. By the same token, they would have been able to communicate back to the Chinese heartland a more realistic and less frightening picture of European civilization and society.

The same yearning for community is hinted at in Mao Zedong's most famous poem, where he compared himself with China's great emperors of the past—including Qin:

> North country scene:
> A hundred leagues locked in ice,
> A thousand leagues of whirling snow.
> Both sides of the Great Wall
> One single white immensity.

The Chinese do not say very much about

their Great Wall, and a superficial judgment of their literature might infer a certain detachment. But that is not to say that they take it for granted. It is a fundamental core image in the mind of the Chinese, representing their own unity, civilization, and rich history. Nor are they callous as to its cost. Many modern Chinese would echo the stanza of Ezra Pound:

Great works by oppression
By splendid oppression.
The Wall was from Yulin to Tse-ho
And a million men worked on that Wall.

It was a common judgment heard in China when Westerners first began to visit that the Great Wall was "the ruin of one generation and the salvation of thousands." Perhaps in the twentieth century the Chinese have become less certain about the salvation, while the catastrophes of the present make it unnatural and difficult to contemplate the troubles of a pre-Christian century.

And so the wall is sometimes seen as a mere monument of memories. Ho Chifang (He Jifang) conveyed this in his poem, The Ancient City, *written in 1934.*

There was a traveller back from beyond the passes
Who said the Great Wall is like a long column of galloping horses
Which just when rearing their necks and snorting were turned to stone . . .

There is one more level of meaning for the Great Wall. It was built to keep enemies out, and the fact that it stands today, more than two millennia later, is an indication that China still hopes to keep foreigners out. For most of the duration of the People's Republic of China, the authorities have been highly selective in letting foreigners in and allowing the Chinese out, even on such nationally justifiable missions as technical study or consultation. In the past few years this policy has been liberalized, but only to a certain extent, and with priority for the remunerative tourist industry. It is still difficult for professional persons or academic specialists outside China to make real and meaningful contact with their opposite numbers within China.

A critic of the Chinese Communist party complained during the Hundred Flowers Campaign in 1957 that political campaign had succeeded political campaign in the

1950s, *"each one leaving behind a Great Wall in its wake, a wall which estranges one man from another."*

Fifteen years later another critic, the poet Huang Xiang, wrote a poem called Confessions of the Great Wall, *depicting it equally as an ideological barrier between individuals and between peoples. The poem had the Great Wall first describing itself as the American astronauts had seen it:*

The earth is small and blue,
I am a little crack in it.

But this Great Wall acknowledged that:

My young sons and grandsons dislike me.
To them, I am a stubborn grandfather.

And the Great Wall knows why the younger generation does not like it. It is because

I divide the great land into numerous small pieces,
Divide the land into many small, suffocating courtyards.
My body lies stretched out among the people
Dividing this group from that,
So that they are constantly guarding against each other,
Can never see the faces of their neighbors,
And cannot even hear their conversation.

The Wall accepts that its days are numbered, and that it is to the younger generation that the future belongs:

A generation of sons and grandsons are moving me into the museum . . .

(Garside, Coming Alive, China After Mao, *pp. 291–293).*

In a sense there is still a Great Wall, a non-material one, which protects China from too fast and too indigestible an invasion of foreign modes and ideas.

One can detect an element of affection in the Chinese attitude to the Great Wall, and a measure of this is its popularity as a brand name. In China's shops you can buy Great Wall ties, Great Wall suitcases, Great Wall cashmere scarves, and Great Wall jam. There are tee-shirts with the words "Great Wall of China" emblazoned upon them. From about 1983 you will be able to stay in a luxury 1000-room Great Wall Hotel in Beijing, thanks to Cyrus Eaton Jr. and his Chinese business partners. Since it will cater primarily for foreign tourists, we can take it that the Emperor Qin would not have approved. Connoisseurs in various

Overleaf: The Great Wall was used for the last time in the war against the Japanese: it was an ideal route for the Chinese soldiers, but it was no longer a means of defense. Today, the old dragon only carries Chinese and foreign tourists on his back; he keeps his terrible memories to himself and, like a tired soldier, he bounces his carefree grandchildren on his knee.

Western capitals are now buying a Great Wall wine made from the deliciously lemon-scented longyan *grapes which grow on the southern slopes of the wall. Thus is the wall popularized and vulgarized, as its virtue seeps inexorably down in a democratic age to the common people.*

Understandably, the wall is now being physically exploited by Chinese diplomacy. A brick from it, similar in appearance and size to the one in Dr. Johnson's house in London, was displayed in Japan in 1981 as part of the Chinese contribution to an international exhibition, at the request of the host city of Kobe. It remained on permanent display in the Kobe museum afterward.

It would be a nasty trick of history if weak judgment or diplomacy were to lead China and the Soviet Union into a future fight. Only in that unlikely circumstance could the Great Wall ever come into its own again as a front line of defense—and quite an important one, because the strategists agree that such a war, if it were to come, would be largely fought on the ground, by soldiers and tanks. But this is to carry speculation to the point of alarmism. Neither could win such a war, and both would be uselessly drained by it. They will almost certainly agree tacitly to avoid it.

So the wall which the emperor Qin built before the Anglo-Saxons were even civilized, by an effort comparable to that of building thirty Great Pyramids all at once, will be left in peace to decay with dignity. Some of its already fallen stones will be cannibalized to make modern buildings and dams, a few might be distributed abroad as visible evidence of China's cultural superiority. It will last long enough to be photographed from the moon, and people will always come to gaze and marvel at it. The Great Wall of China was the wonder of its day, and it remains the wonder of the world. Nowhere else is there a work of man so immense, so ambitious, and so movingly symbolic.

CHRONOLOGY

B.C.	ca. 4000	Yangshao culture, Henan; Banpo Village, Shaanxi
	ca. 1500	Ruins of Yin at Xiaotun, province of Henan
	early 11th c.	Chang'an (Xi'an) capital of the Western Zhou
	1108	Building of Luoyang begun by Prince Jidan of Zhou
	770	Zhou capital moved from Chang'an to Luoyang
	551—479	Confucius
	513	Introduction of iron smelting
	ca. 400	*First walls built for defense by the Warring Kingdoms*
	343—278	Qu Yuan, China's first major poet
	221	Unification of China under Qin rule ends the Warring Kingdoms period
	214	*Walls of Qin, Zhao, and Yan linked to form the Great Wall*
	209	Death of Qin Shi huangdi, first emperor of all China
A.D.	67	Introduction of Buddhism in China
	ca. 105	Invention of paper
	366	Mogao caves, Dunhuang
	460—490	Yunggang grottoes
	5th c.	Longmeng grottoes
	581	Reunion of China under the Sui dynasty
	early 7th c.	Construction of the Grand Canal
	7th c.	Invention of printing from type
	627—649	Reign of the Tang emperor Tai Zong, perhaps the high point of ancient Chinese history
	701—762	Li Bai (Li Po), poet
	712—770	Du Fu, poet
	960	Reunion of China under the Song dynasty
	10th c.	Rockets with niter powder produced
	early 11th c.	Gunpowder used for firing
	12th c.	Development of printing and porcelain
	1175	The Sleeping Buddha of Dazu begun
	1211	Beginning of Mongol invasions; devastation of North China
	1215	Beijing sacked by Genghis Khan
	1268—1279	Conquest of all China by Kublai Khan
	1274—1291	Marco Polo in Dadu (Beijing)
	1368—1398	Mongols driven from China by the first Ming emperor
	ca. 1400	Ming capital transferred from Nanjing to Beijing
	1403—1424	*The Great Wall extended and rebuilt*
	1405—1433	Seven crossings of the Western Ocean to East Africa and Red Sea by Zheng He
	15th/16th c.	Great period of Ming porcelain; development of acupuncture
	early 17th c.	Matteo Ricci in China; encouragement of Jesuit missionaries
	1644	Peasant uprising under Li Zichan captures Beijing
	1662—1722	Emperor Kang Xi (Qing dynasty), famous as military commander, statesman, and scholar
	18th c.	Greatest territorial expansion of China
	1840—1842	The Opium War; China opened to the Western world
	1860	Beijing occupied by French and English troops
	1895	Formation of the Tung Meng Hui Society (later the Kuomintang Party) by Sun Yat-sen
	1900	The Boxer Rebellion, popular revolt against foreigners
	1911	The Double Ten uprising in Guangdong (Canton); China proclaimed a republic, with Sun Yat-sen as president
	1916—1926	Wars of the warlords for Beijing in northern China
	1919	Demonstration of Beijing students against the peace treaty with Japan and the Western powers; beginning of the May 4 Movement and the abandonment of Confucianism
	1921	Formation of the Communist Party of China
	1925—1927	National revolution, led by Chiang Kai-shek
	1927	Break between the Communists and the Kuomintang (Chiang Kai-shek); foundation of the Red Army
	1927—1936	Rule of the Kuomintang
	1931	Mao Zedong elected president of the first Chinese Soviet Republic
	1934—1935	The Long March of the Red Army from Jiangxi to Yan'an
	1937—1945	The Sino-Japanese War
	1949	Proclamation of the People's Republic of China with Mao Zedong as president (October 1)
	1976	Death of Mao Zedong Death of Zhou Enlai Hua Guofeng president of China

THE CHINESE DYNASTIES

XIA	23rd(?)—18th century B.C. (quasi-legendary)
SHANG	18th(?)—11th century B.C.
ZHOU	11th—6th century B.C.
WARRING KINGDOMS	ca. 500—221 B.C.
QIN	221—206 B.C
HAN	206 B.C.—A.D. 200
WESTERN HAN	206 B.C.—A.D. 9
EASTERN HAN	A.D. 25—220
THREE KINGDOMS (WEI, SHU, WU)	220—280(?)
WEI	220—264
QIN	265—419
WESTERN QIN	265—317
EASTERN QIN	317—419
SOUTHERN AND NORTHERN DYNASTIES (SONG, XI, LING, QEN)	420—589
SUI	589—618
TANG	618—907
FIVE DYNASTIES	907—960
SONG	960—1280
NORTHERN SONG	960—1127
SOUTHERN SONG	1127—1280
JIN (JÜRCHEN, IN NORTH)	1115—1254
YUAN (MONGOL)	1277—1367
MING	1368—1644
QING (MANCHU)	1644—1912

SELECTED BIBLIOGRAPHY

Bodde, Derk. *China's First Unifier: A Study of the Ch'in Dynasty as Seen in the Life of Li Ssu (280?—208).* Leiden, Holland: Brill, 1938.

Bodde, Derk. *Statesman, Patriot, and General in Ancient China.* New Haven: American Oriental Society, 1940.

Chavannes, Edouard. *Les Documents chinois découverts par Aurel Stein dans les sables du Turkestan oriental.* Oxford, 1913.

Chavannes, Edouard. *Les Mémoires historiques de Se-ma Ts'ien.* Paris: A. Maisonneuve, 1967—1979. 6 vols.

Fryer, Jonathan. *The Great Wall of China.* London: New English Library, 1975.

Geil, W.E. *The Great Wall of China.* London: John Murray, 1909.

Gernet, Jacques. *Le Monde chinois.* Paris: A. Colin, 1972.

Gernet, Jacques. *Ancient China: From the Beginnings to the Empire.* Trans. Raymond Rudorff. Berkeley, University of California Press, 1968.

Lattimore, Owen. *Inner Asian Frontiers of China.* New York, 1940.

Lattimore, Owen. *Studies in Frontier History.* London and New York: Oxford University Press, 1962.

Luo Zewen. *The Great Wall.* Beijing: Cultural Relics Publishing House, 1980.

Maspero, Henri. *Les Documents chinois de la troisième expédition de Sir Aurel Stein en Asie centrale.* London, 1953.

Needham, Joseph. *Science and Civilization in China.* Vol. 4, part III. Cambridge University Press, 1971.

Stein, Aurel. *Serindia.* Oxford: Clarendon Press, 1921. 4 vols.

Watson, Burton. *Records of the Grand Historians of China.* New York: Columbia University Press, 1961. 2 vols.

Yü Ying-shih. *Trade and Expansion in Han China.* Berkeley, University of California Press, 1967.

PICTURE CREDITS

Original Artwork:
Coray, Franz, Lucerne: 69, 130 top, 132/133, 136, 137, 147 top, 148/149 top, 150 center, 151 above right; all drawn maps, and wall diagram
Luzi, Werner, Lucerne: 138 below

From Published Works:
Allom, T., *China, its Scenery, Architecture, Social Habits ect.,* London 1840: 176
Bauer, Wolfgang, *China und die Fremden,* Munich 1980: 174 center left
Biedermann, Hans, *Medicina Magica,* Graz 1972: 172 left
Boerschmann, Ernst, *Baukunst und Landschaft in China,* Berlin 1923: 122 top
Chavannes, E., *Les documents chinois découverts par Aurel Stein dans les sables du Turkestan oriental,* Oxford 1913: 38 below
Chhi Chhi Thu Shuo, 1627: 135 right
Fryer, Jonathan, *The Great Wall of China,* London 1975, 25 (map)
Fuchs, Walter, *Der Jesuiten-Atlas der Kanghsi-Zeit,* Peking 1943: 62/63, 107 above right
Geil, William Edgar, *The Great Wall of China,* London 1909: 2 left, 3 right, 8 left, 28 top, 62 left, 70 center below, 120 below, 126 center left, 128, 150 below
Guangyu Tü, Ming edition: 64 left

Kürschner, Joseph, *China,* Leipzig 1901: 7
Le Coq, A.V., *Chotscho,* Berlin 1913: 158 bottom
Linyu Xian Zhi, Peiping 1929: 65 top
Manzhou Shilu, original Qing edition: 50 right, 51, 151 below
Map: People's Republic of China, ONC G-9, Defense Mapping Agency Aerospace Center, St. Louis Air Force Station, Missouri, May 1974: 81
Mémoires concernant l'histoire... des Chinois, Paris 1776—1791: 22 above right
San Cai Tu Hui (catalogue), vol. II: 23 left, 26 above right, 152 top left and top right, 153 above right and bottom, 154 bottom center and bottom right, 162 top, 163 top center left
Shuntian Fuzhi (annals of the Beijing region) 1593: 60 above left
Tiangong Kaiwu, 1637: 173 bottom center
T'ien-kung K'ai-wu, 1637: 173 bottom right

Photographic Sources:
Bibliothèque Nationale, Paris: 2 center, 27, 36 right, 92, 95 center, 135 left
British Museum, London: 56 above, 61, 118 above, 168 bottom, 175 center
Cambridge University Library, Cambridge: 43, 174 top
Cultural Relics Publishing House, Beijing: 2 right, 4/5, 6, 8/12, 13, 14, 16, 17, 18 below, 19, 20, 21, 22 top and bottom, 23 right, 24, 25 left and top, 28 center left and bottom left, 30 left, 31 bottom, 32 above and bottom left, 33, 34, 35, 38 top, 39, 40, 41, 42, 44, 45 below, 46 right, 47, 48, 49, 50 left, 52, 53, 54, 55, 57, 60 above center and bottom, 66 above left, 67 bottom right, 68, 70 center above and bottom, 71, 72, 73, 74, 75, 76 above, 76/77, 78, 79 above and below right, 80, 81 top and bottom, 82, 83 top, center left and right, 84, 84/85, 86, 88 above, 89, 90, 91, 93, 94, 95 top left, top right and bottom, 96, 97 top, 98/99, 99

right, 100, 101, 102/103, 103, 104, 105, 106, 107 above left and below left, 108, 109, 110, 110/111, 111, 112, 112/113, 113, 114, 115, 116, 117, 118 bottom, 119 top left and bottom, 120 above, 122 bottom, 123, 124, 125 right, 126 top and center, 127, 130 left, 131, 132, 133, 134, 138 top, 138/139, 140, 141, 142, 143, 146, 147 center, 150 top, 151 top left, 152 top center and below left, 153 left, 154 above left and center left, 154/155, 155, 156/157, 158 top, 159, 162 below, 163 top left, top center right, top right and bottom, 166, 167, 169, 173 center and center right, 174/175, 175 top and bottom, 180, 181, 185
Darbois, Dominique, Paris: 36 top, 37, 171
Dräyer, Walter, Zurich: 30 bottom center and bottom right
Eros Data Center, Sioux Falls: 87 left, 98 left, 121
E.T. Archive, London: 26 bottom, 174 bottom
Freeman, John, London: 129
Giraudon, Paris: 32 bottom right, 164
Harvard Yenching Library, Cambridge, Massachusetts: 65 bottom, 66 bottom, 122 center, 124/125, 144/145 above, 148 bottom, 149 center and bottom
Keystone-Press, Zurich: 184
Lateran Museum, Rome: 64/65, 76 below, 79 below left, 83 bottom
Metropolitan Museum of Art, New York (Gift of the Dillon Fund, 1973): 45 above
Museum of Fine Arts, Boston: 26 above left, 172/173
Réunion des Musées Nationaux, Paris: 36 left, 58/59
Roger-Viollet, Paris: 56 below
Sheridan, Ronald, London: 173 top
Tholstrup, Else, Copenhagen: 28 center right, 29
Topkapi Saray Museum, Istanbul: 168 top
Werner Forman Archive, London: 46 left
Yugoslav Review, Belgrade: 15, 31 top, 88 below, 97 center and bottom, 119 top right, 160/161, 164/165, 170 bottom

ACKNOWLEDGMENTS

The McGraw-Hill Co-Publishing Division wishes to thank the following persons without whose kind help and cooperation this book could not have been produced:

The authors, Luo Zewen, Dai Wenbao, Dick Wilson, and Jean-Pierre Drège, for the chapters they contributed to this book; and Hubert Delahaye who provided advice and expertise, and who wrote the picture captions.

Professor Jacques Gernet for his valuable advice and for contributing the Foreword.

Nebojša Tomašević, director and editor in chief of Jugoslevenska Revija (The Yugoslav Review), for providing counsel and liaison.

Xu Liyi, deputy director of the National Publishing Association, Beijing, who helped to get the project under way.

Wang Fangzi, Wang Daiwen, Han Zhongmin, Sun Banchang, Luo Zewen, and Yu Jin of the Cultural Relics Publishing House, Beijing, who provided so much of the textual and illustrative contents of this book.

Jörg Bühler of the Eidgenössische Technische Hochschule, Zurich, for painstaking help with maps.

Pierre Tobler, for his editorial assistance with maps.

Jörg Schumacher, of the Ostasiastisches Seminar, University of Zurich, for his help with translations.

And all others, both those mentioned in the front of the book and any who may have been overlooked.

INDEX

Page numbers in *italic* refer to illustrations.

189

INDEX

Page numbers in *italic* refer to illustrations.